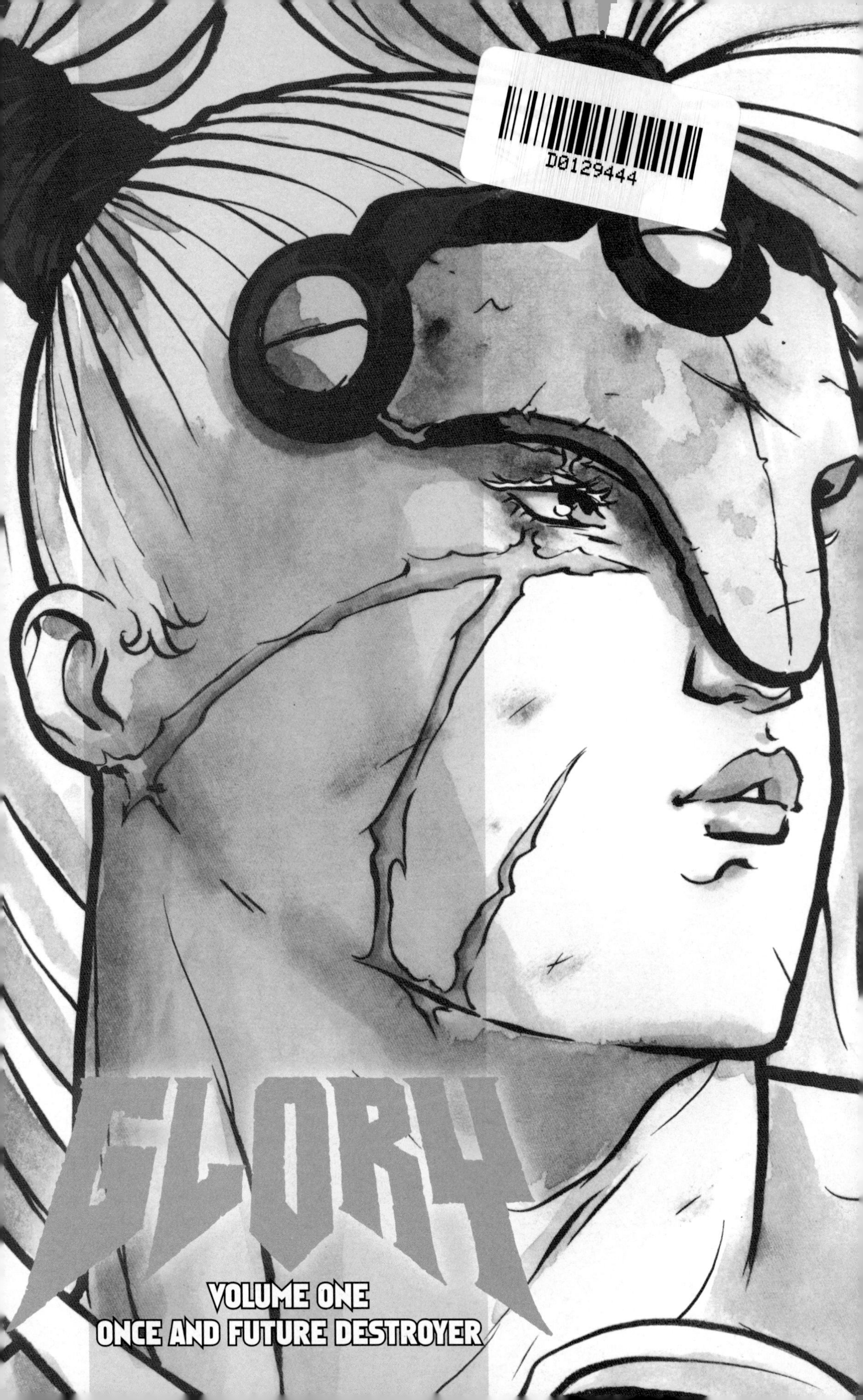
GLORY
VOLUME ONE
ONCE AND FUTURE DESTROYER

GLORY

written by JOE KEATINGE
illustrated by ROSS CAMPBELL
colors by Ms. SHATIA HAMILTON,
JOSEPH BERGIN III,
&
OWEN GIENI with CHARIS SOLIS
letters by DOUGLAS E. SHERWOOD
edited by ERIC STEPHENSON

image®

IMAGE COMICS, INC.

ROBERT KIRKMAN - chief operating officer
ERIK LARSEN - chief financial officer
TODD MCFARLANE - president
MARC SILVESTRI - chief executive officer
JIM VALENTINO - vice-president

ERIC STEPHENSON - publisher
TODD MARTINEZ - sales & licensing coordinator
JENNIFER DE GUZMAN - pr & marketing director
BRANWYN BIGGLESTONE - accounts manager
EMILY MILLER - administrative assistant
JAMIE PARRENO - marketing assistant
SARAH deLAINE - events coordinator
KEVIN YUEN - digital rights coordinator
JONATHAN CHAN - production manager
DREW GILL - art director
MONICA GARCIA - production artist
VINCENT KUKUA - production artist
JANA COOK - production artist
www.imagecomics.com

Glory Volume 1 Trade Paperback.
September 2012. FIRST PRINTING. ISBN: 978-1-60706-604-0. $16.99

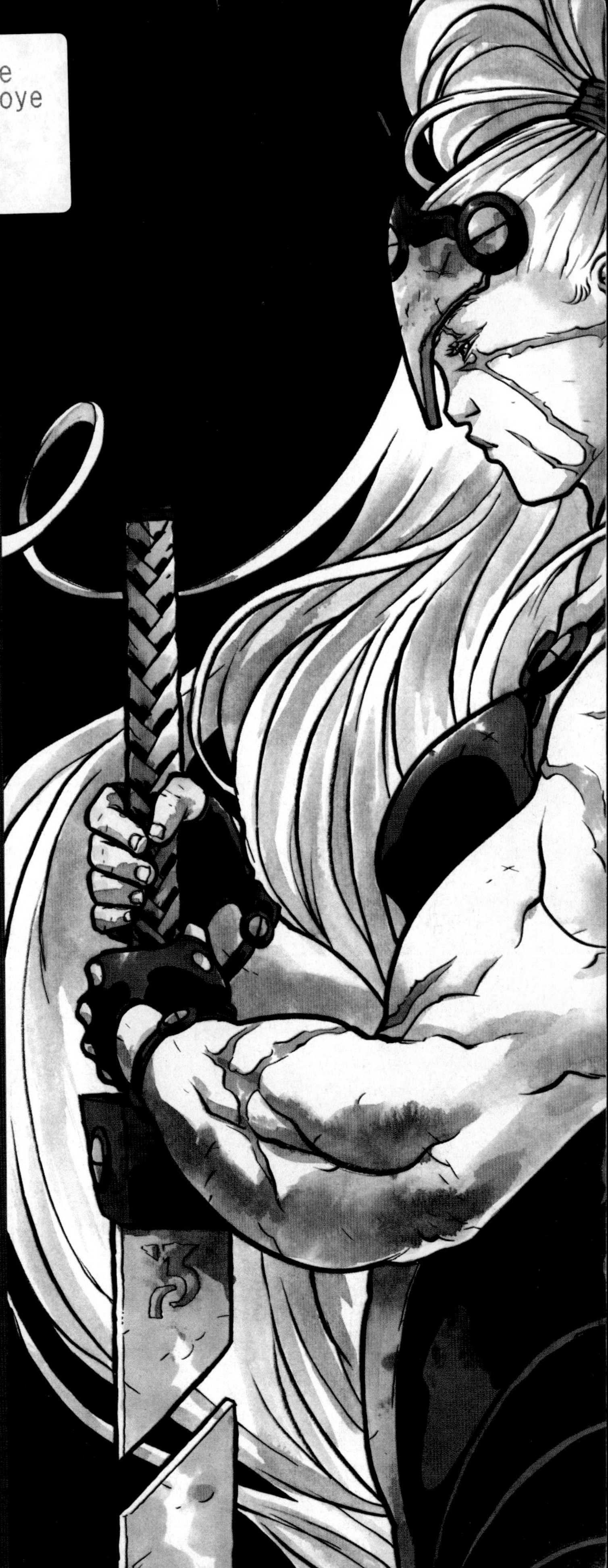

JOE KEATINGE -
To my Mom, Step-Mom, Grandmothers, Sister, Aunts, Cousins, Lovers and Friends for proving the `strong female character´ isn´t an exception to compliment, it´s the rule to follow.

ROSS CAMPBELL -
Thanks to mom, dad, Kelly Thompson, Zach Smith, Fawn LaRoche, Kaylie McDougal, everyone at The Dragon, everyone who reads my comics, Rob Liefeld for trusting me with Glory, and of course Joe for bringing me on board and putting up with me.

Chapter One

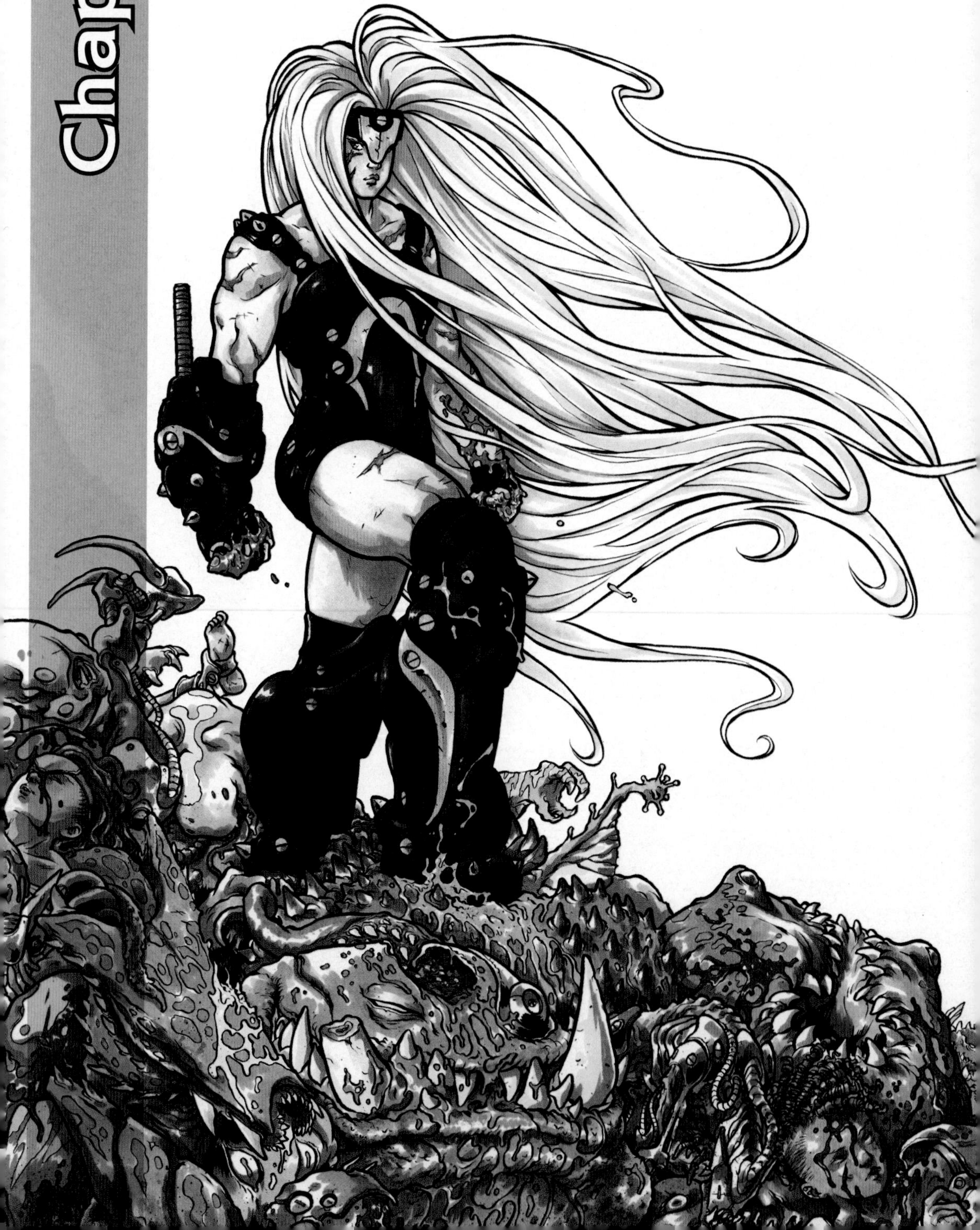

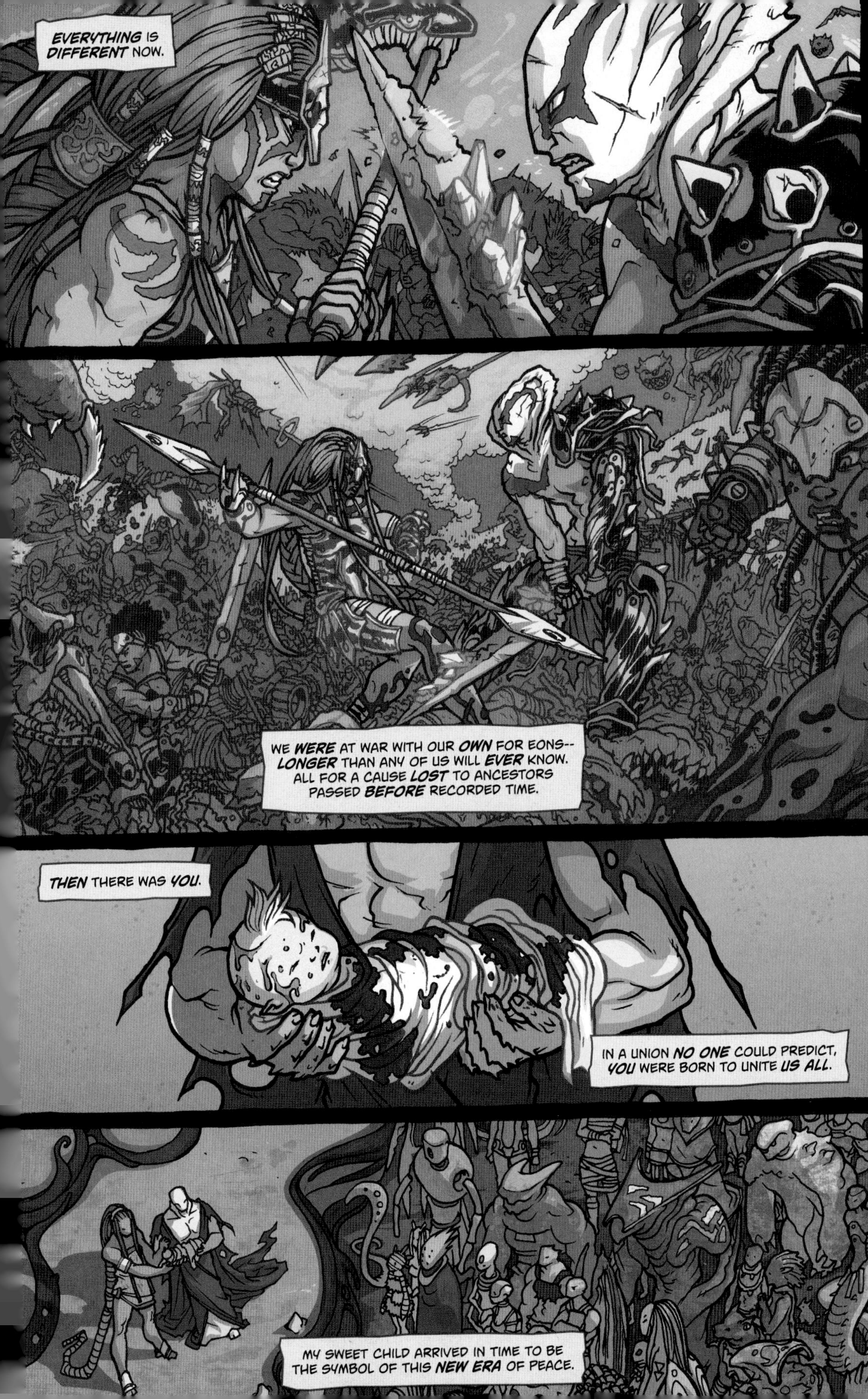
EVERYTHING IS DIFFERENT NOW.
WE WERE AT WAR WITH OUR OWN FOR EONS-- LONGER THAN ANY OF US WILL EVER KNOW. ALL FOR A CAUSE LOST TO ANCESTORS PASSED BEFORE RECORDED TIME.
THEN THERE WAS YOU.
IN A UNION NO ONE COULD PREDICT, YOU WERE BORN TO UNITE US ALL.
MY SWEET CHILD ARRIVED IN TIME TO BE THE SYMBOL OF THIS NEW ERA OF PEACE.

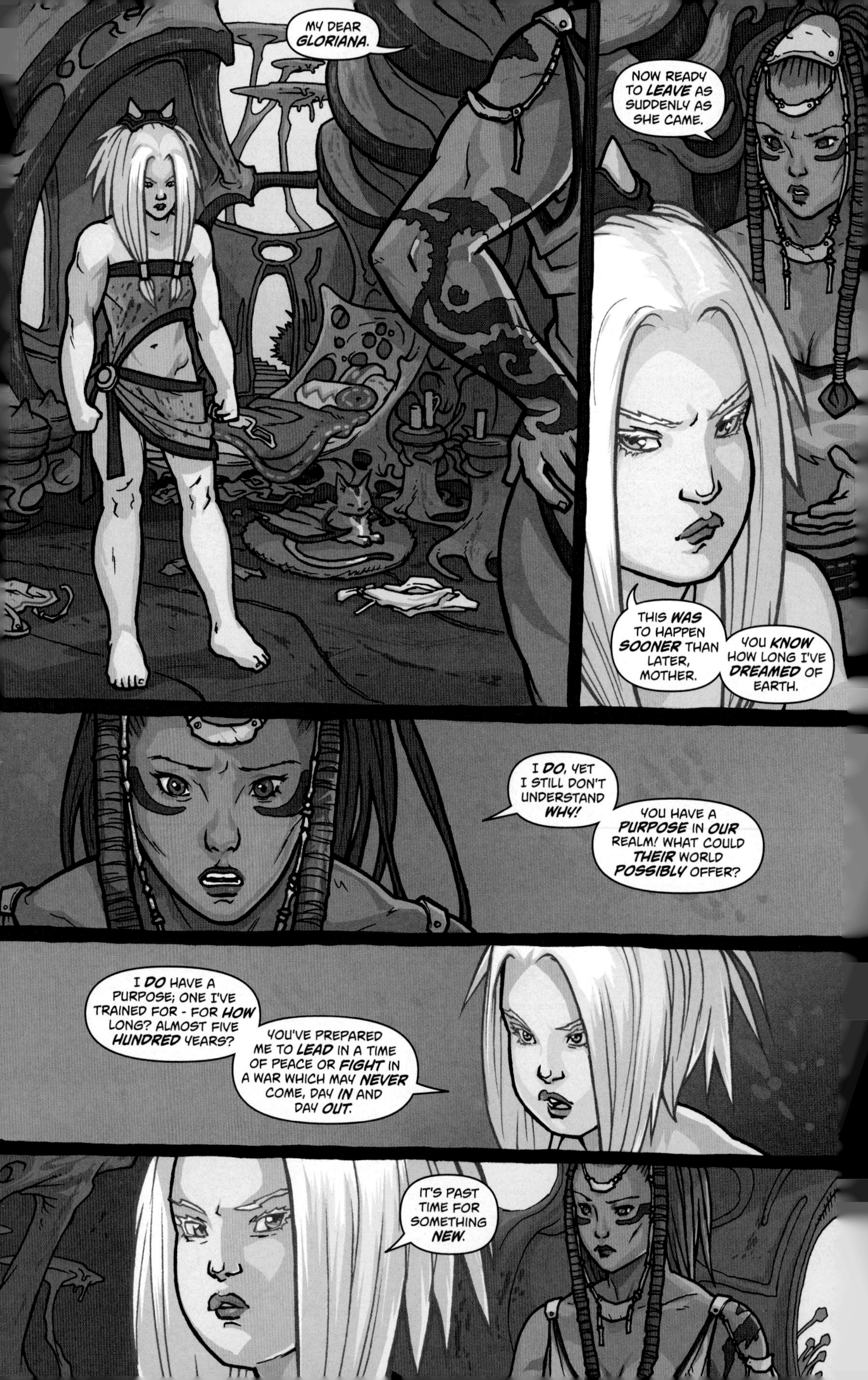
MY DEAR GLORIANA.
NOW READY TO LEAVE AS SUDDENLY AS SHE CAME.
THIS WAS TO HAPPEN SOONER THAN LATER, MOTHER.
YOU KNOW HOW LONG I'VE DREAMED OF EARTH.
I DO, YET I STILL DON'T UNDERSTAND WHY!
YOU HAVE A PURPOSE IN OUR REALM! WHAT COULD THEIR WORLD POSSIBLY OFFER?
I DO HAVE A PURPOSE; ONE I'VE TRAINED FOR - FOR HOW LONG? ALMOST FIVE HUNDRED YEARS?
YOU'VE PREPARED ME TO LEAD IN A TIME OF PEACE OR FIGHT IN A WAR WHICH MAY NEVER COME, DAY IN AND DAY OUT.
IT'S PAST TIME FOR SOMETHING NEW.

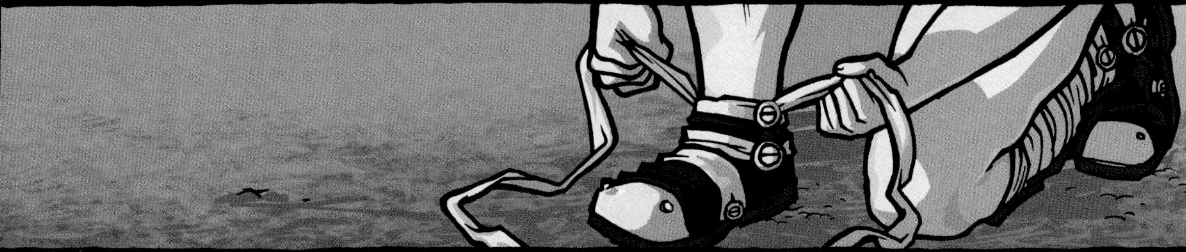

IMAGE COMICS PRESENTS

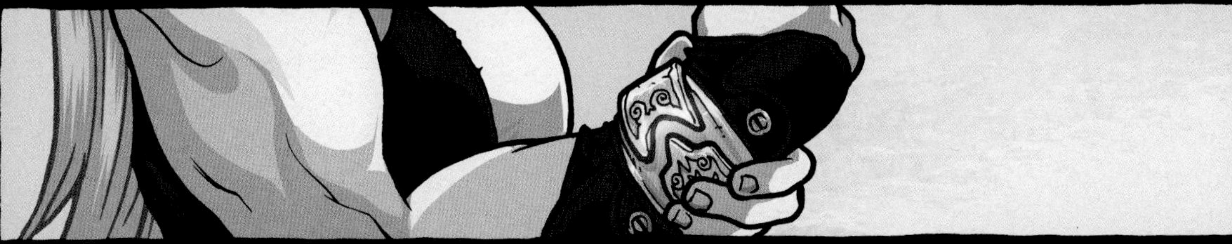

JOE KEATINGE
WRITER

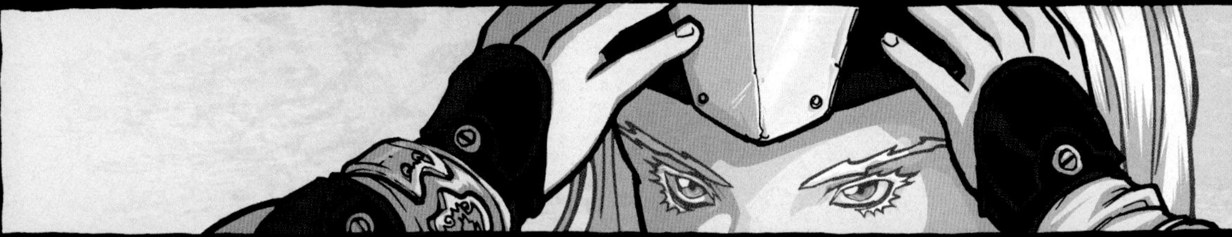

ROSS CAMPBELL
ARTIST

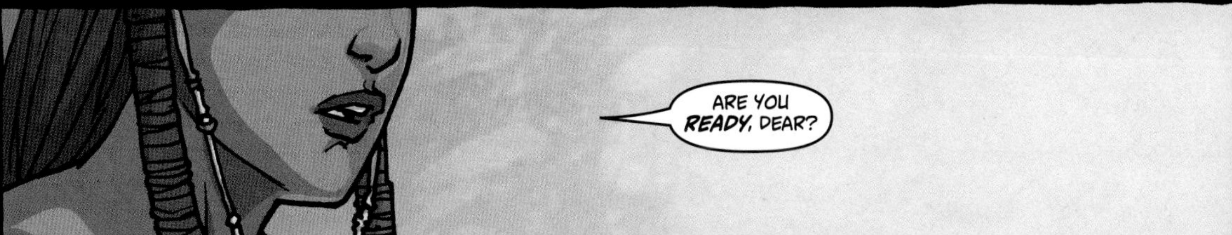
ARE YOU *READY*, DEAR?

MS,SHATIA HAMILTON COLORIST

DOUGLAS E. SHERWOOD LETTERER

ERIC STEPHENSON EDITOR

VARIANT COVER BY **ROB LIEFELD & MATT YACKEY**

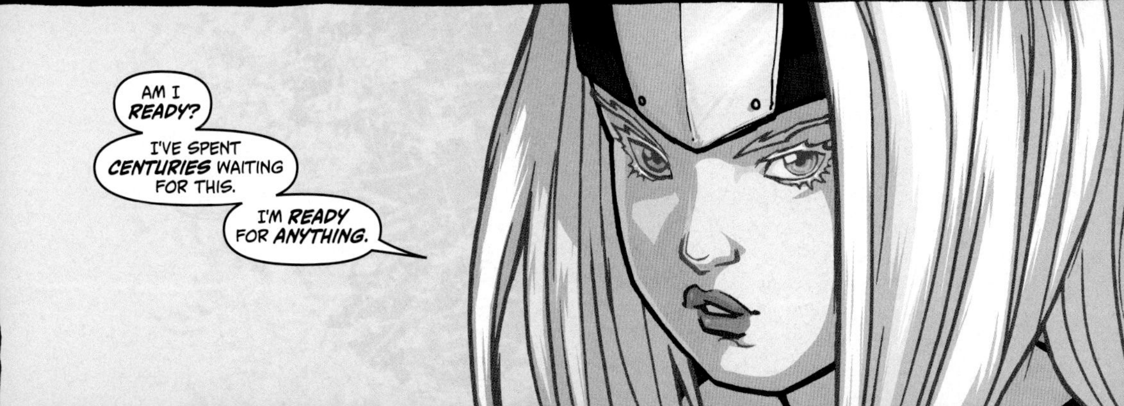
AM I *READY?*
I'VE SPENT *CENTURIES* WAITING FOR THIS.
I'M *READY* FOR *ANYTHING.*

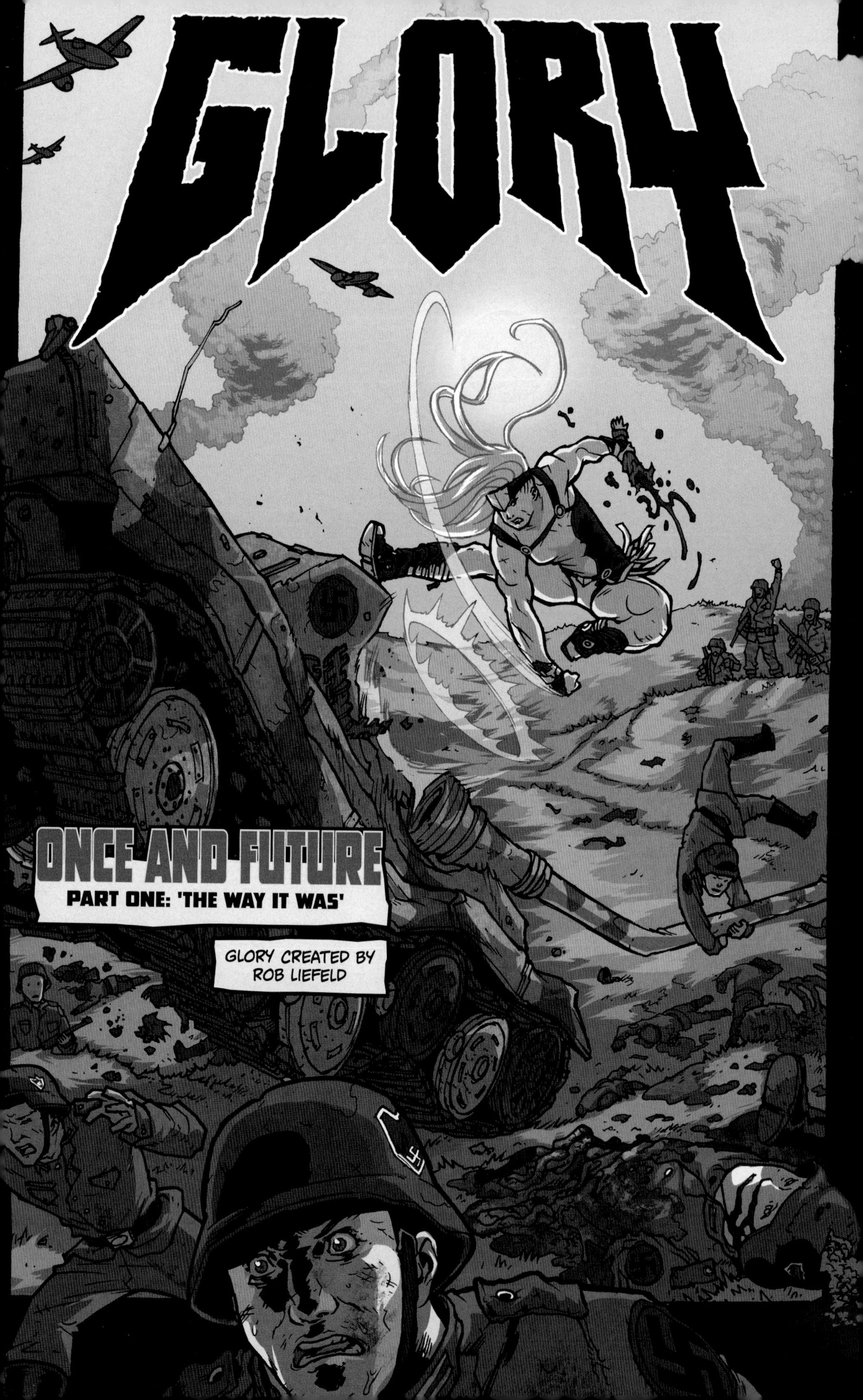
GLORY
ONCE AND FUTURE
PART ONE: 'THE WAY IT WAS'
GLORY CREATED BY
ROB LIEFELD

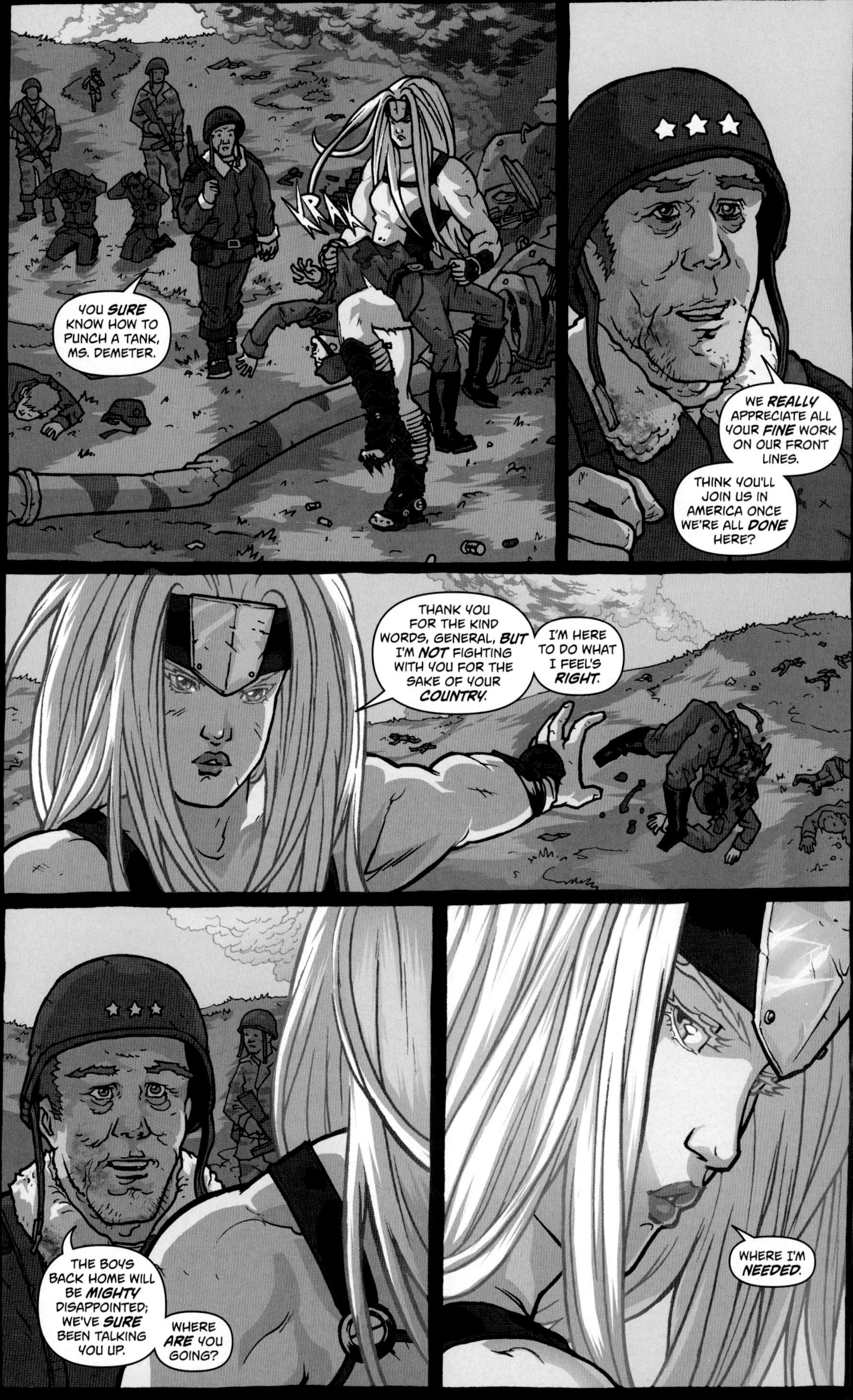
VRAK
YOU SURE KNOW HOW TO PUNCH A TANK, MS. DEMETER.
WE REALLY APPRECIATE ALL YOUR FINE WORK ON OUR FRONT LINES.
THINK YOU'LL JOIN US IN AMERICA ONCE WE'RE ALL DONE HERE?
THANK YOU FOR THE KIND WORDS, GENERAL, BUT I'M NOT FIGHTING WITH YOU FOR THE SAKE OF YOUR COUNTRY.
I'M HERE TO DO WHAT I FEEL'S RIGHT.
THE BOYS BACK HOME WILL BE MIGHTY DISAPPOINTED; WE'VE SURE BEEN TALKING YOU UP.
WHERE ARE YOU GOING?
WHERE I'M NEEDED.

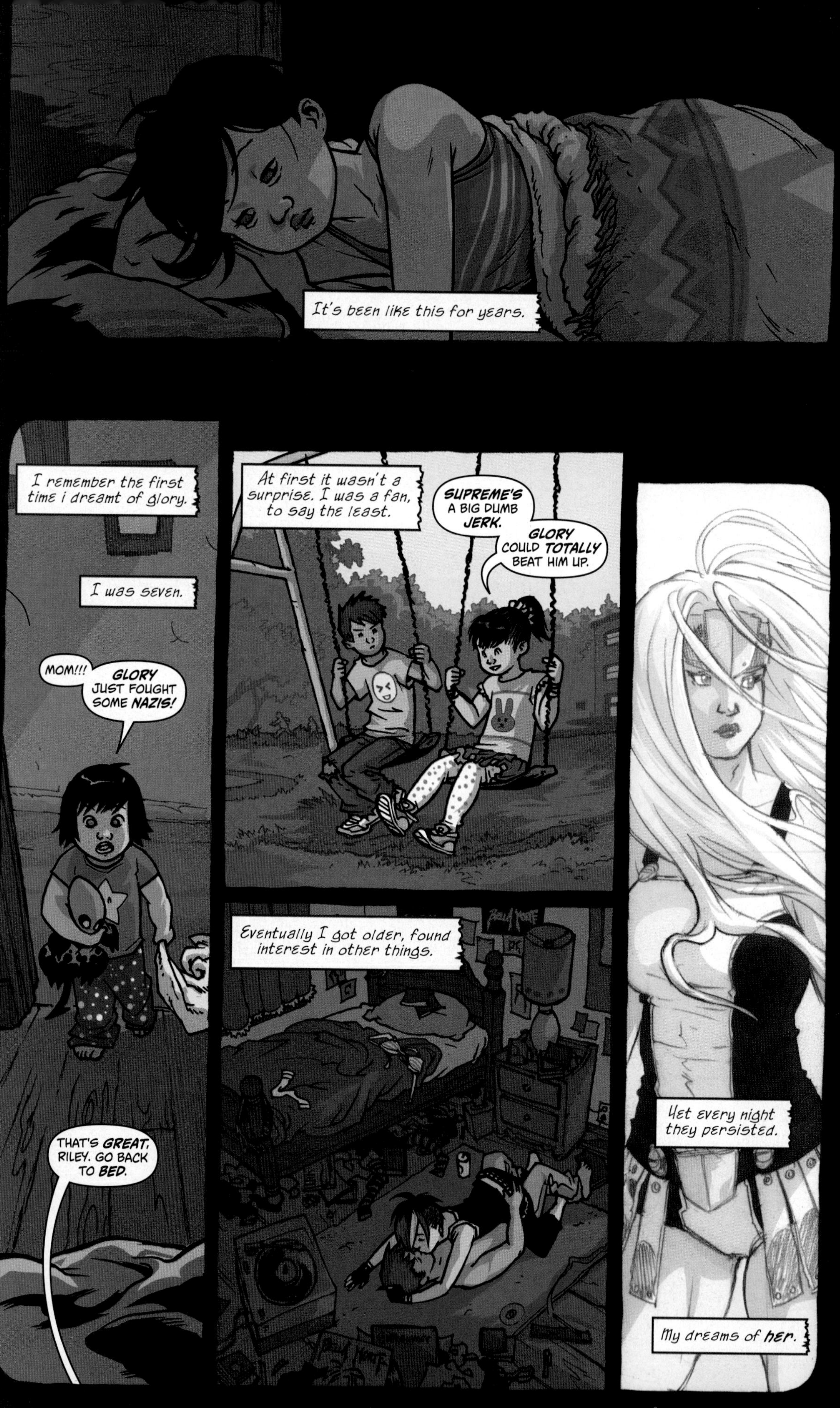
It's been like this for years.
I remember the first time i dreamt of glory.
I was seven.
MOM!!!
GLORY JUST FOUGHT SOME NAZIS!
THAT'S GREAT, RILEY. GO BACK TO BED.
At first it wasn't a surprise. I was a fan, to say the least.
SUPREME'S A BIG DUMB JERK.
GLORY COULD TOTALLY BEAT HIM UP.
Eventually I got older, found interest in other things.
Yet every night they persisted.
My dreams of her.

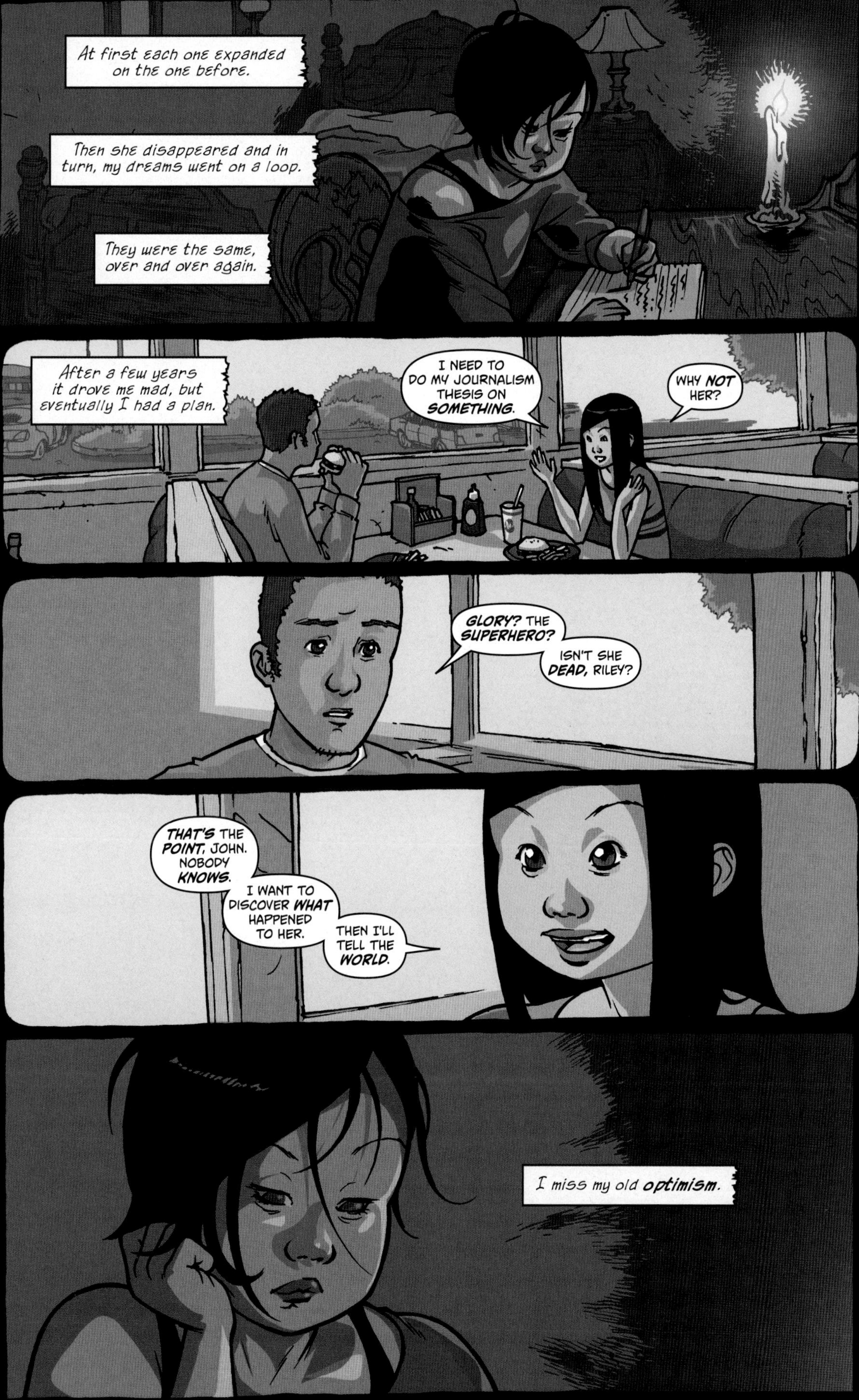
At first each one expanded on the one before.
Then she disappeared and in turn, my dreams went on a loop.
They were the same, over and over again.
After a few years it drove me mad, but eventually I had a plan.
I NEED TO DO MY JOURNALISM THESIS ON SOMETHING.
WHY NOT HER?
GLORY? THE SUPERHERO?
ISN'T SHE DEAD, RILEY?
THAT'S THE POINT, JOHN. NOBODY KNOWS.
I WANT TO DISCOVER WHAT HAPPENED TO HER.
THEN I'LL TELL THE WORLD.
I miss my old optimism.

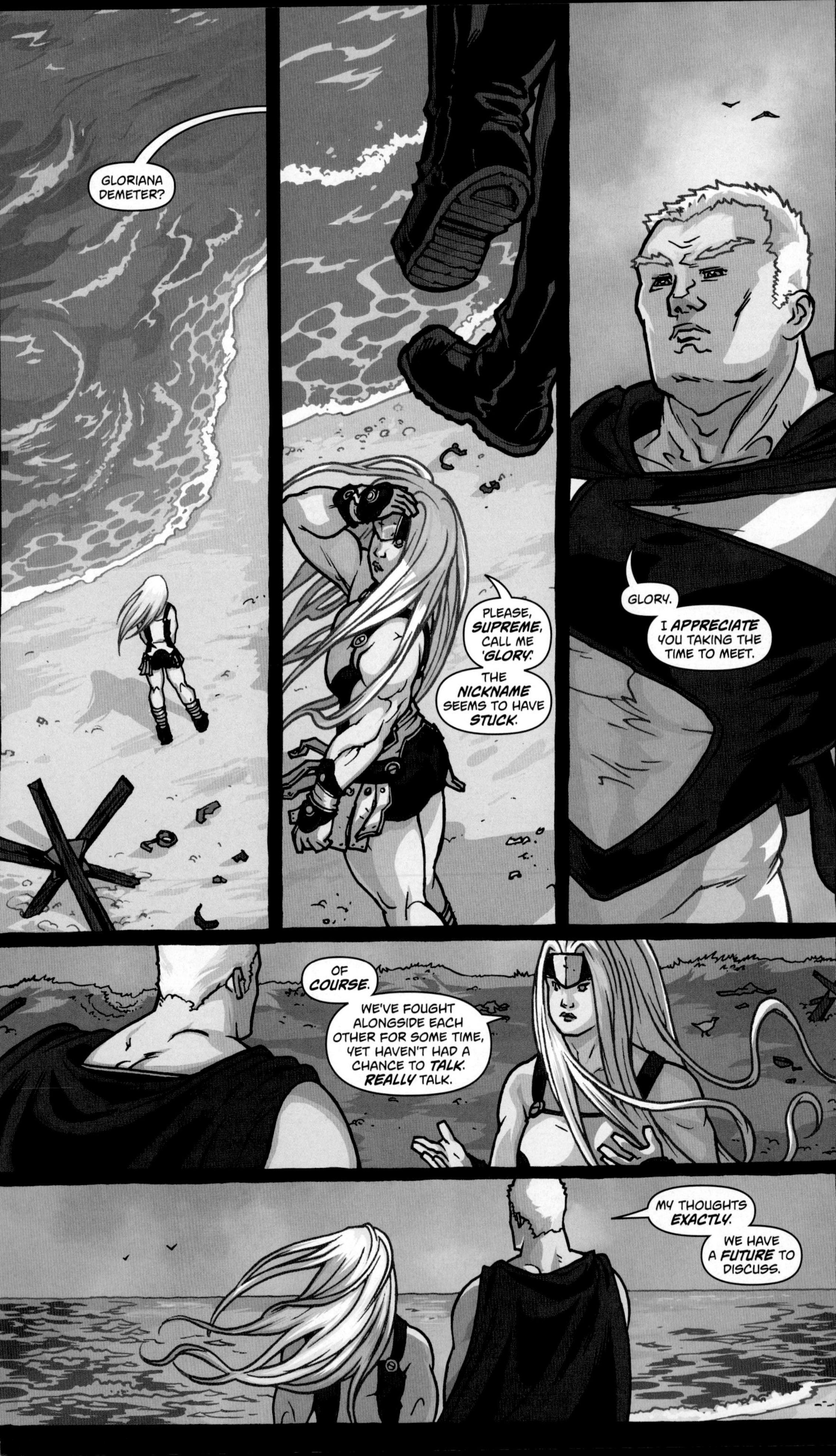
GLORIANA DEMETER?
PLEASE, SUPREME, CALL ME 'GLORY'.
THE NICKNAME SEEMS TO HAVE STUCK.
GLORY.
I APPRECIATE YOU TAKING THE TIME TO MEET.
OF COURSE.
WE'VE FOUGHT ALONGSIDE EACH OTHER FOR SOME TIME, YET HAVEN'T HAD A CHANCE TO TALK. REALLY TALK.
MY THOUGHTS EXACTLY.
WE HAVE A FUTURE TO DISCUSS.

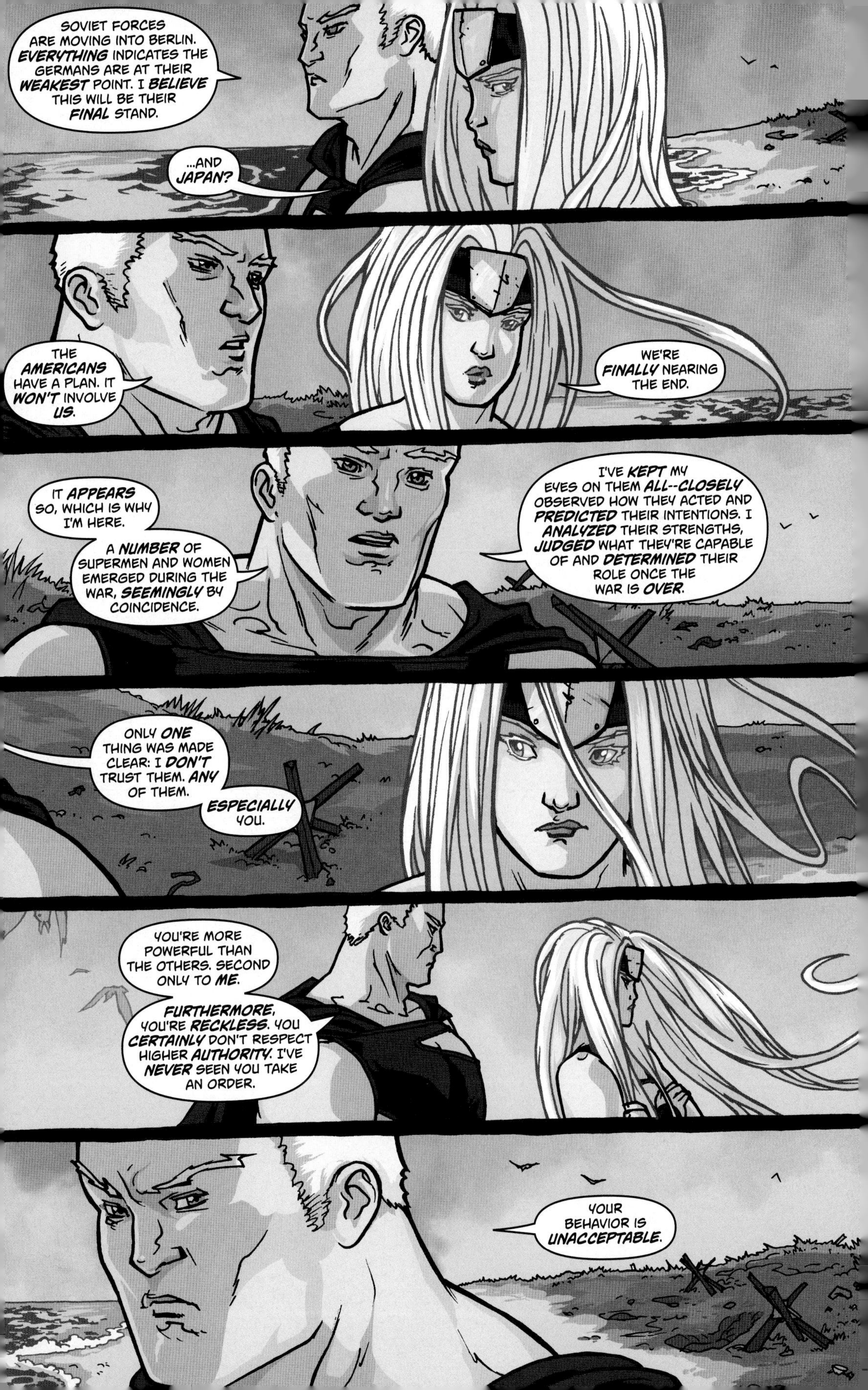
SOVIET FORCES ARE MOVING INTO BERLIN. EVERYTHING INDICATES THE GERMANS ARE AT THEIR WEAKEST POINT. I BELIEVE THIS WILL BE THEIR FINAL STAND.
...AND JAPAN?
THE AMERICANS HAVE A PLAN. IT WON'T INVOLVE US.
WE'RE FINALLY NEARING THE END.
IT APPEARS SO, WHICH IS WHY I'M HERE.
A NUMBER OF SUPERMEN AND WOMEN EMERGED DURING THE WAR, SEEMINGLY BY COINCIDENCE.
I'VE KEPT MY EYES ON THEM ALL--CLOSELY OBSERVED HOW THEY ACTED AND PREDICTED THEIR INTENTIONS. I ANALYZED THEIR STRENGTHS, JUDGED WHAT THEY'RE CAPABLE OF AND DETERMINED THEIR ROLE ONCE THE WAR IS OVER.
ONLY ONE THING WAS MADE CLEAR: I DON'T TRUST THEM. ANY OF THEM.
ESPECIALLY YOU.
YOU'RE MORE POWERFUL THAN THE OTHERS. SECOND ONLY TO ME.
FURTHERMORE, YOU'RE RECKLESS. YOU CERTAINLY DON'T RESPECT HIGHER AUTHORITY. I'VE NEVER SEEN YOU TAKE AN ORDER.
YOUR BEHAVIOR IS UNACCEPTABLE.

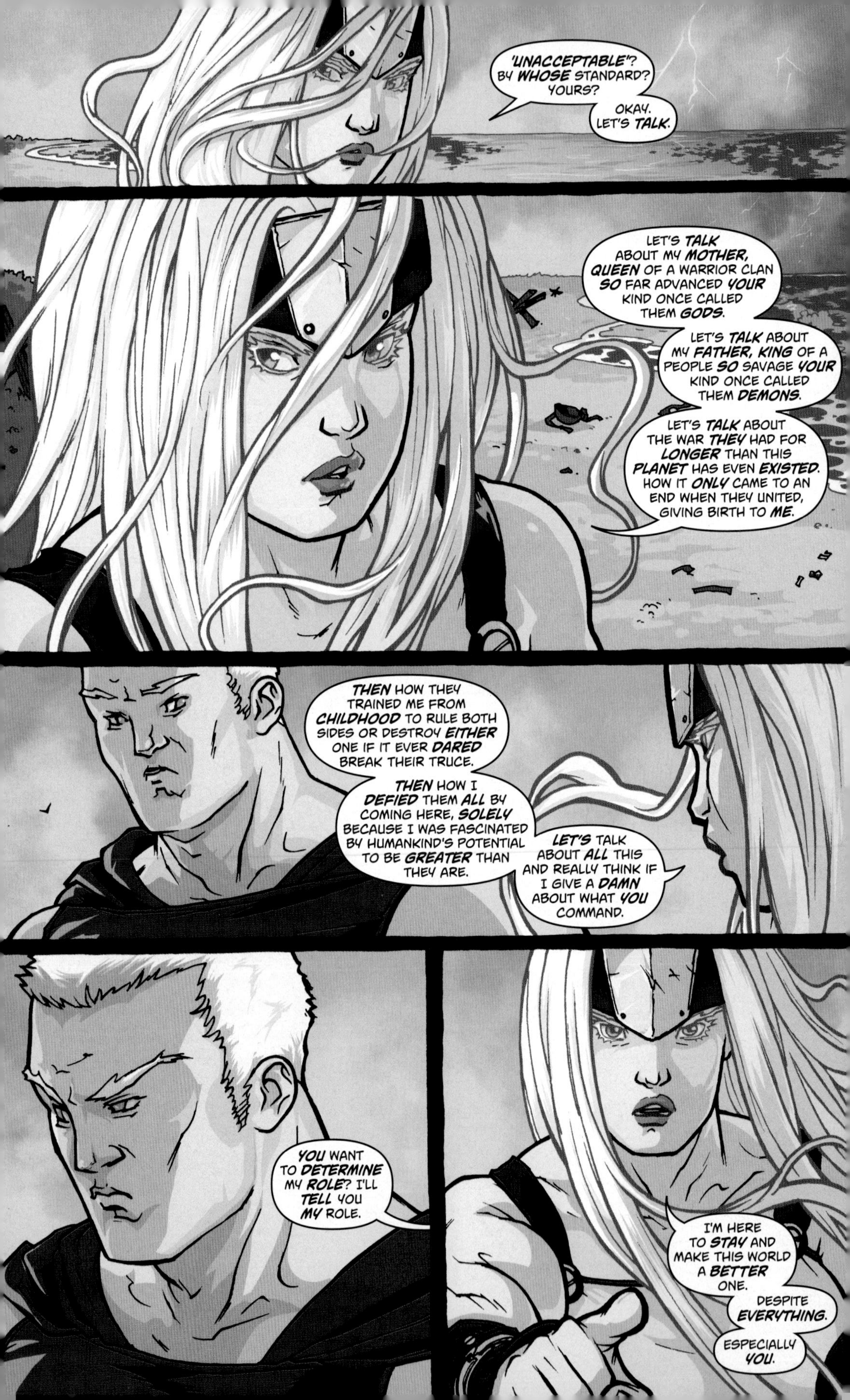
'UNACCEPTABLE'? BY WHOSE STANDARD? YOURS?
OKAY. LET'S TALK.
LET'S TALK ABOUT MY MOTHER, QUEEN OF A WARRIOR CLAN SO FAR ADVANCED YOUR KIND ONCE CALLED THEM GODS.
LET'S TALK ABOUT MY FATHER, KING OF A PEOPLE SO SAVAGE YOUR KIND ONCE CALLED THEM DEMONS.
LET'S TALK ABOUT THE WAR THEY HAD FOR LONGER THAN THIS PLANET HAS EVEN EXISTED. HOW IT ONLY CAME TO AN END WHEN THEY UNITED, GIVING BIRTH TO ME.
THEN HOW THEY TRAINED ME FROM CHILDHOOD TO RULE BOTH SIDES OR DESTROY EITHER ONE IF IT EVER DARED BREAK THEIR TRUCE.
THEN HOW I DEFIED THEM ALL BY COMING HERE, SOLELY BECAUSE I WAS FASCINATED BY HUMANKIND'S POTENTIAL TO BE GREATER THAN THEY ARE.
LET'S TALK ABOUT ALL THIS AND REALLY THINK IF I GIVE A DAMN ABOUT WHAT YOU COMMAND.
YOU WANT TO DETERMINE MY ROLE? I'LL TELL YOU MY ROLE.
I'M HERE TO STAY AND MAKE THIS WORLD A BETTER ONE.
DESPITE EVERYTHING.
ESPECIALLY YOU.

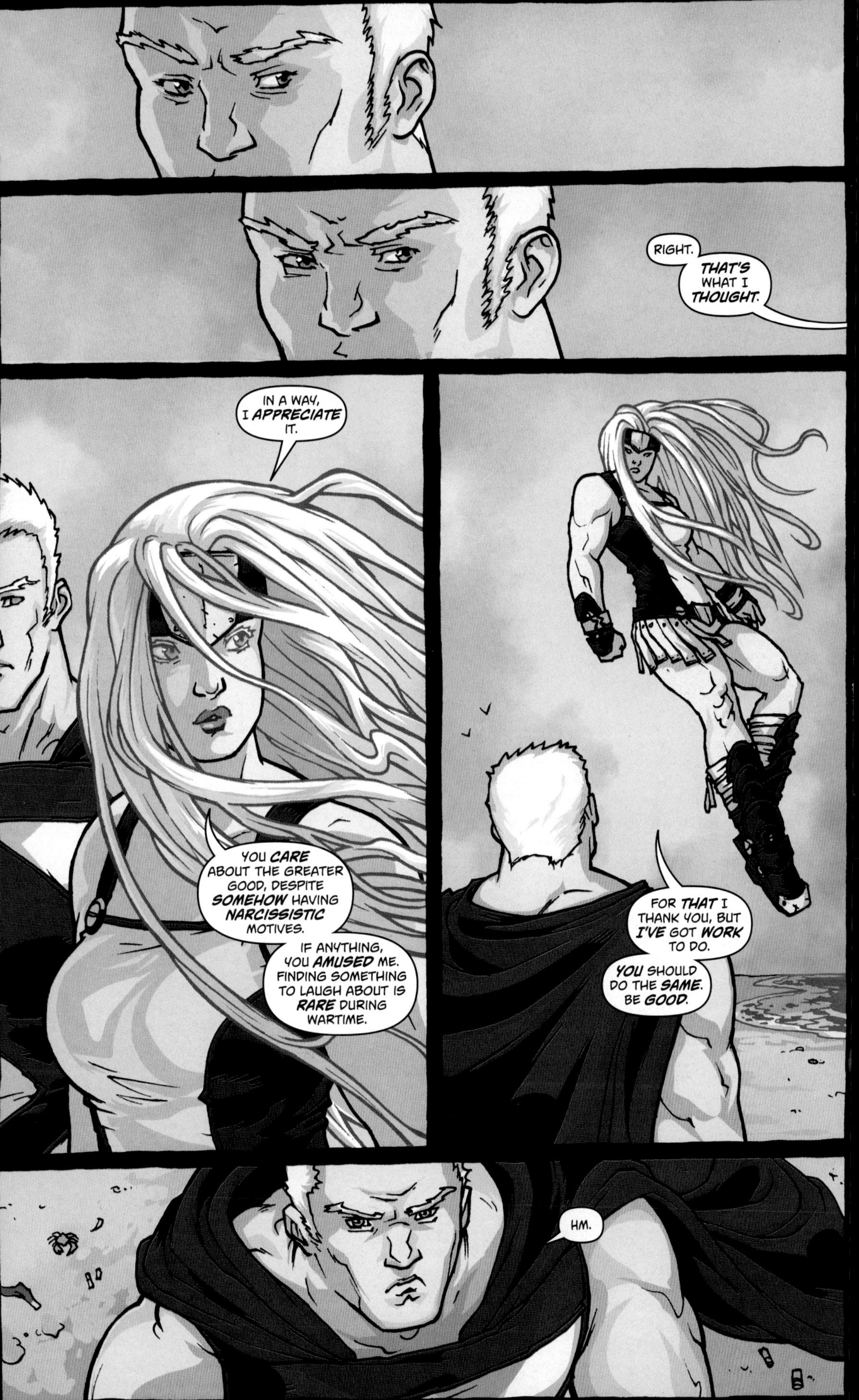

RIGHT. THAT'S WHAT I THOUGHT.
IN A WAY, I APPRECIATE IT.
YOU CARE ABOUT THE GREATER GOOD, DESPITE SOMEHOW HAVING NARCISSISTIC MOTIVES.
IF ANYTHING, YOU AMUSED ME. FINDING SOMETHING TO LAUGH ABOUT IS RARE DURING WARTIME.
FOR THAT I THANK YOU, BUT I'VE GOT WORK TO DO.
YOU SHOULD DO THE SAME. BE GOOD.
HM.

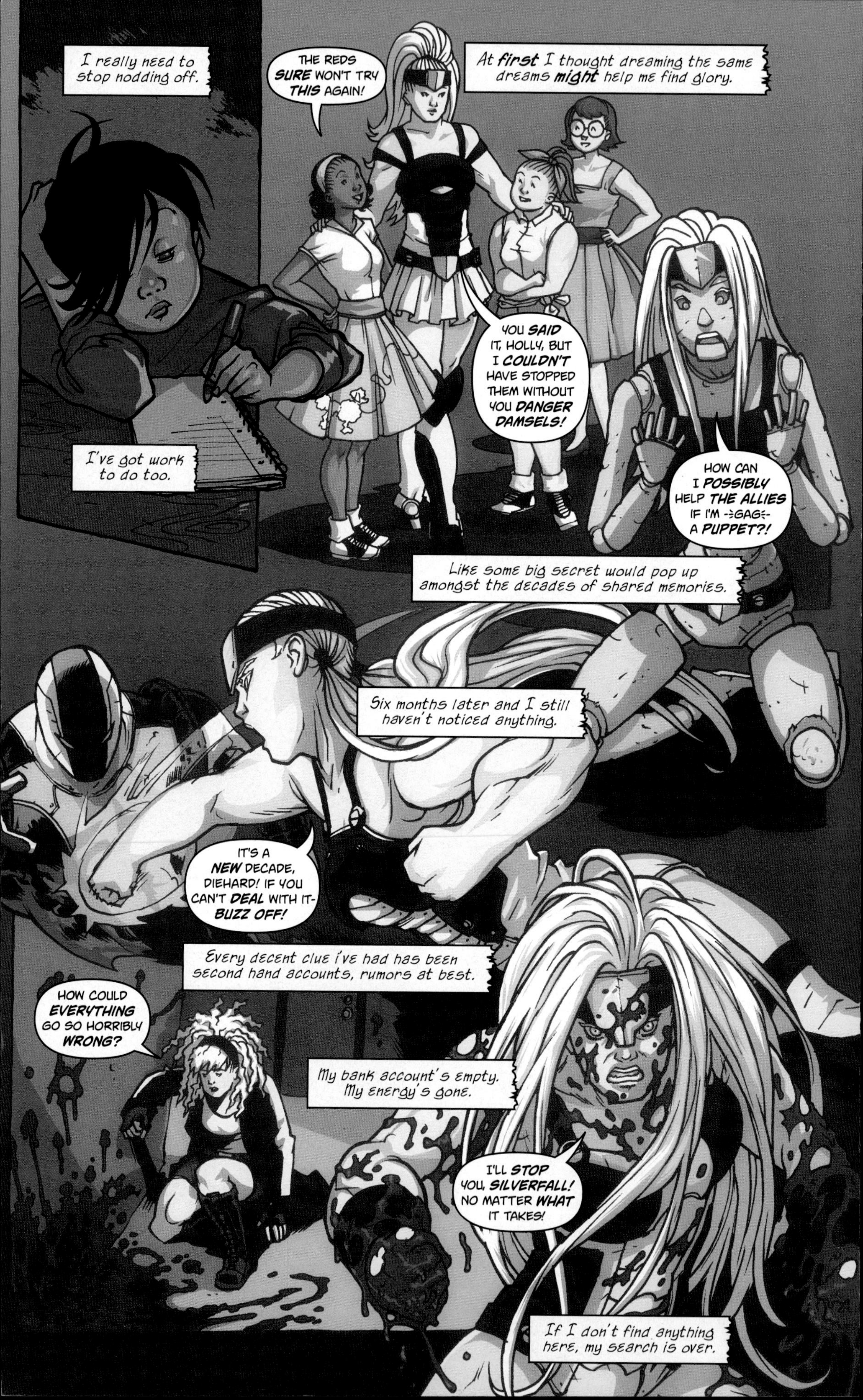
I really need to stop nodding off.
THE REDS SURE WON'T TRY THIS AGAIN!
At first I thought dreaming the same dreams might help me find glory.
YOU SAID IT, HOLLY, BUT I COULDN'T HAVE STOPPED THEM WITHOUT YOU DANGER DAMSELS!
I've got work to do too.
HOW CAN I POSSIBLY HELP THE ALLIES IF I'M -GAG- A PUPPET?!
Like some big secret would pop up amongst the decades of shared memories.
Six months later and I still haven't noticed anything.
IT'S A NEW DECADE, DIEHARD! IF YOU CAN'T DEAL WITH IT- BUZZ OFF!
Every decent clue i've had has been second hand accounts, rumors at best.
HOW COULD EVERYTHING GO SO HORRIBLY WRONG?
My bank account's empty. My energy's gone.
I'LL STOP YOU, SILVERFALL! NO MATTER WHAT IT TAKES!
If I don't find anything here, my search is over.

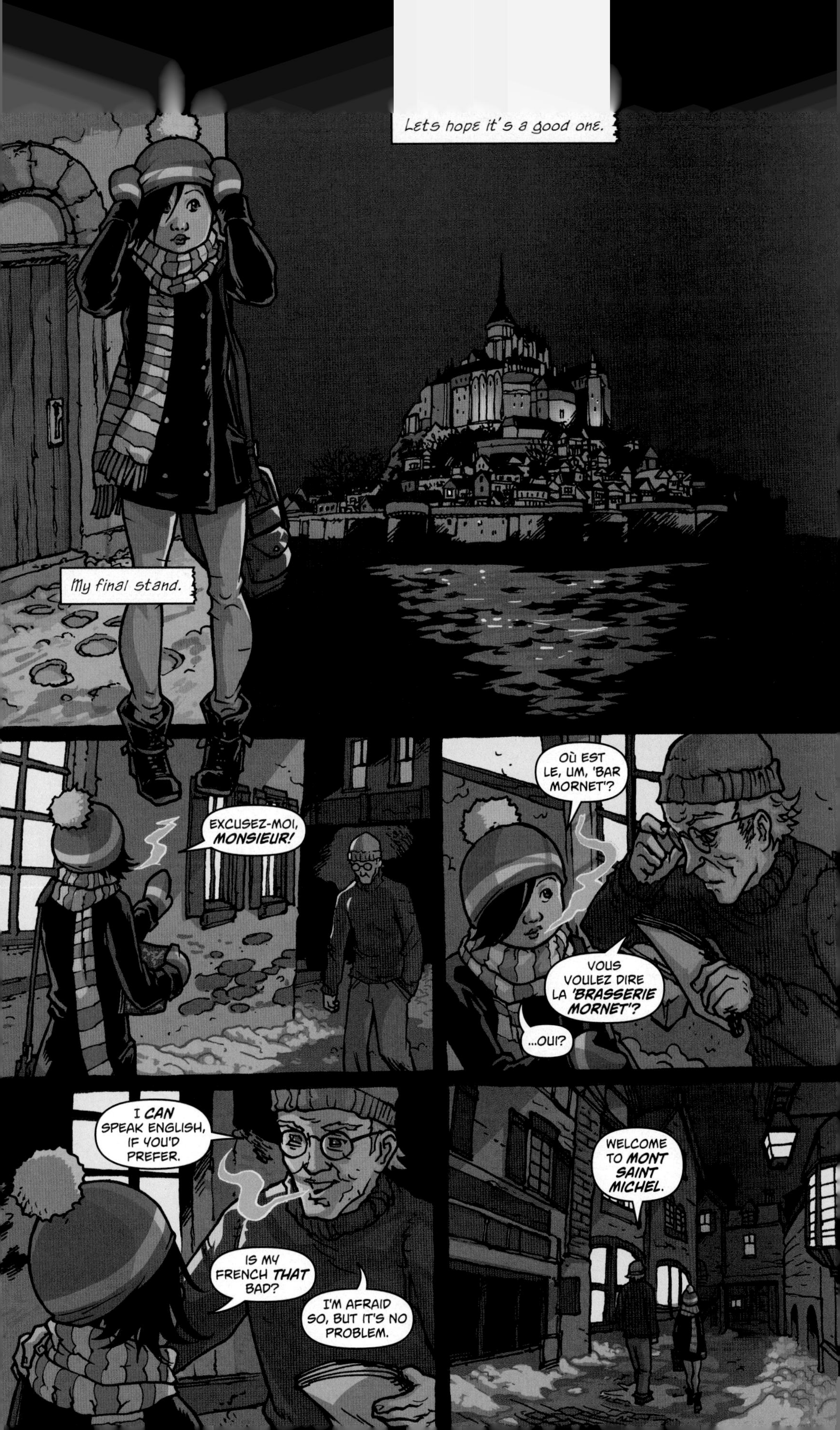
Lets hope it's a good one.
My final stand.
EXCUSEZ-MOI, MONSIEUR!
OÙ EST LE, UM, 'BAR MORNET'?
VOUS VOULEZ DIRE LA 'BRASSERIE MORNET'?
...OUI?
I CAN SPEAK ENGLISH, IF YOU'D PREFER.
IS MY FRENCH THAT BAD?
I'M AFRAID SO, BUT IT'S NO PROBLEM.
WELCOME TO MONT SAINT MICHEL.

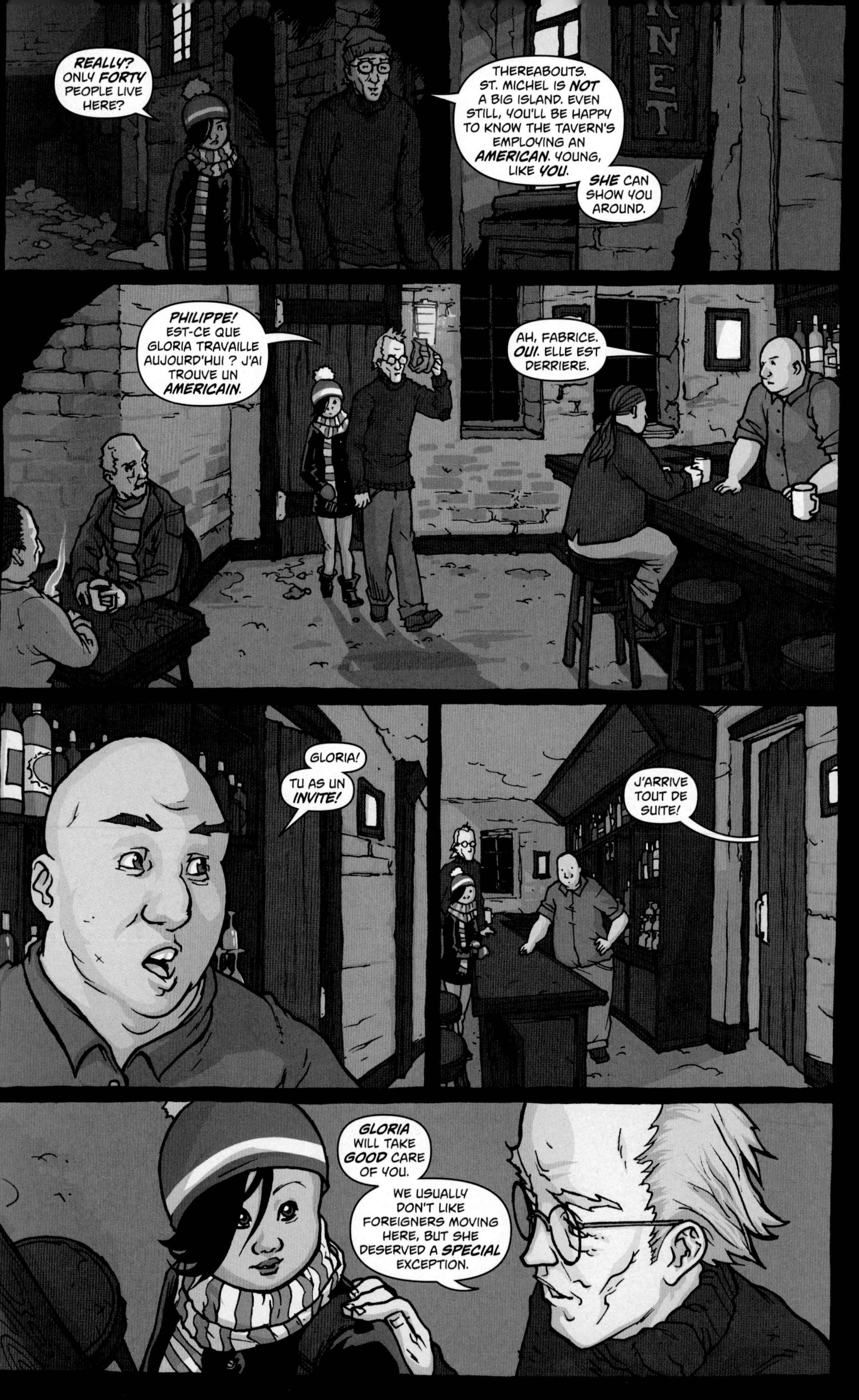

REALLY? ONLY FORTY PEOPLE LIVE HERE?
THEREABOUTS. ST. MICHEL IS NOT A BIG ISLAND. EVEN STILL, YOU'LL BE HAPPY TO KNOW THE TAVERN'S EMPLOYING AN AMERICAN. YOUNG, LIKE YOU.
SHE CAN SHOW YOU AROUND.
PHILIPPE! EST-CE QUE GLORIA TRAVAILLE AUJOURD'HUI ? J'AI TROUVE UN AMERICAIN.
AH, FABRICE. OUI. ELLE EST DERRIERE.
GLORIA!
TU AS UN INVITE!
J'ARRIVE TOUT DE SUITE!
GLORIA WILL TAKE GOOD CARE OF YOU.
WE USUALLY DON'T LIKE FOREIGNERS MOVING HERE, BUT SHE DESERVED A SPECIAL EXCEPTION.

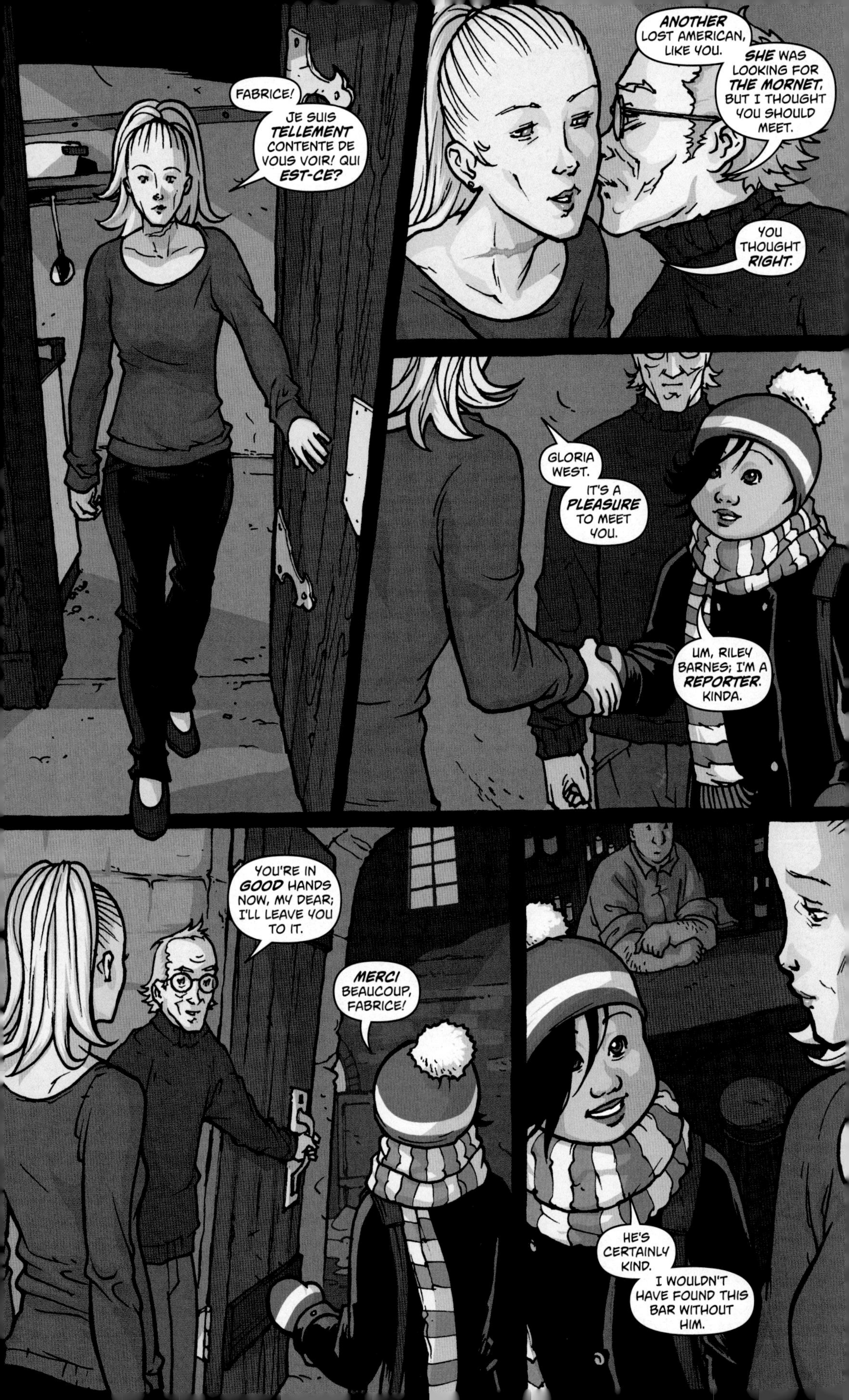
FABRICE!
JE SUIS TELLEMENT CONTENTE DE VOUS VOIR! QUI EST-CE?
ANOTHER LOST AMERICAN, LIKE YOU.
SHE WAS LOOKING FOR THE MORNET, BUT I THOUGHT YOU SHOULD MEET.
YOU THOUGHT RIGHT.
GLORIA WEST.
IT'S A PLEASURE TO MEET YOU.
UM, RILEY BARNES; I'M A REPORTER. KINDA.
YOU'RE IN GOOD HANDS NOW, MY DEAR; I'LL LEAVE YOU TO IT.
MERCI BEAUCOUP, FABRICE!
HE'S CERTAINLY KIND.
I WOULDN'T HAVE FOUND THIS BAR WITHOUT HIM.

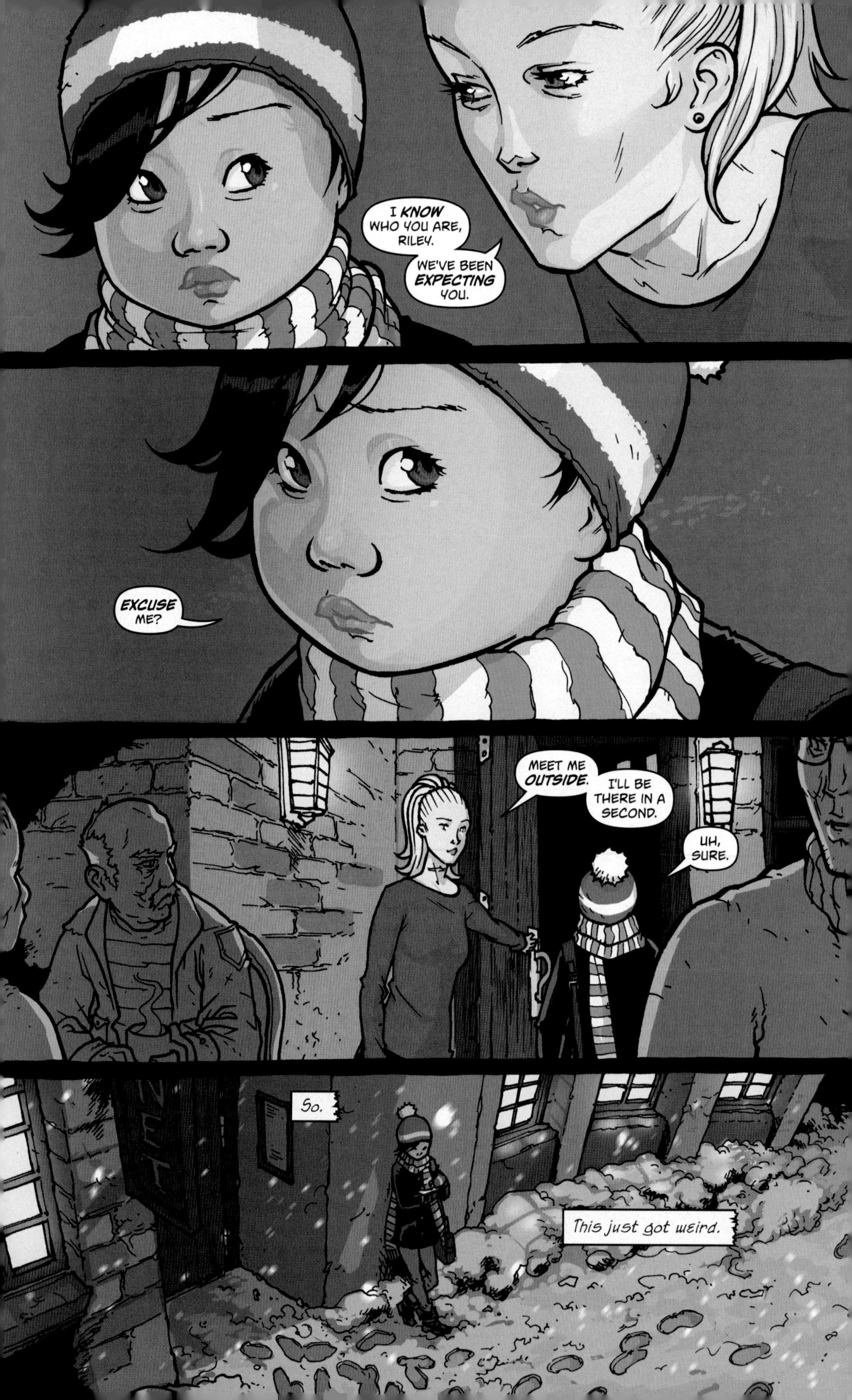
I KNOW WHO YOU ARE, RILEY.
WE'VE BEEN EXPECTING YOU.
EXCUSE ME?
MEET ME OUTSIDE.
I'LL BE THERE IN A SECOND.
UH, SURE.
So.
This just got weird.

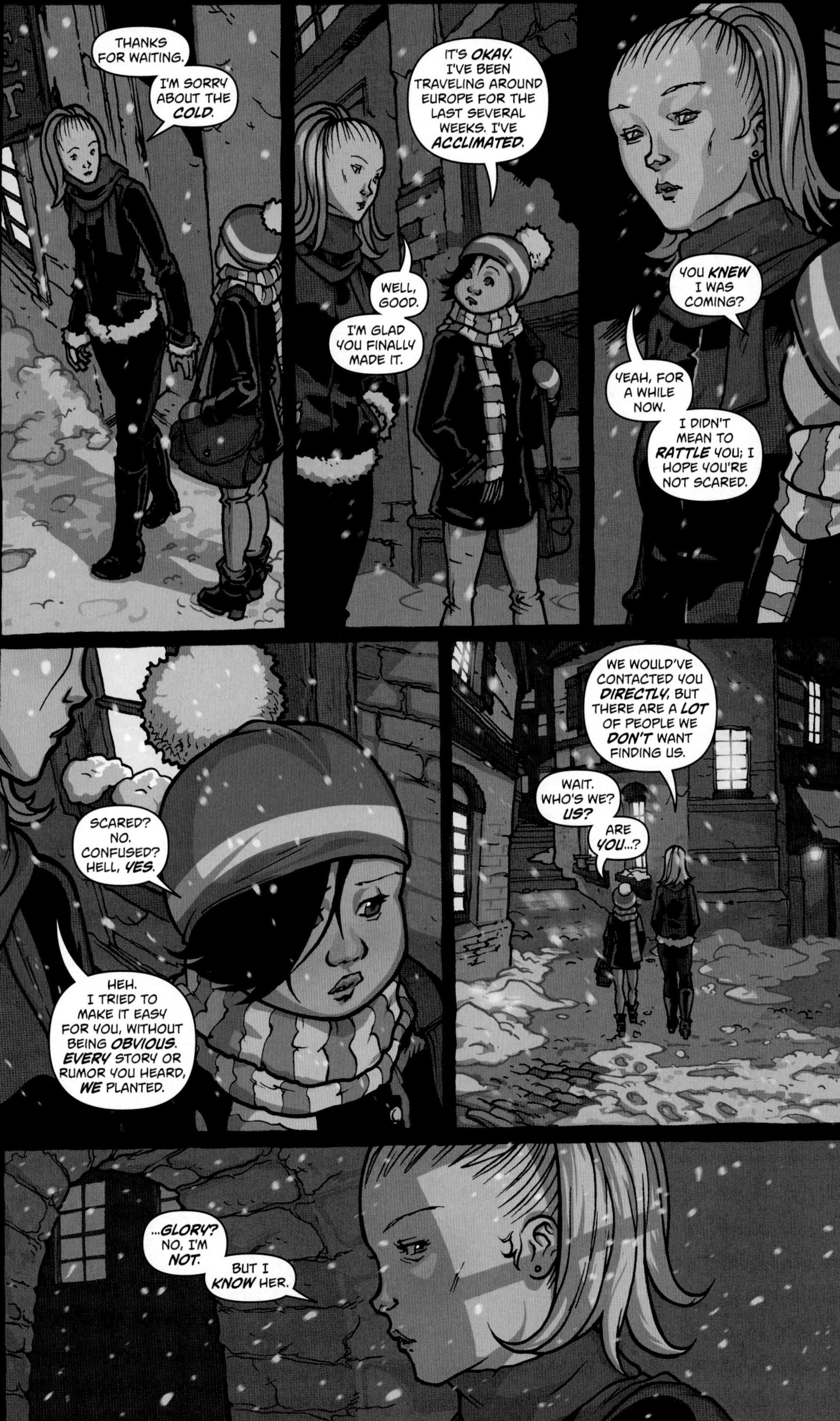

THANKS FOR WAITING.
I'M SORRY ABOUT THE COLD.
IT'S OKAY. I'VE BEEN TRAVELING AROUND EUROPE FOR THE LAST SEVERAL WEEKS. I'VE ACCLIMATED.
WELL, GOOD.
I'M GLAD YOU FINALLY MADE IT.
YOU KNEW I WAS COMING?
YEAH, FOR A WHILE NOW.
I DIDN'T MEAN TO RATTLE YOU; I HOPE YOU'RE NOT SCARED.
SCARED? NO. CONFUSED? HELL, YES.
HEH. I TRIED TO MAKE IT EASY FOR YOU, WITHOUT BEING OBVIOUS. EVERY STORY OR RUMOR YOU HEARD, WE PLANTED.
WE WOULD'VE CONTACTED YOU DIRECTLY, BUT THERE ARE A LOT OF PEOPLE WE DON'T WANT FINDING US.
WAIT. WHO'S WE? US?
ARE YOU...?
...GLORY? NO, I'M NOT.
BUT I KNOW HER.

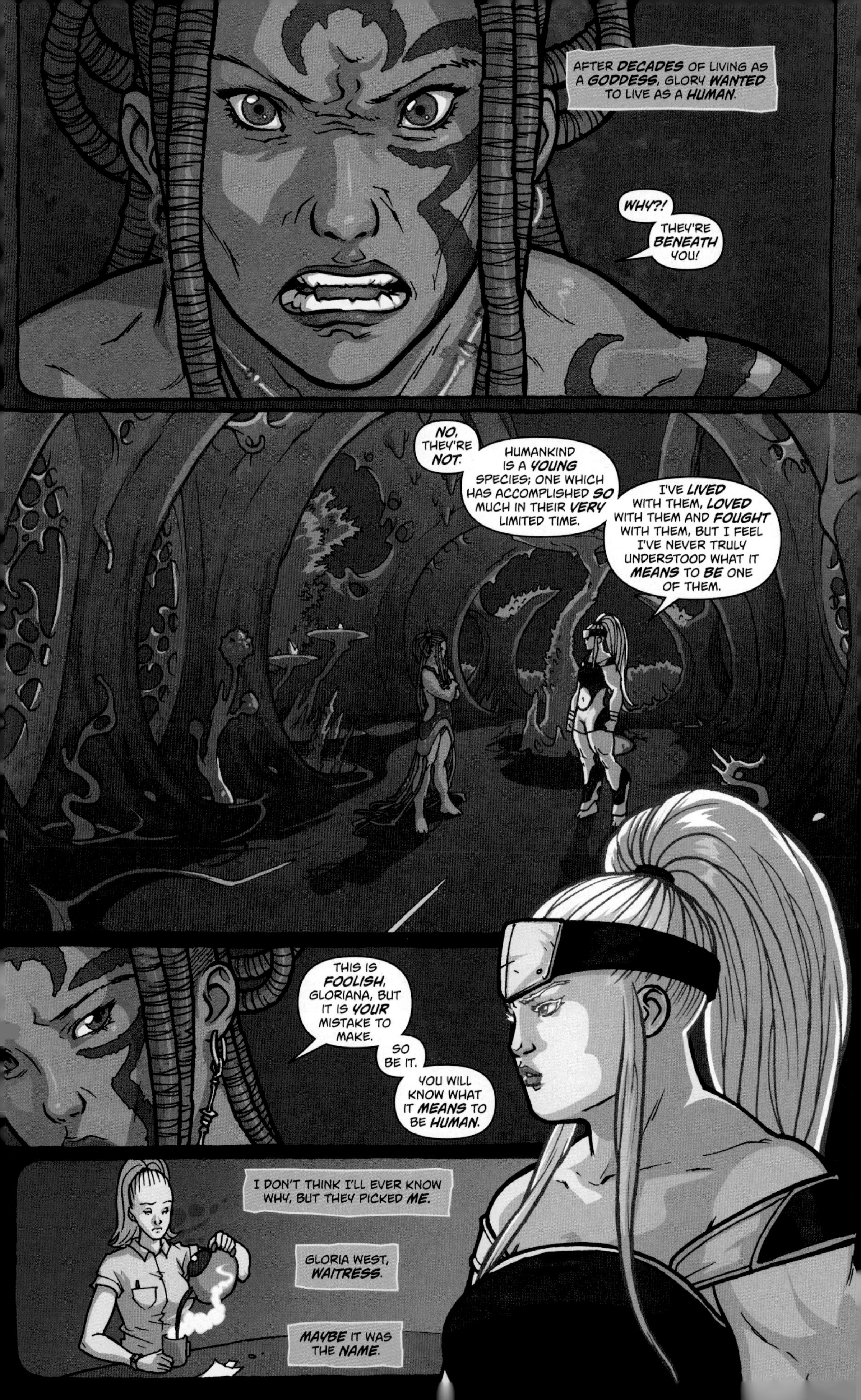
AFTER DECADES OF LIVING AS A GODDESS, GLORY WANTED TO LIVE AS A HUMAN.
WHY?! THEY'RE BENEATH YOU!
NO, THEY'RE NOT.
HUMANKIND IS A YOUNG SPECIES; ONE WHICH HAS ACCOMPLISHED SO MUCH IN THEIR VERY LIMITED TIME.
I'VE LIVED WITH THEM, LOVED WITH THEM AND FOUGHT WITH THEM, BUT I FEEL I'VE NEVER TRULY UNDERSTOOD WHAT IT MEANS TO BE ONE OF THEM.
THIS IS FOOLISH, GLORIANA, BUT IT IS YOUR MISTAKE TO MAKE.
SO BE IT.
YOU WILL KNOW WHAT IT MEANS TO BE HUMAN.
I DON'T THINK I'LL EVER KNOW WHY, BUT THEY PICKED ME.
GLORIA WEST, WAITRESS.
MAYBE IT WAS THE NAME.

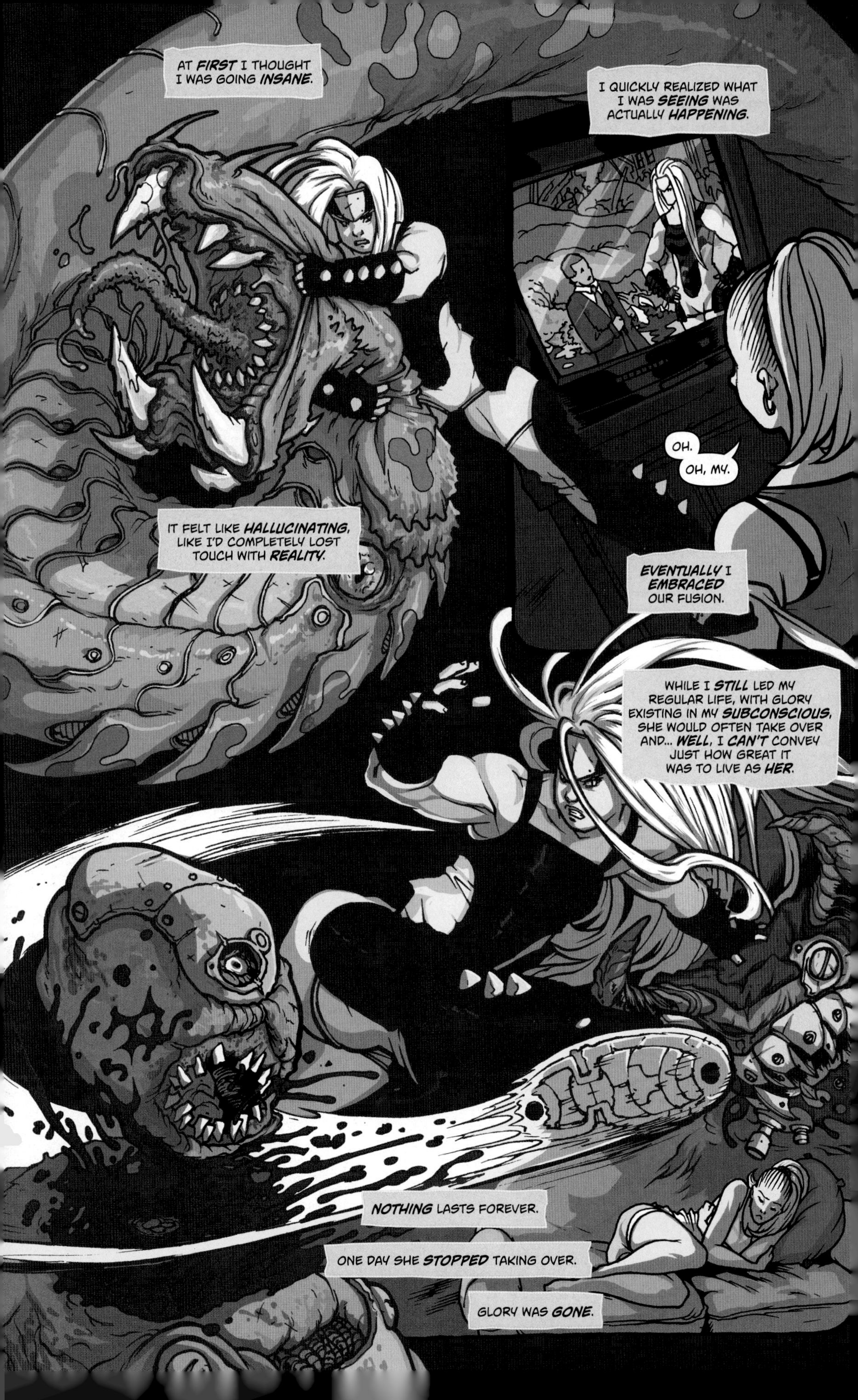
AT FIRST I THOUGHT I WAS GOING INSANE.
I QUICKLY REALIZED WHAT I WAS SEEING WAS ACTUALLY HAPPENING.
OH.
OH, MY.
IT FELT LIKE HALLUCINATING, LIKE I'D COMPLETELY LOST TOUCH WITH REALITY.
EVENTUALLY I EMBRACED OUR FUSION.
WHILE I STILL LED MY REGULAR LIFE, WITH GLORY EXISTING IN MY SUBCONSCIOUS, SHE WOULD OFTEN TAKE OVER AND... WELL, I CAN'T CONVEY JUST HOW GREAT IT WAS TO LIVE AS HER.
NOTHING LASTS FOREVER.
ONE DAY SHE STOPPED TAKING OVER.
GLORY WAS GONE.

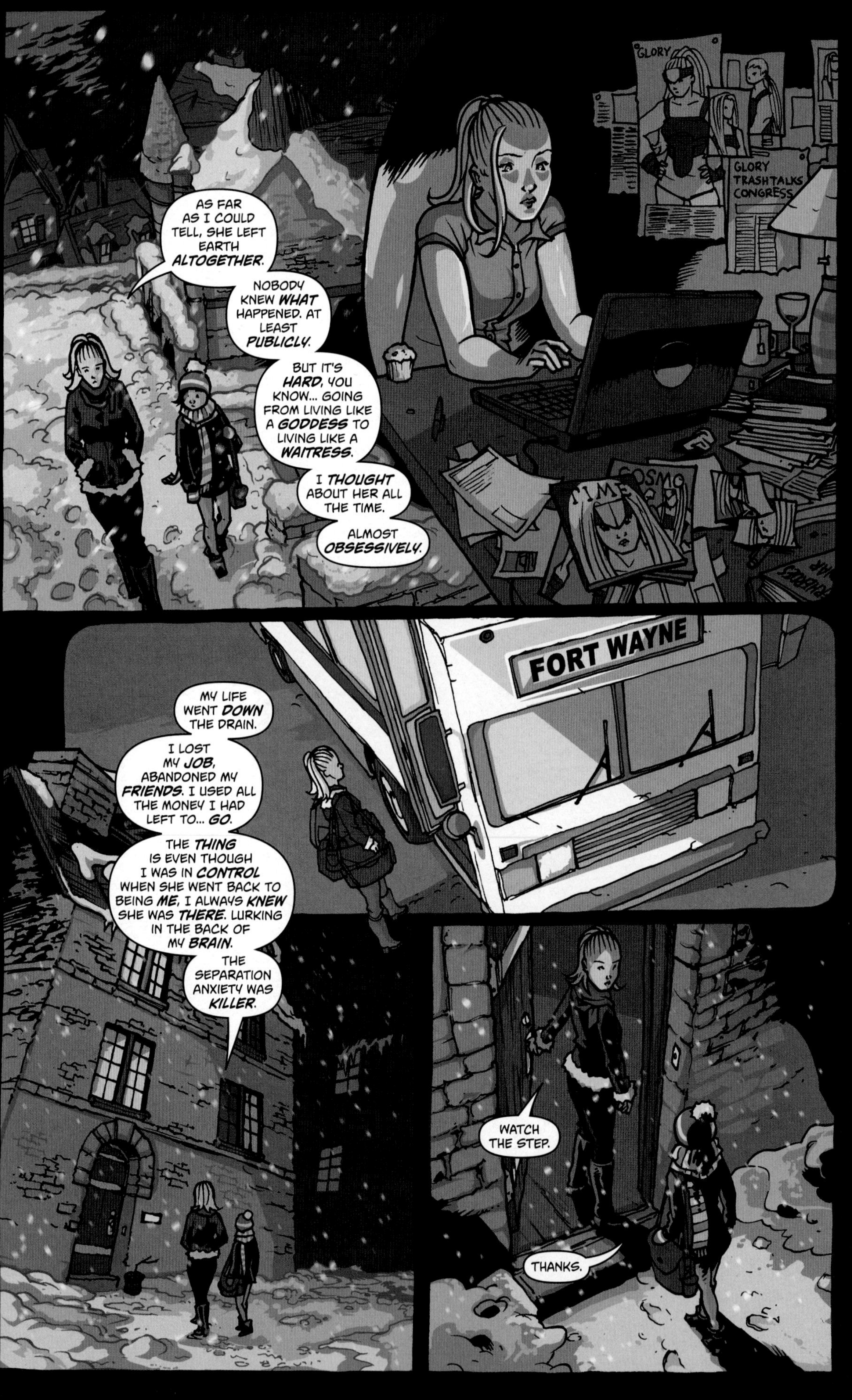

GLORY
GLORY TRASHTALKS CONGRESS
COSMO
TIME
AS FAR AS I COULD TELL, SHE LEFT EARTH ALTOGETHER.
NOBODY KNEW WHAT HAPPENED. AT LEAST PUBLICLY.
BUT IT'S HARD, YOU KNOW... GOING FROM LIVING LIKE A GODDESS TO LIVING LIKE A WAITRESS.
I THOUGHT ABOUT HER ALL THE TIME.
ALMOST OBSESSIVELY.
FORT WAYNE
MY LIFE WENT DOWN THE DRAIN.
I LOST MY JOB, ABANDONED MY FRIENDS. I USED ALL THE MONEY I HAD LEFT TO... GO.
THE THING IS EVEN THOUGH I WAS IN CONTROL WHEN SHE WENT BACK TO BEING ME, I ALWAYS KNEW SHE WAS THERE. LURKING IN THE BACK OF MY BRAIN.
THE SEPARATION ANXIETY WAS KILLER.
WATCH THE STEP.
THANKS.

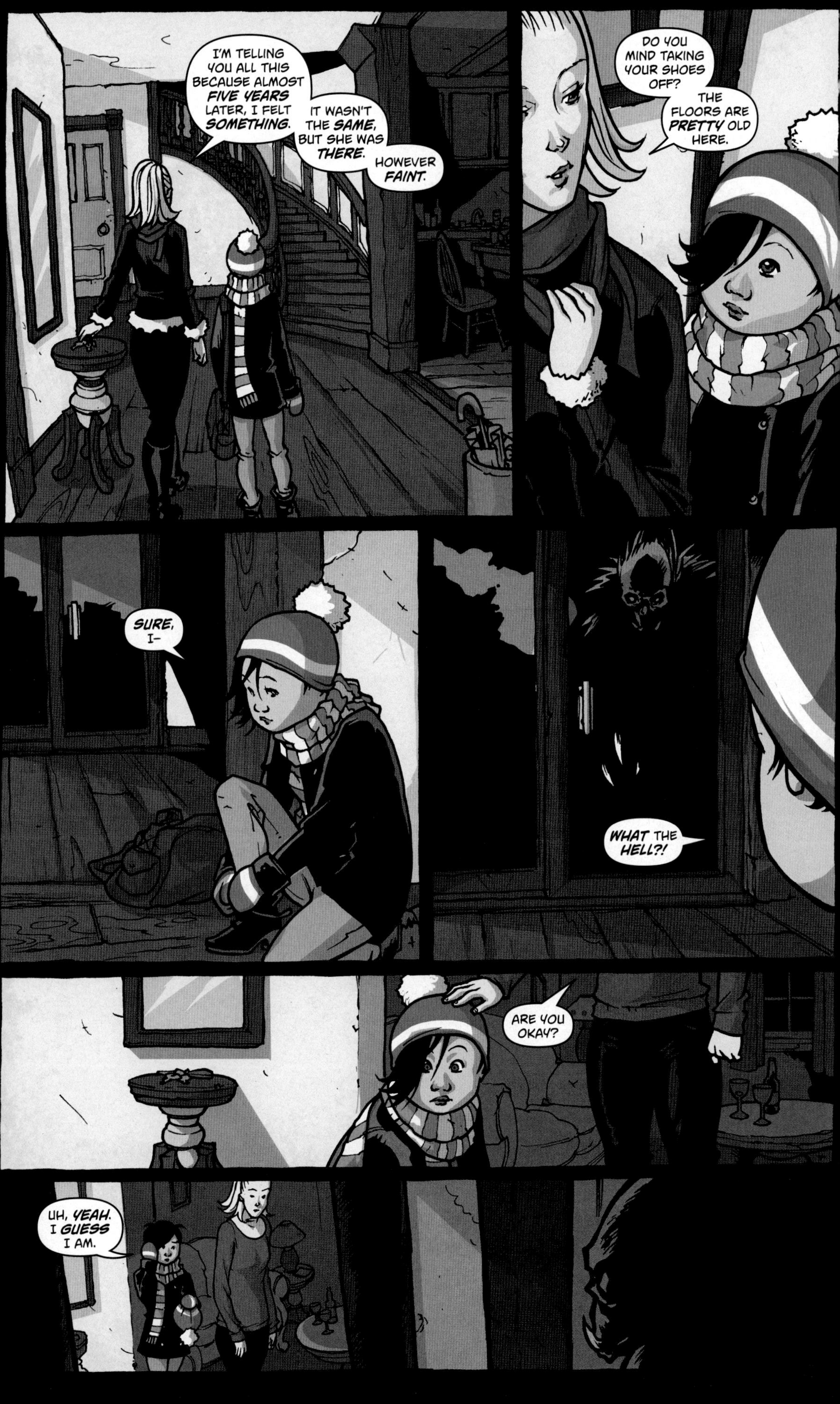
I'M TELLING YOU ALL THIS BECAUSE ALMOST FIVE YEARS LATER, I FELT SOMETHING.
IT WASN'T THE SAME, BUT SHE WAS THERE.
HOWEVER FAINT.
DO YOU MIND TAKING YOUR SHOES OFF?
THE FLOORS ARE PRETTY OLD HERE.
SURE, I–
WHAT THE HELL?!
ARE YOU OKAY?
UH, YEAH. I GUESS I AM.

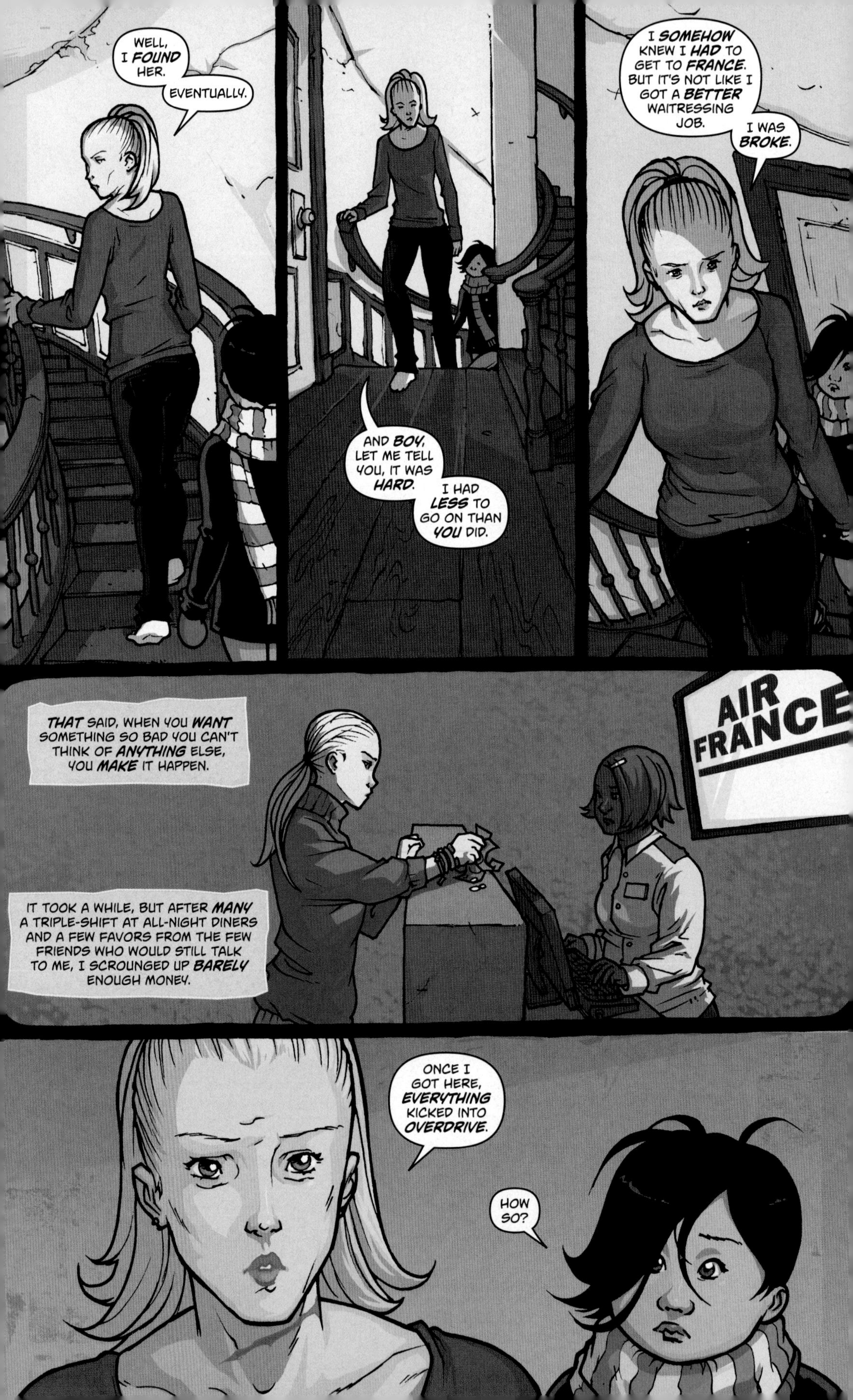
WELL, I FOUND HER.
EVENTUALLY.
AND BOY, LET ME TELL YOU, IT WAS HARD.
I HAD LESS TO GO ON THAN YOU DID.
I SOMEHOW KNEW I HAD TO GET TO FRANCE. BUT IT'S NOT LIKE I GOT A BETTER WAITRESSING JOB.
I WAS BROKE.
THAT SAID, WHEN YOU WANT SOMETHING SO BAD YOU CAN'T THINK OF ANYTHING ELSE, YOU MAKE IT HAPPEN.
AIR FRANCE
IT TOOK A WHILE, BUT AFTER MANY A TRIPLE-SHIFT AT ALL-NIGHT DINERS AND A FEW FAVORS FROM THE FEW FRIENDS WHO WOULD STILL TALK TO ME, I SCROUNGED UP BARELY ENOUGH MONEY.
ONCE I GOT HERE, EVERYTHING KICKED INTO OVERDRIVE.
HOW SO?

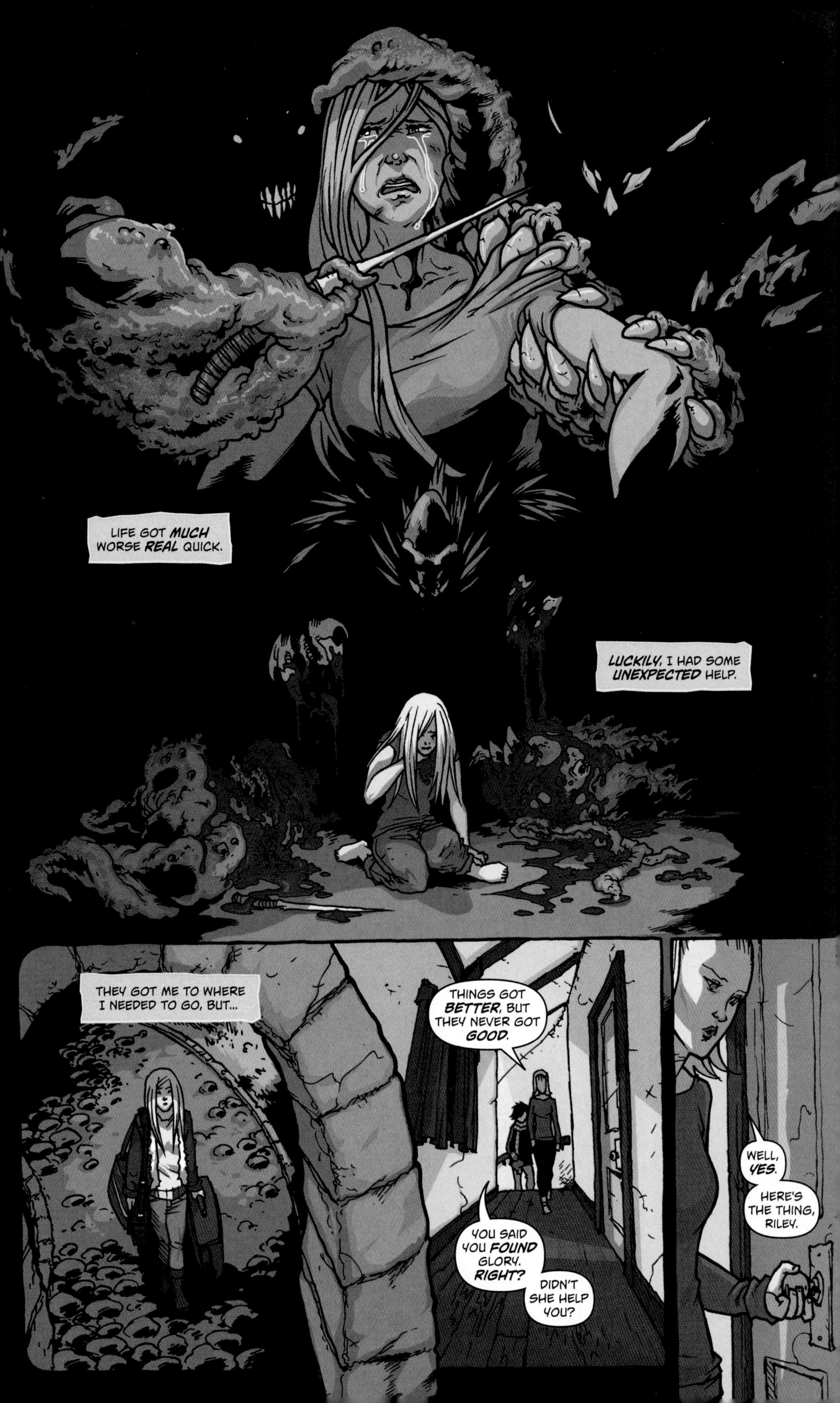
LIFE GOT MUCH WORSE REAL QUICK.
LUCKILY, I HAD SOME UNEXPECTED HELP.
THEY GOT ME TO WHERE I NEEDED TO GO, BUT...
THINGS GOT BETTER, BUT THEY NEVER GOT GOOD.
YOU SAID YOU FOUND GLORY. RIGHT?
DIDN'T SHE HELP YOU?
WELL, YES.
HERE'S THE THING, RILEY.

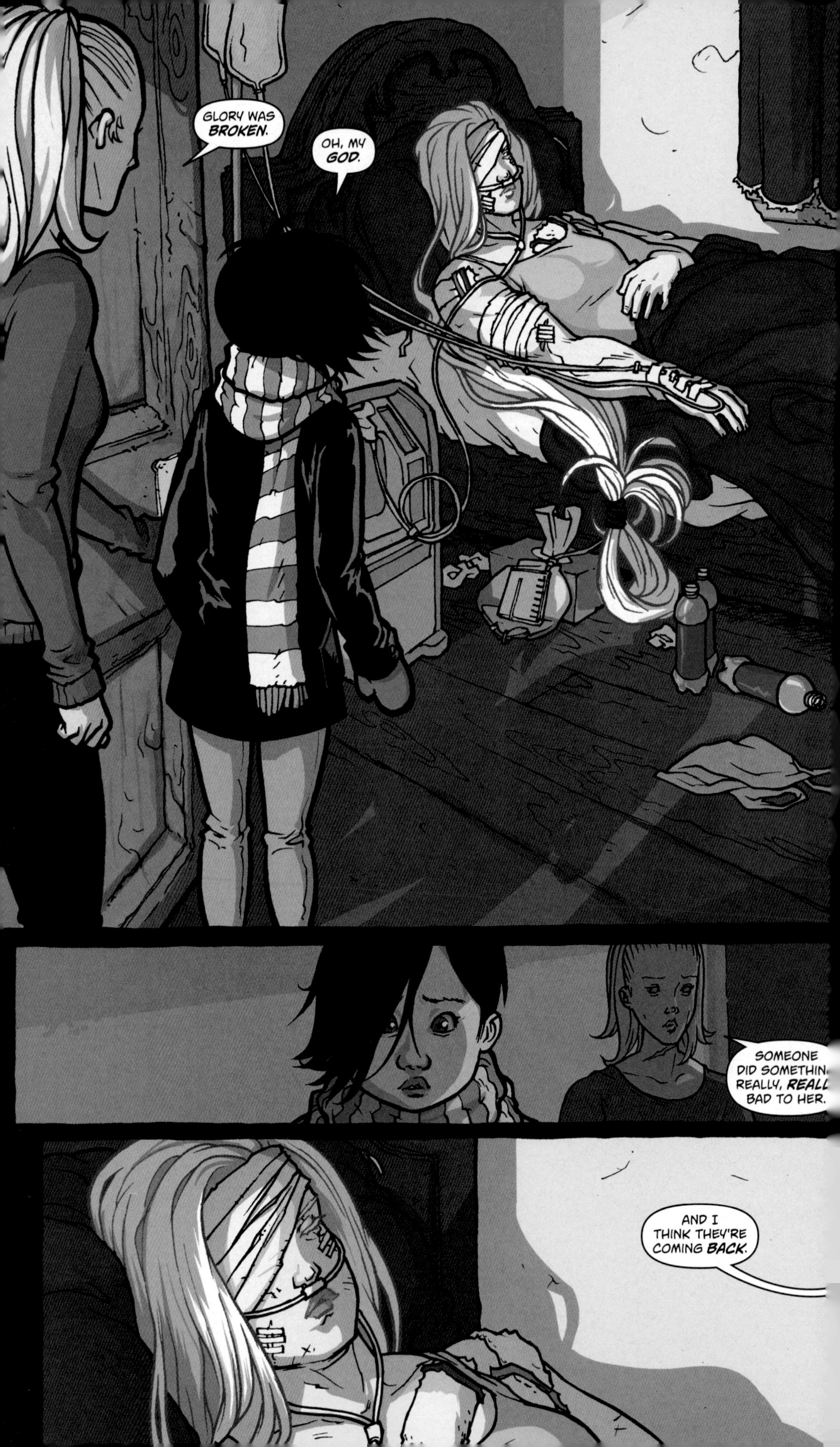
GLORY WAS BROKEN.
OH, MY GOD.
SOMEONE DID SOMETHIN REALLY, REALL BAD TO HER.
AND I THINK THEY'RE COMING BACK.

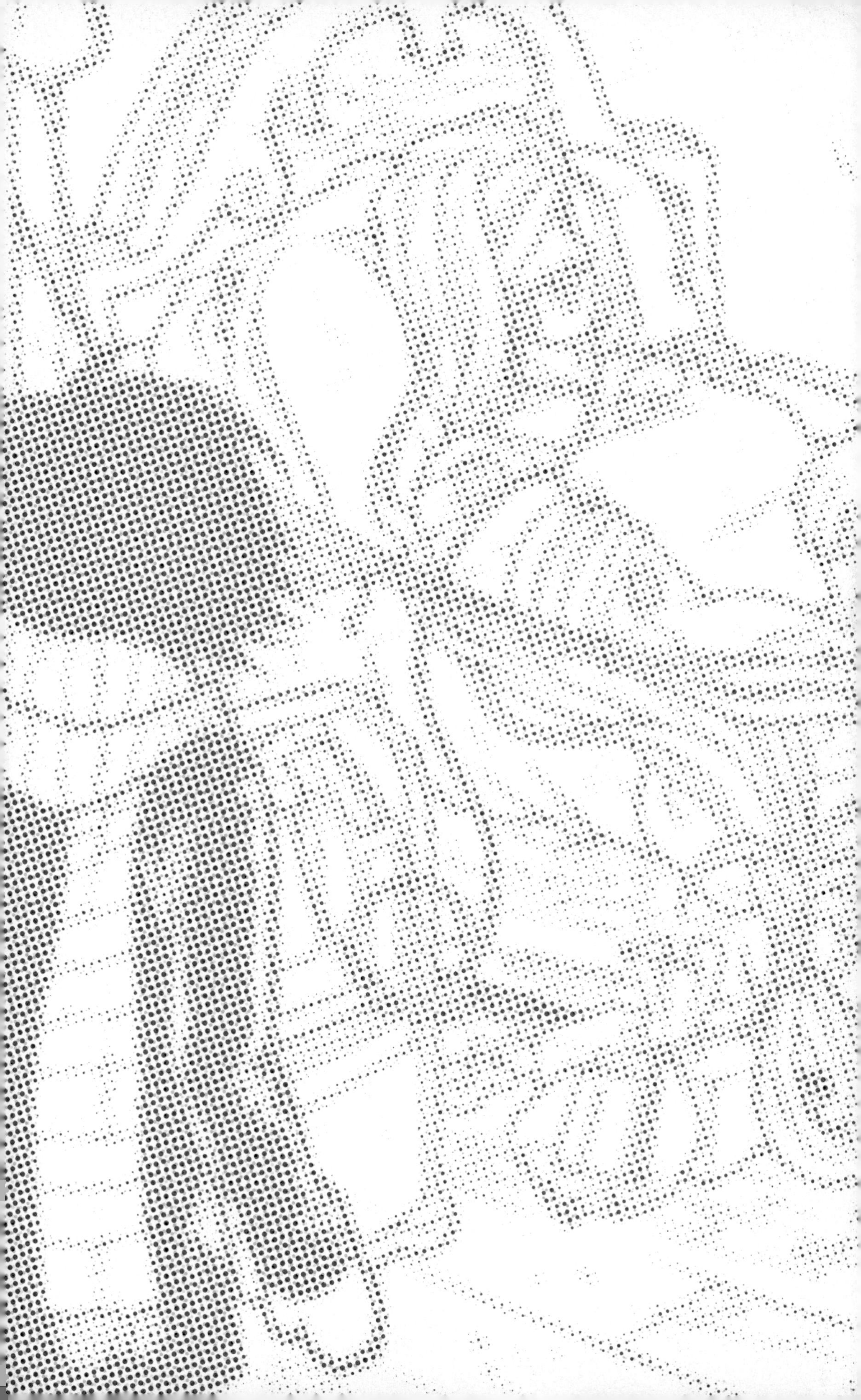

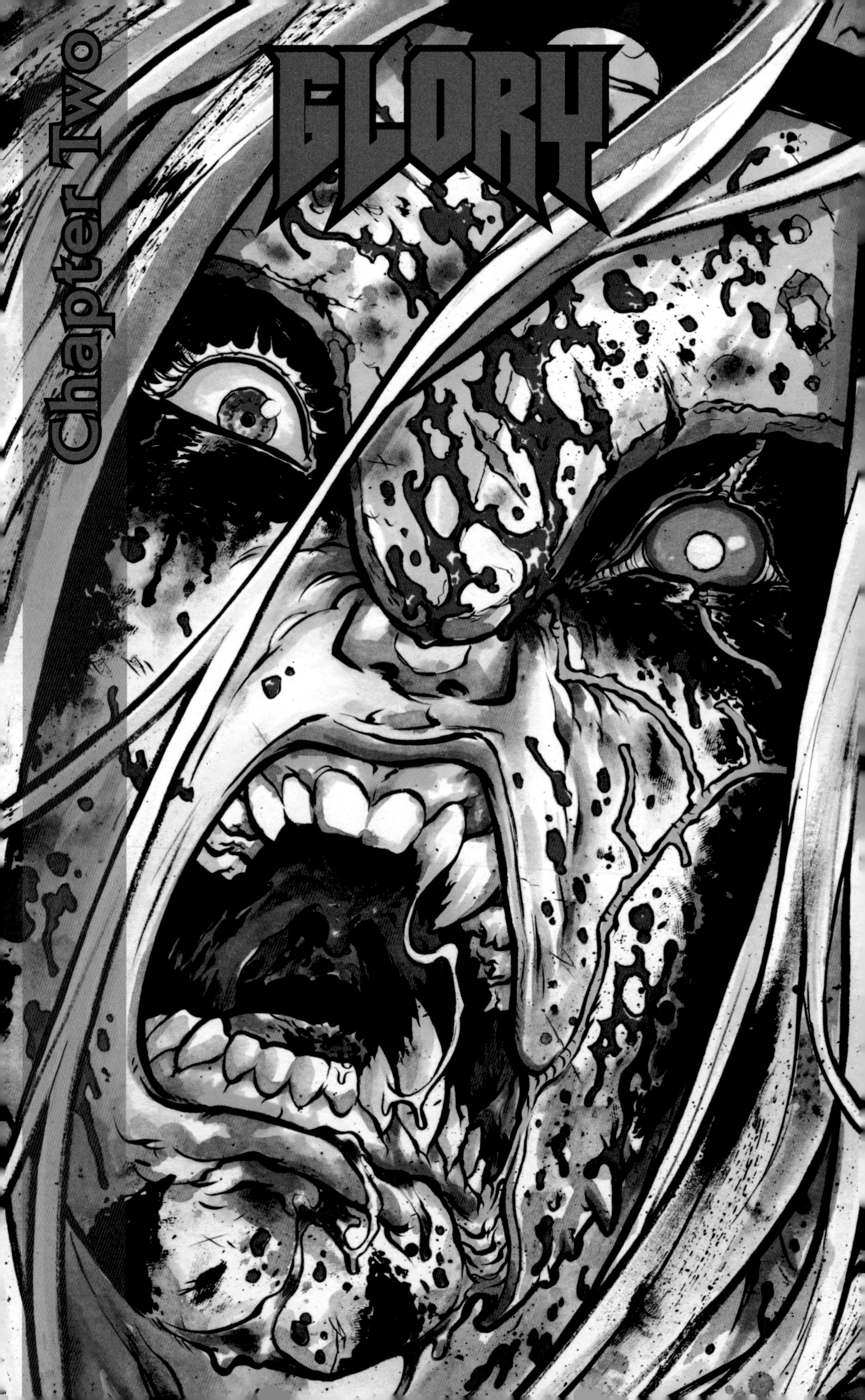
GLORY
Chapter Two

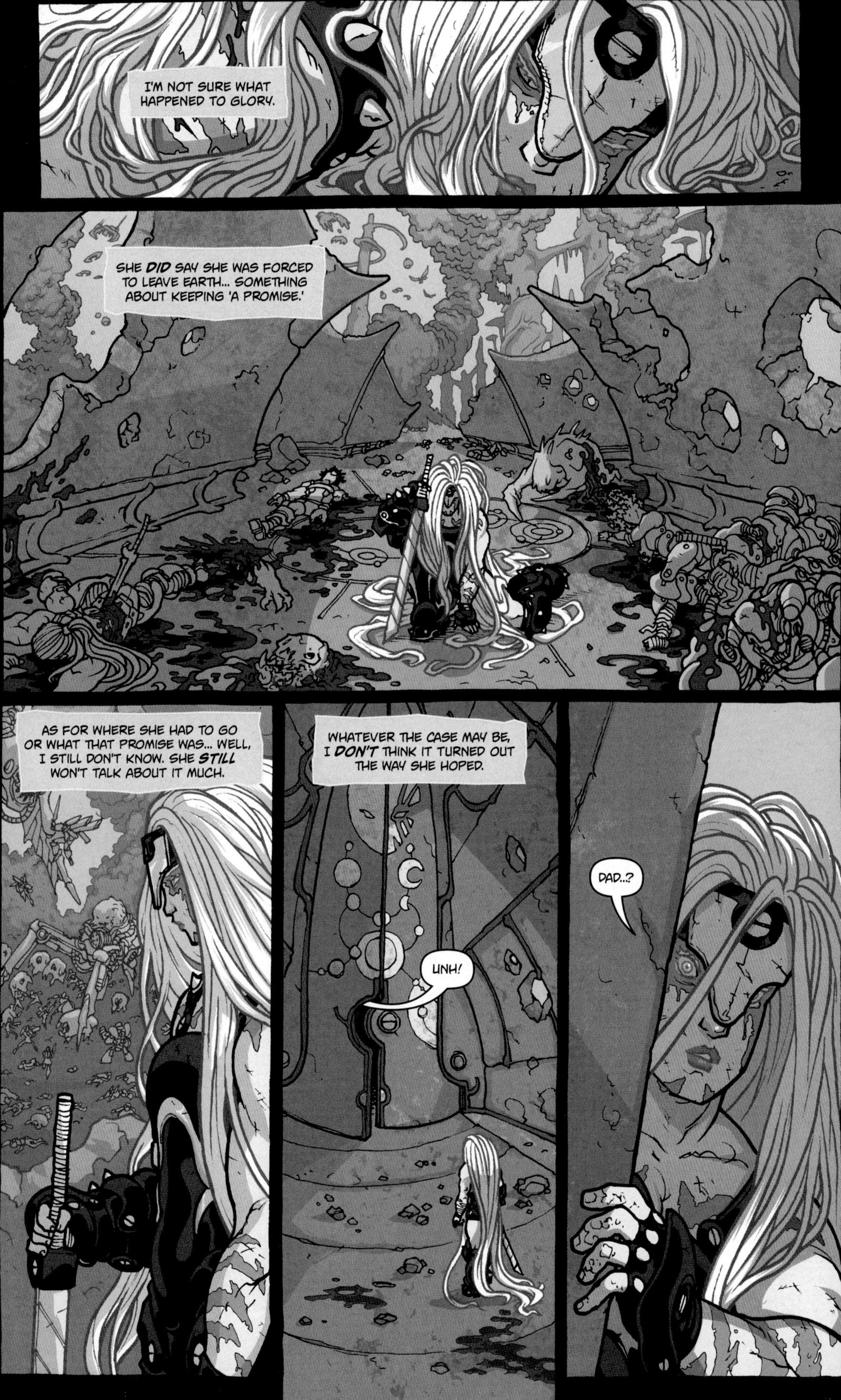
I'M NOT SURE WHAT HAPPENED TO GLORY.
SHE DID SAY SHE WAS FORCED TO LEAVE EARTH... SOMETHING ABOUT KEEPING 'A PROMISE.'
AS FOR WHERE SHE HAD TO GO OR WHAT THAT PROMISE WAS... WELL, I STILL DON'T KNOW. SHE STILL WON'T TALK ABOUT IT MUCH.
WHATEVER THE CASE MAY BE, I DON'T THINK IT TURNED OUT THE WAY SHE HOPED.
UNH!
DAD..?

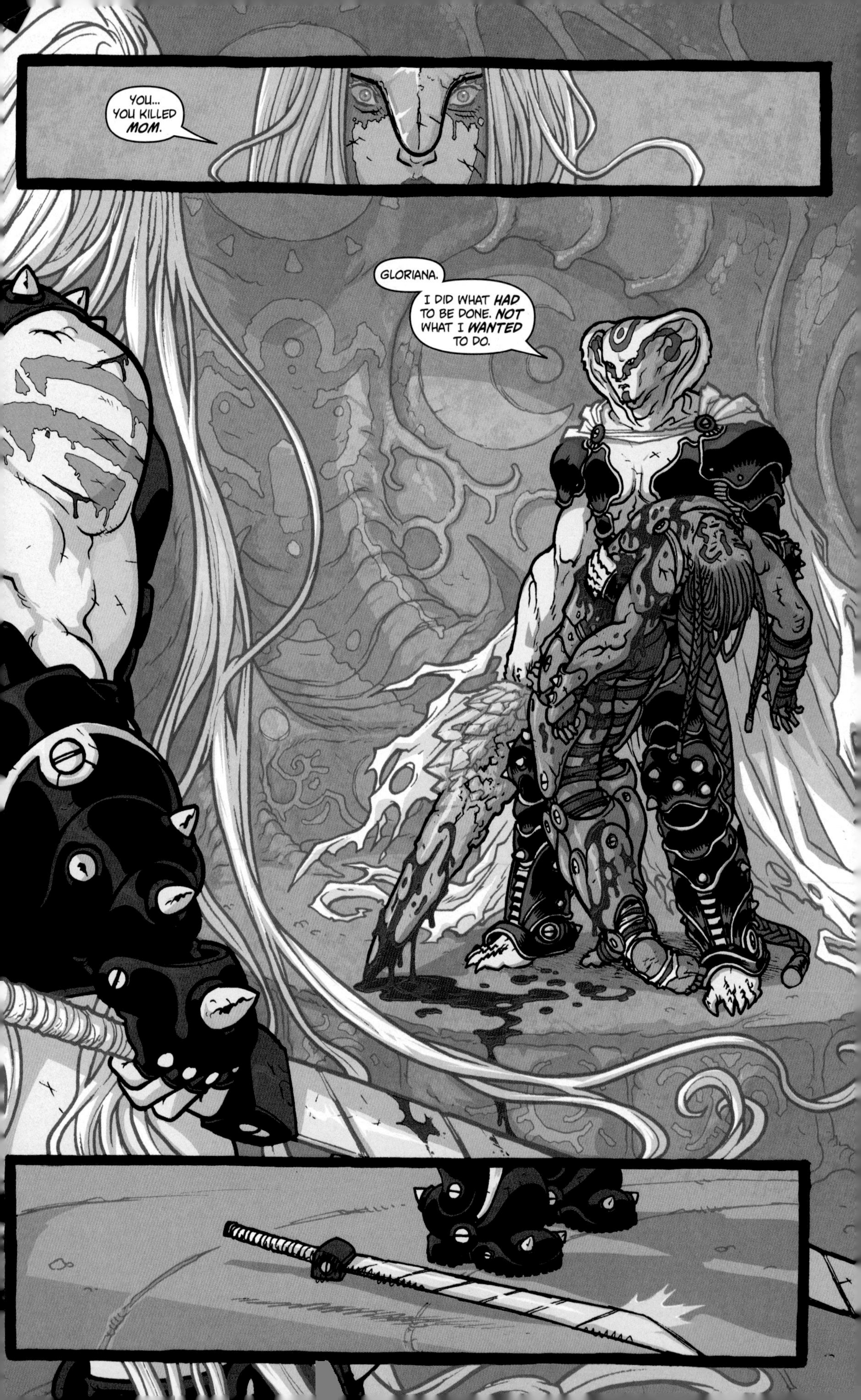
YOU... YOU KILLED MOM.
GLORIANA.
I DID WHAT HAD TO BE DONE. NOT WHAT I WANTED TO DO.

WHAT *HAD* TO BE DONE?!

IMAGE COMICS PRESENTS

SHE FOUGHT FOR *PEACE!* YOU FOUGHT FOR *GREED!* YOU WANTED TO *CONTROL* THULE... CONTROL *EARTH!*

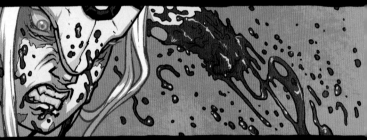

JOE KEATINGE
WRITER

CONTROL FOR *WHAT?* WHY? THE *'BETTER WAY'* YOU ALWAYS GO ON ABOUT? LOOK WHERE IT'S GOTTEN YOU!

ROSS CAMPBELL
ARTIST

MS,SHATIA HAMILTON
COLORIST

DOUGLAS E. SHERWOOD
LETTERER

ERIC STEPHENSON
EDITOR

SHE ENDED UP *DIFFERENT.*

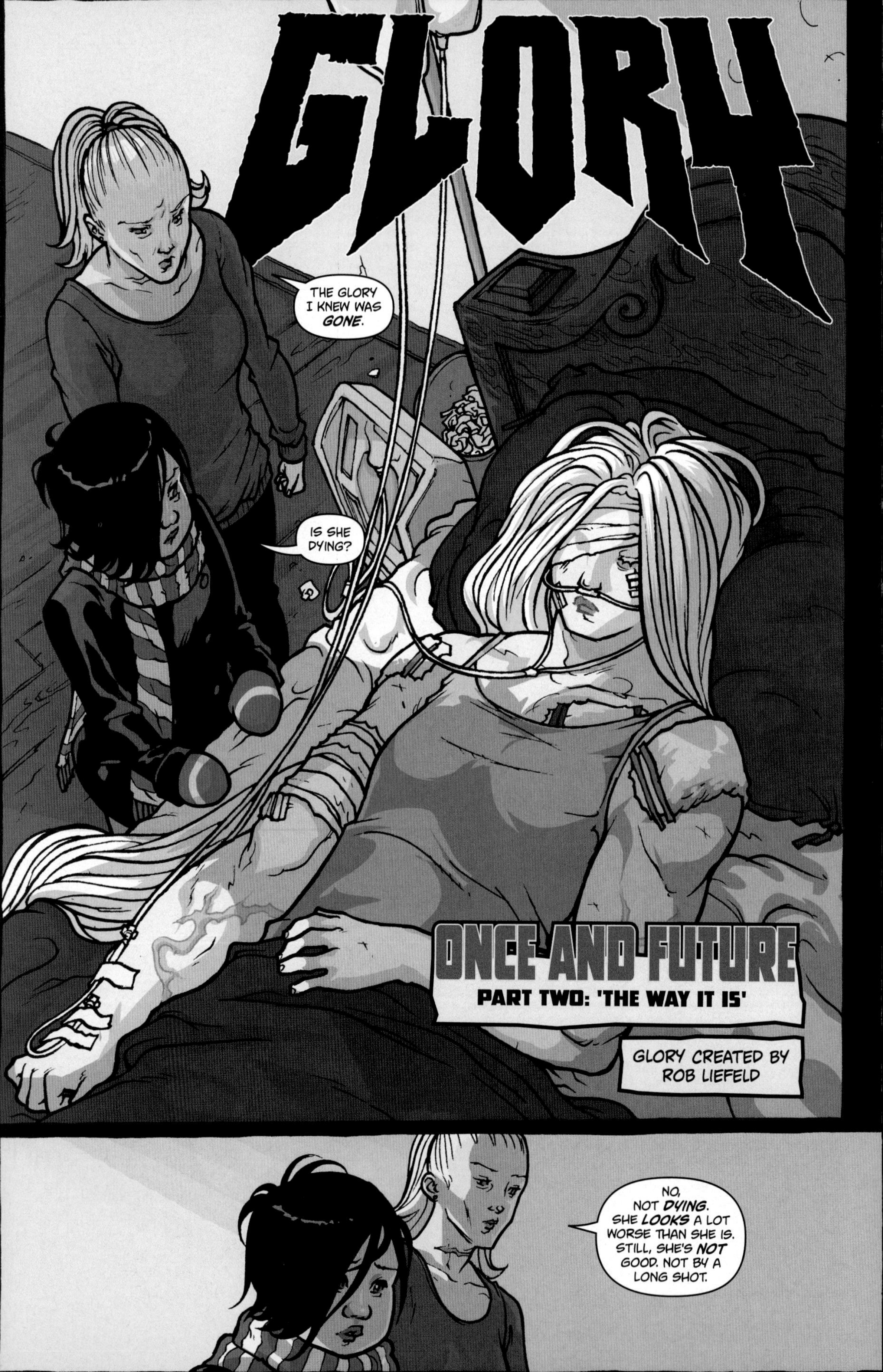
GLORY
THE GLORY I KNEW WAS *GONE*.
IS SHE DYING?
ONCE AND FUTURE
PART TWO: 'THE WAY IT IS'
GLORY CREATED BY ROB LIEFELD
NO, NOT *DYING*. SHE *LOOKS* A LOT WORSE THAN SHE IS. STILL, SHE'S *NOT* GOOD. NOT BY A LONG SHOT.

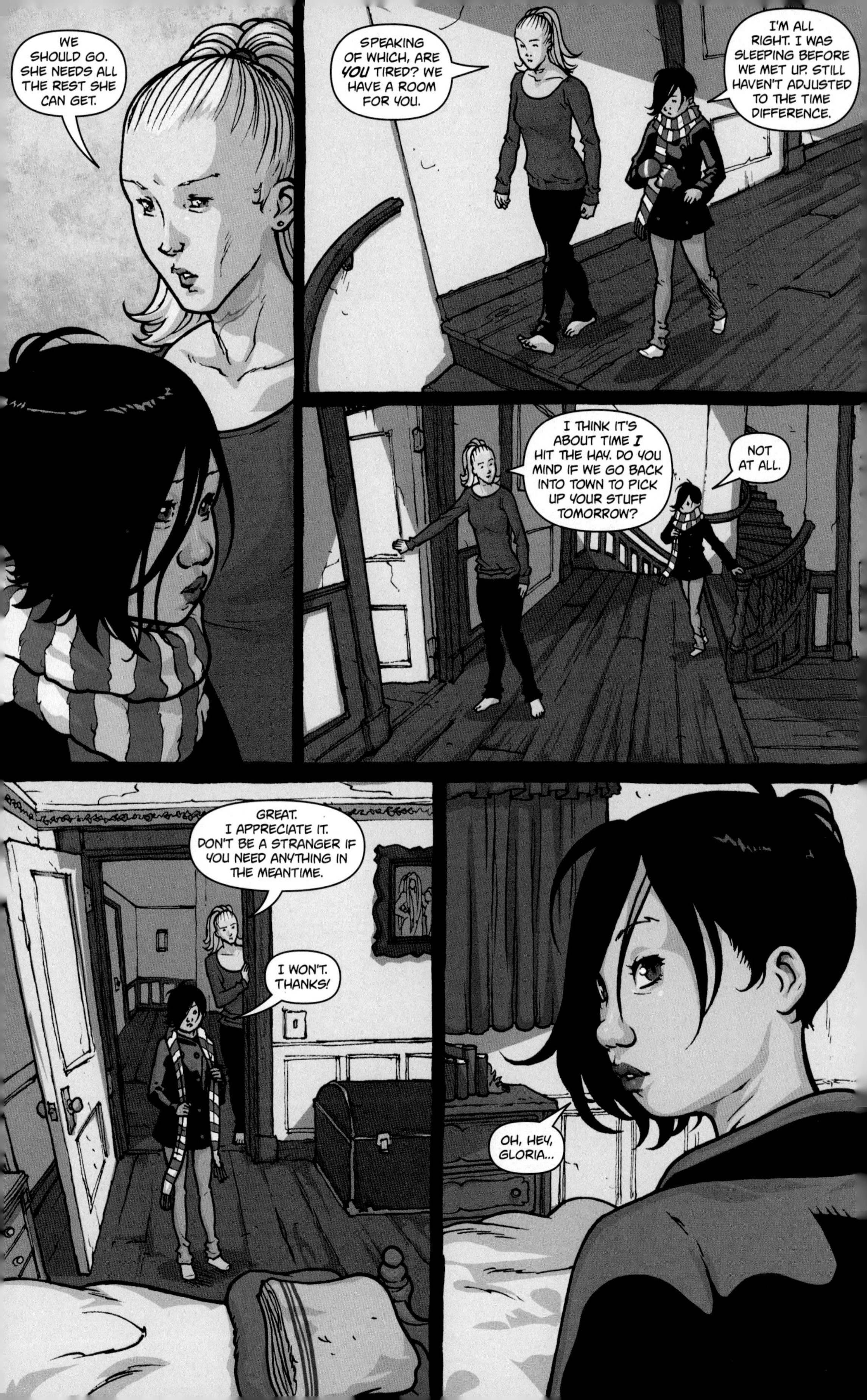
WE SHOULD GO. SHE NEEDS ALL THE REST SHE CAN GET.
SPEAKING OF WHICH, ARE *YOU* TIRED? WE HAVE A ROOM FOR YOU.
I'M ALL RIGHT. I WAS SLEEPING BEFORE WE MET UP. STILL HAVEN'T ADJUSTED TO THE TIME DIFFERENCE.
I THINK IT'S ABOUT TIME *I* HIT THE HAY. DO YOU MIND IF WE GO BACK INTO TOWN TO PICK UP YOUR STUFF TOMORROW?
NOT AT ALL.
GREAT. I APPRECIATE IT. DON'T BE A STRANGER IF YOU NEED ANYTHING IN THE MEANTIME.
I WON'T. THANKS!
OH, HEY, GLORIA...

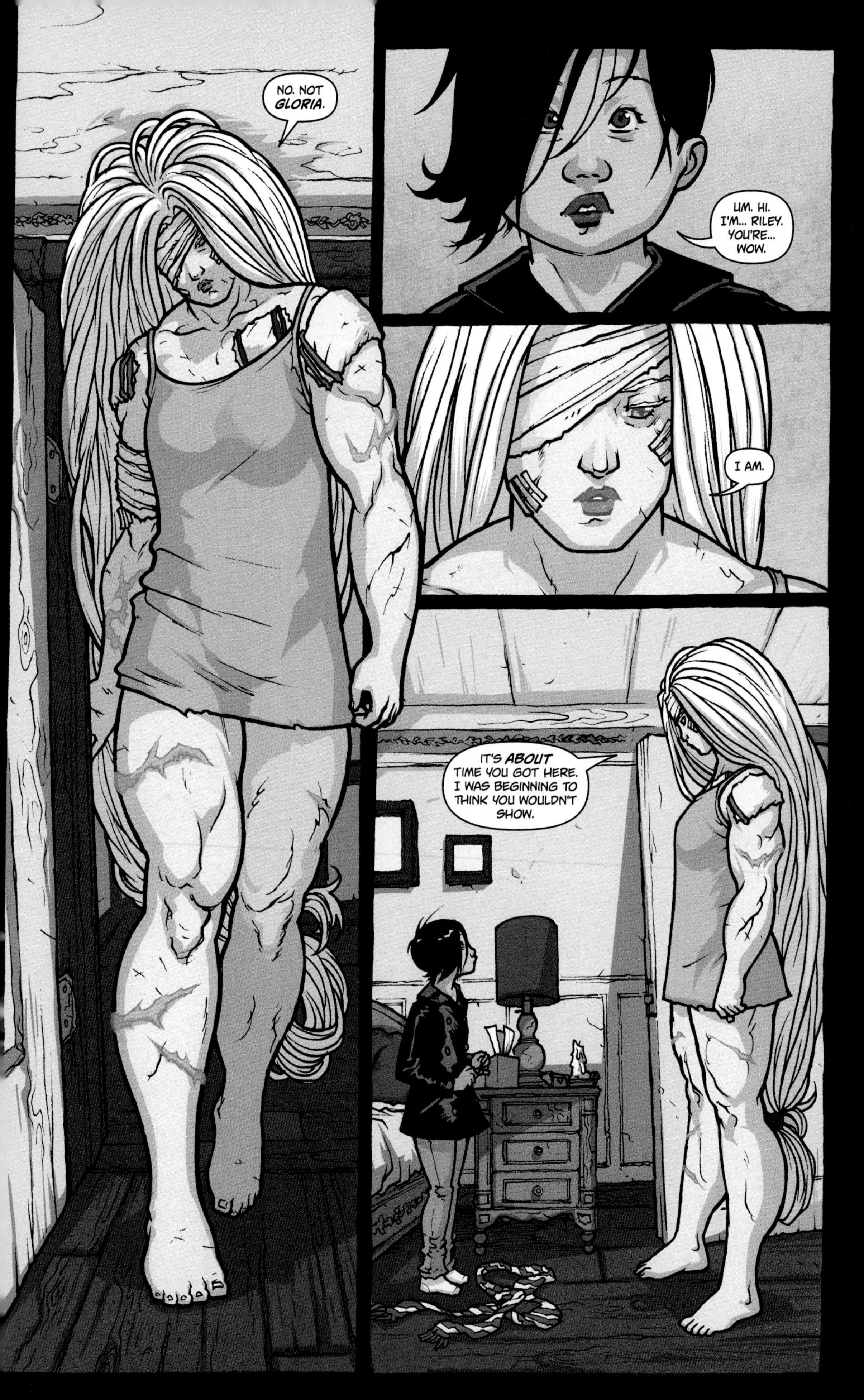
NO. NOT GLORIA.
UM. HI. I'M... RILEY. YOU'RE... WOW.
I AM.
IT'S ABOUT TIME YOU GOT HERE. I WAS BEGINNING TO THINK YOU WOULDN'T SHOW.

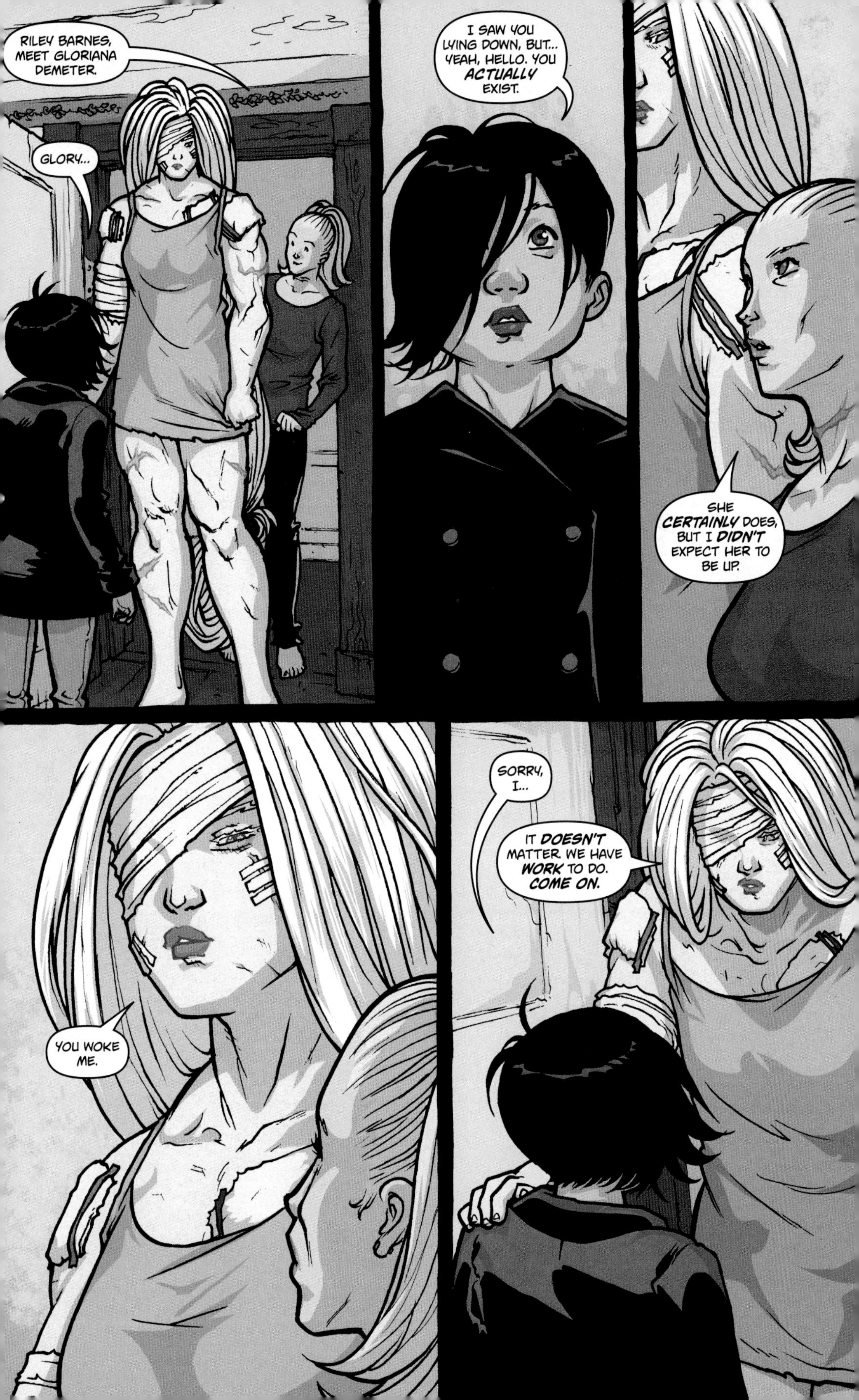
RILEY BARNES, MEET GLORIANA DEMETER.
GLORY...
I SAW YOU LYING DOWN, BUT... YEAH, HELLO. YOU ACTUALLY EXIST.
SHE CERTAINLY DOES, BUT I DIDN'T EXPECT HER TO BE UP.
YOU WOKE ME.
SORRY, I...
IT DOESN'T MATTER. WE HAVE WORK TO DO. COME ON.

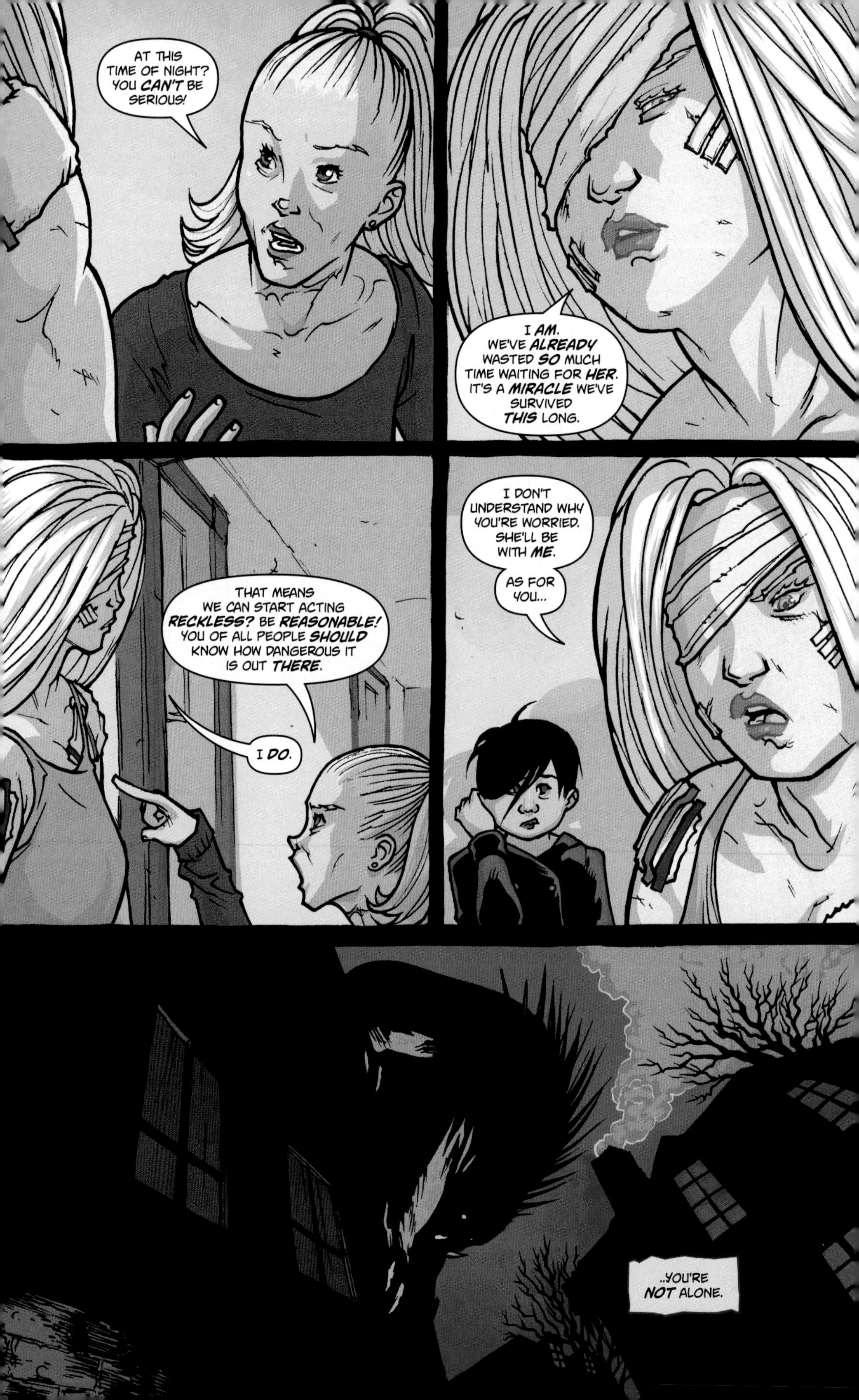
AT THIS TIME OF NIGHT? YOU CAN'T BE SERIOUS!
I AM. WE'VE ALREADY WASTED SO MUCH TIME WAITING FOR HER. IT'S A MIRACLE WE'VE SURVIVED THIS LONG.
THAT MEANS WE CAN START ACTING RECKLESS? BE REASONABLE! YOU OF ALL PEOPLE SHOULD KNOW HOW DANGEROUS IT IS OUT THERE.
I DO.
I DON'T UNDERSTAND WHY YOU'RE WORRIED. SHE'LL BE WITH ME.
AS FOR YOU...
..YOU'RE NOT ALONE.

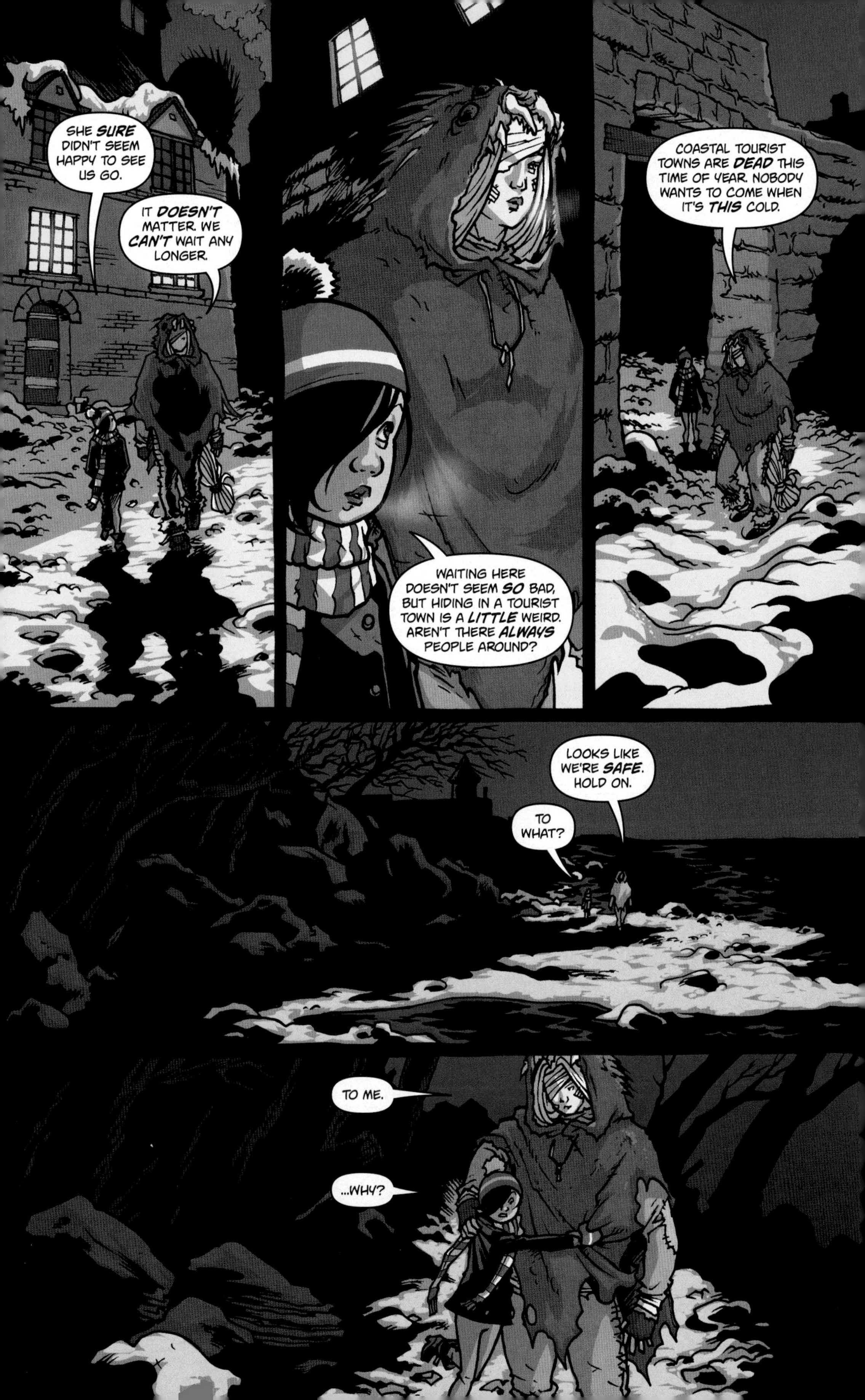
SHE SURE DIDN'T SEEM HAPPY TO SEE US GO.
IT DOESN'T MATTER. WE CAN'T WAIT ANY LONGER.
WAITING HERE DOESN'T SEEM SO BAD, BUT HIDING IN A TOURIST TOWN IS A LITTLE WEIRD. AREN'T THERE ALWAYS PEOPLE AROUND?
COASTAL TOURIST TOWNS ARE DEAD THIS TIME OF YEAR. NOBODY WANTS TO COME WHEN IT'S THIS COLD.
LOOKS LIKE WE'RE SAFE. HOLD ON.
TO WHAT?
TO ME.
...WHY?

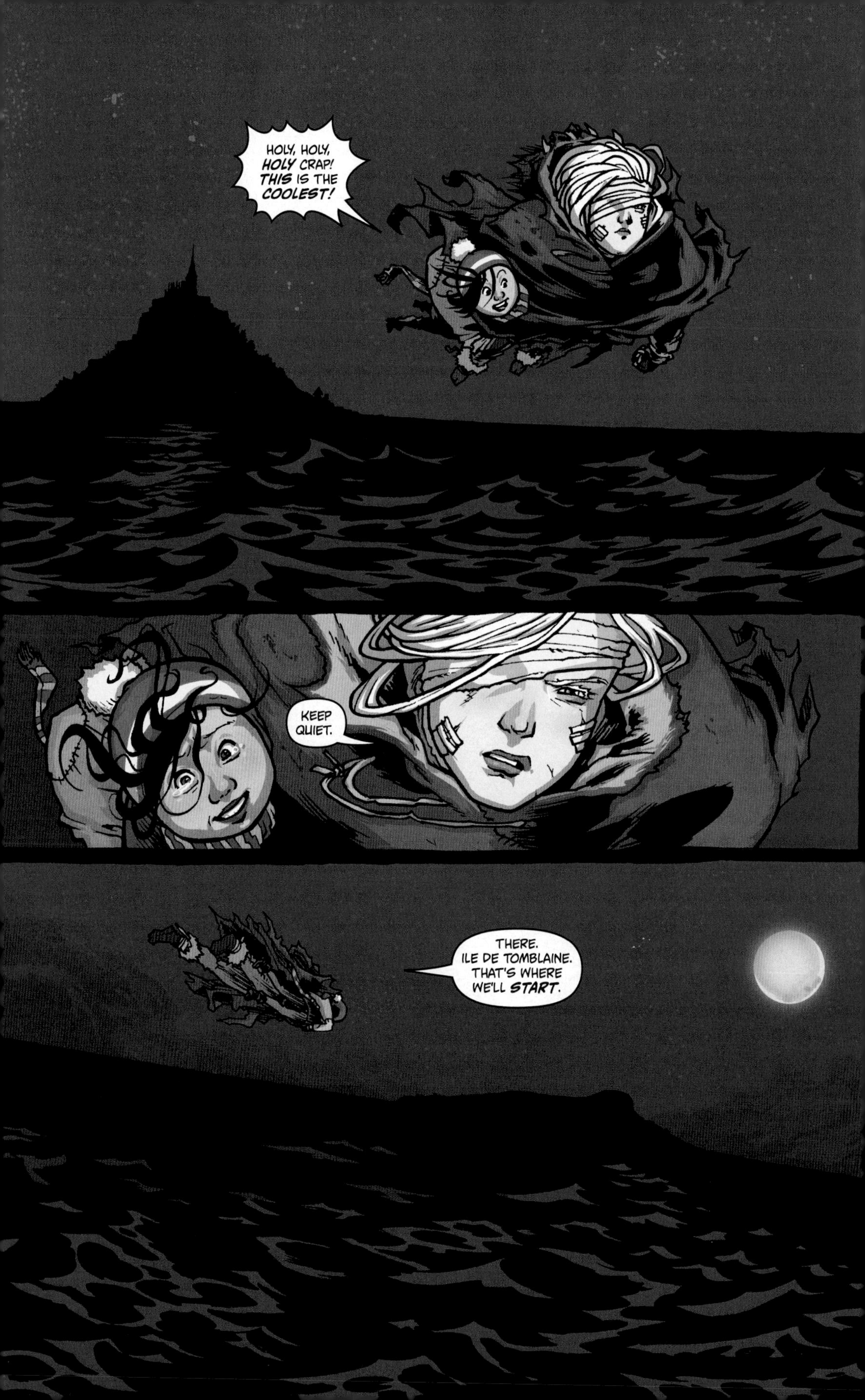
HOLY, HOLY, HOLY CRAP! THIS IS THE COOLEST!
KEEP QUIET.
THERE. ILE DE TOMBLAINE. THAT'S WHERE WE'LL START.

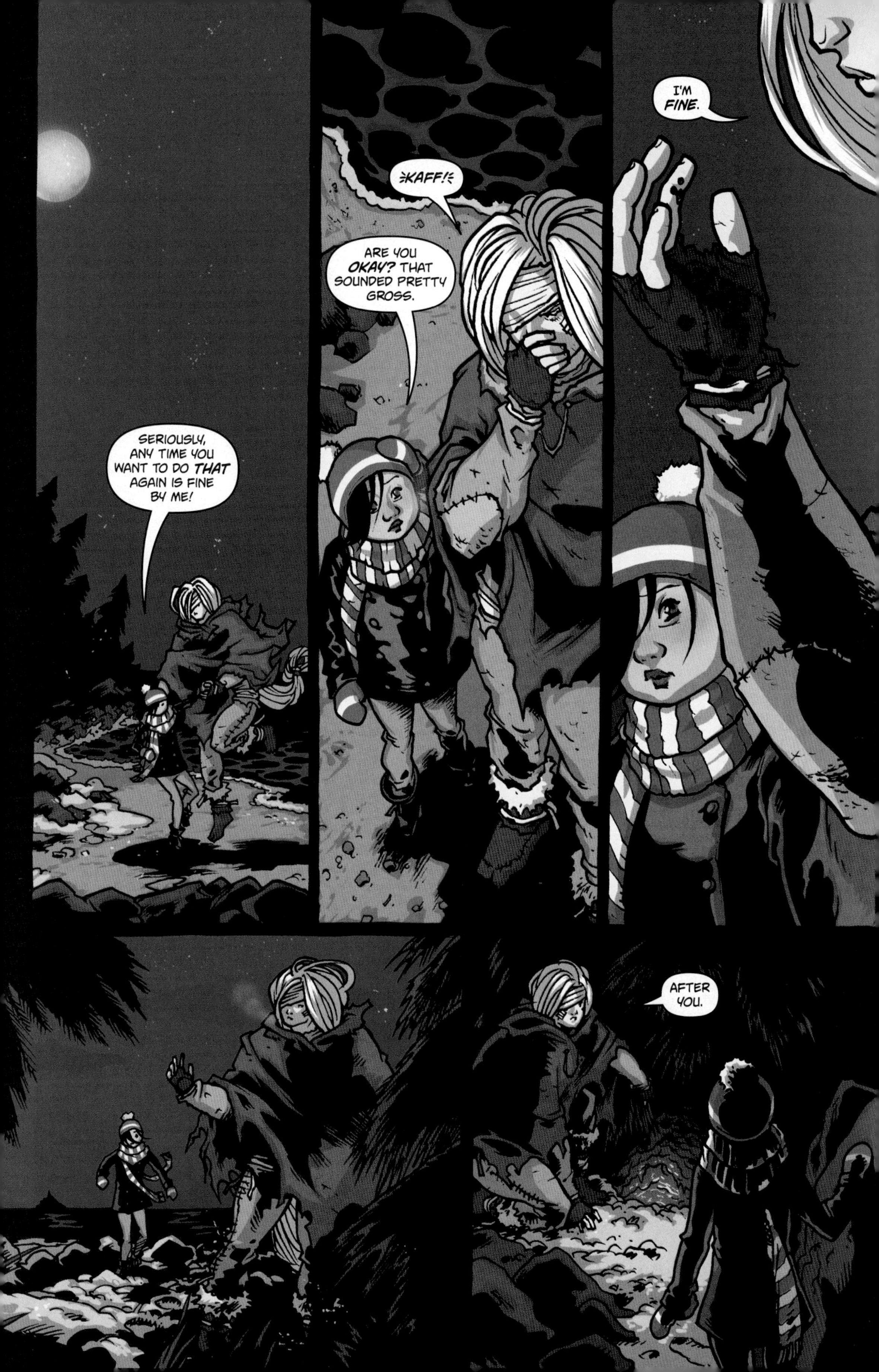
SERIOUSLY, ANY TIME YOU WANT TO DO THAT AGAIN IS FINE BY ME!
KAFF!
ARE YOU OKAY? THAT SOUNDED PRETTY GROSS.
I'M FINE.
AFTER YOU.

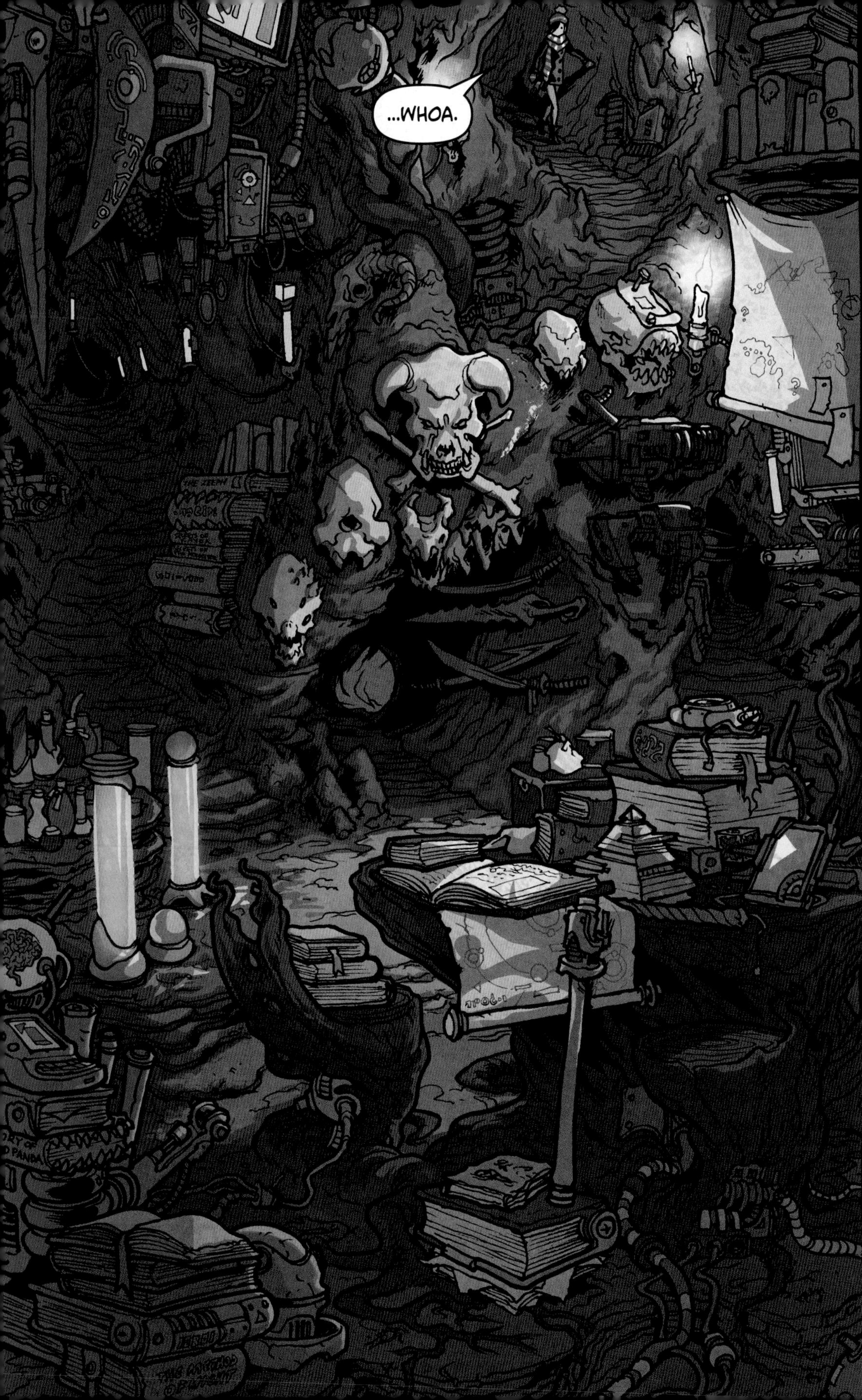
...WHOA.

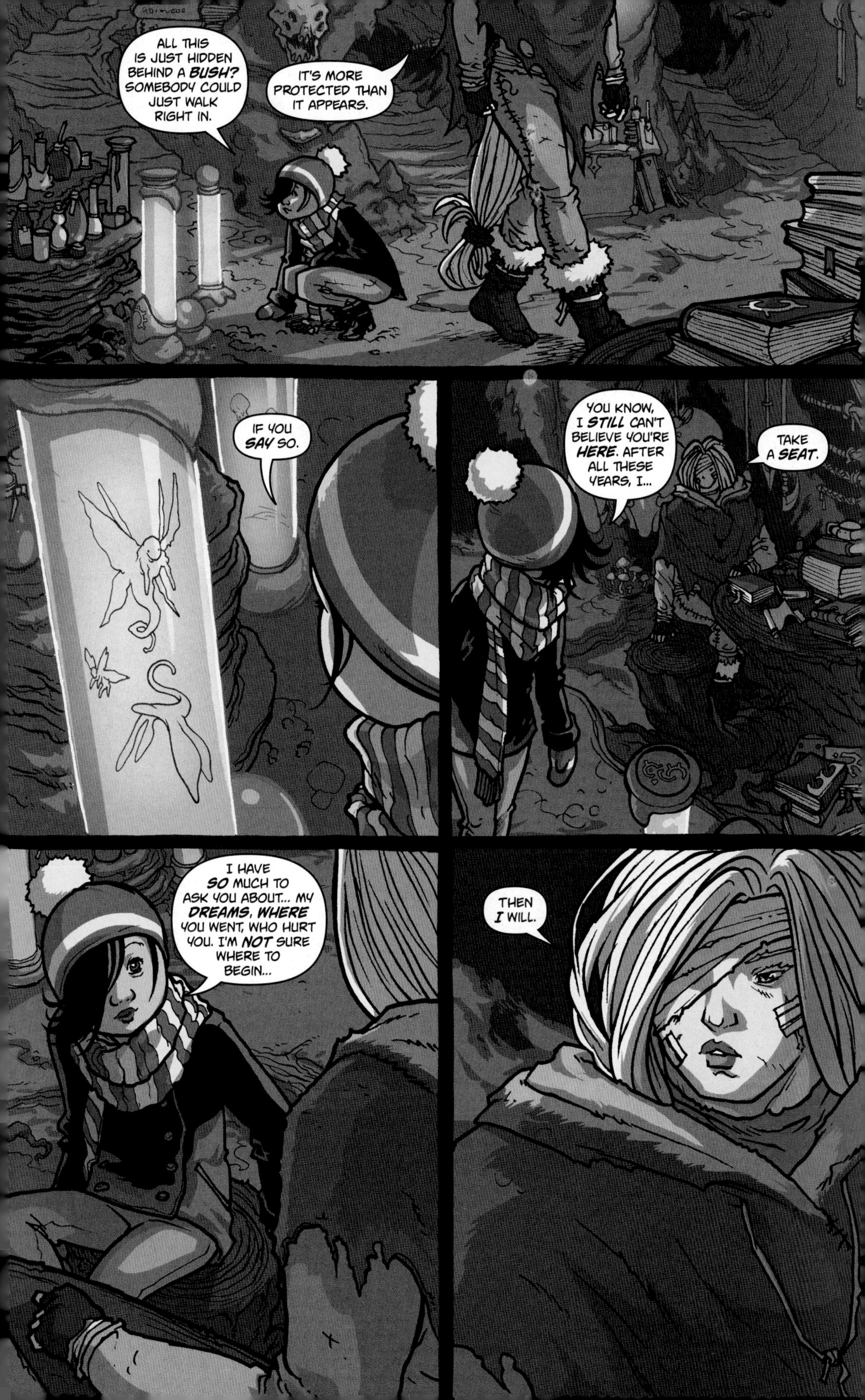
ALL THIS IS JUST HIDDEN BEHIND A BUSH? SOMEBODY COULD JUST WALK RIGHT IN.
IT'S MORE PROTECTED THAN IT APPEARS.
IF YOU SAY SO.
YOU KNOW, I STILL CAN'T BELIEVE YOU'RE HERE. AFTER ALL THESE YEARS, I...
TAKE A SEAT.
I HAVE SO MUCH TO ASK YOU ABOUT... MY DREAMS, WHERE YOU WENT, WHO HURT YOU. I'M NOT SURE WHERE TO BEGIN...
THEN I WILL.

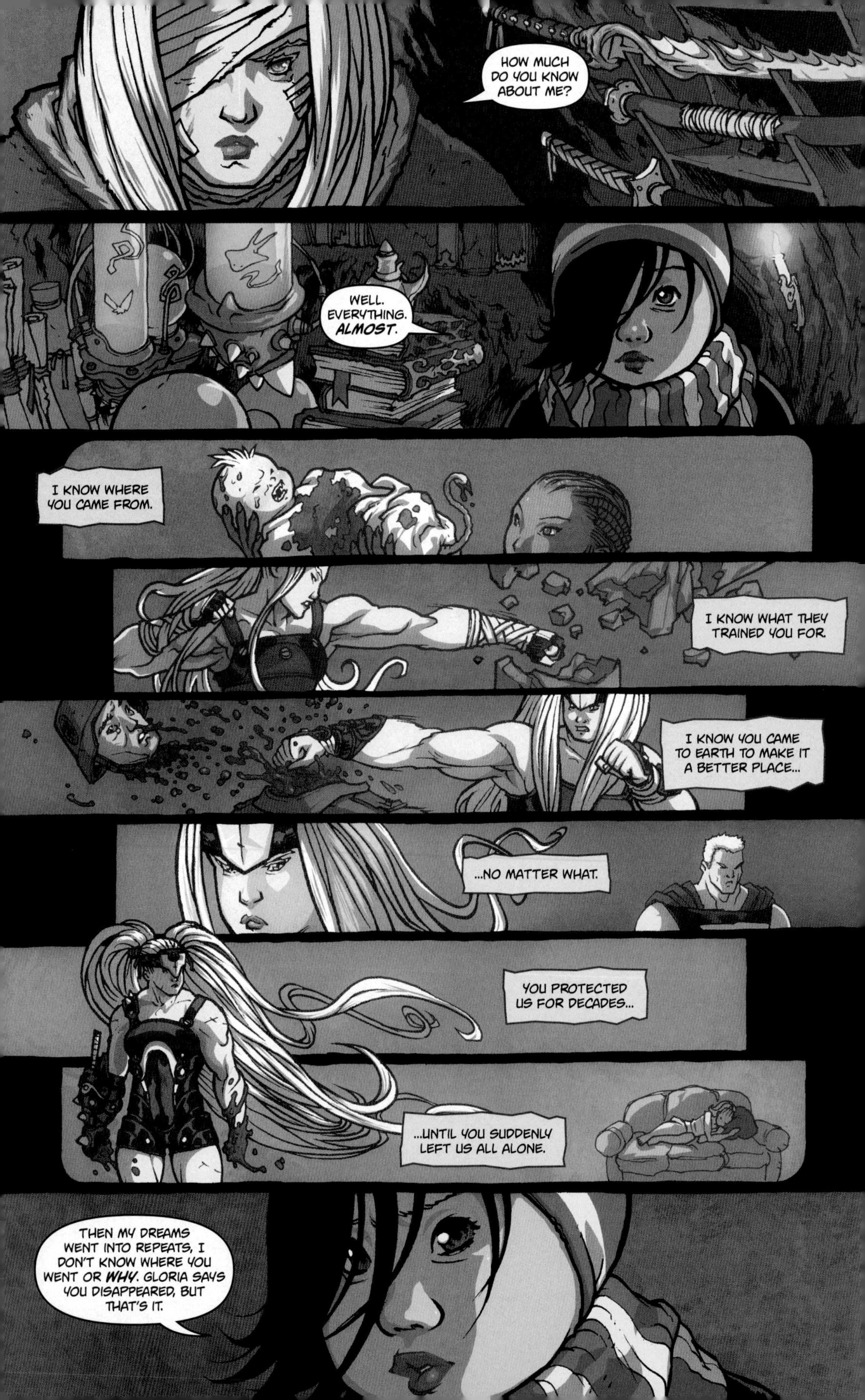
HOW MUCH DO YOU KNOW ABOUT ME?
WELL. EVERYTHING. ***ALMOST***.
I KNOW WHERE YOU CAME FROM.
I KNOW WHAT THEY TRAINED YOU FOR.
I KNOW YOU CAME TO EARTH TO MAKE IT A BETTER PLACE...
...NO MATTER WHAT.
YOU PROTECTED US FOR DECADES...
...UNTIL YOU SUDDENLY LEFT US ALL ALONE.
THEN MY DREAMS WENT INTO REPEATS, I DON'T KNOW WHERE YOU WENT OR ***WHY***. GLORIA SAYS YOU DISAPPEARED, BUT THAT'S IT.

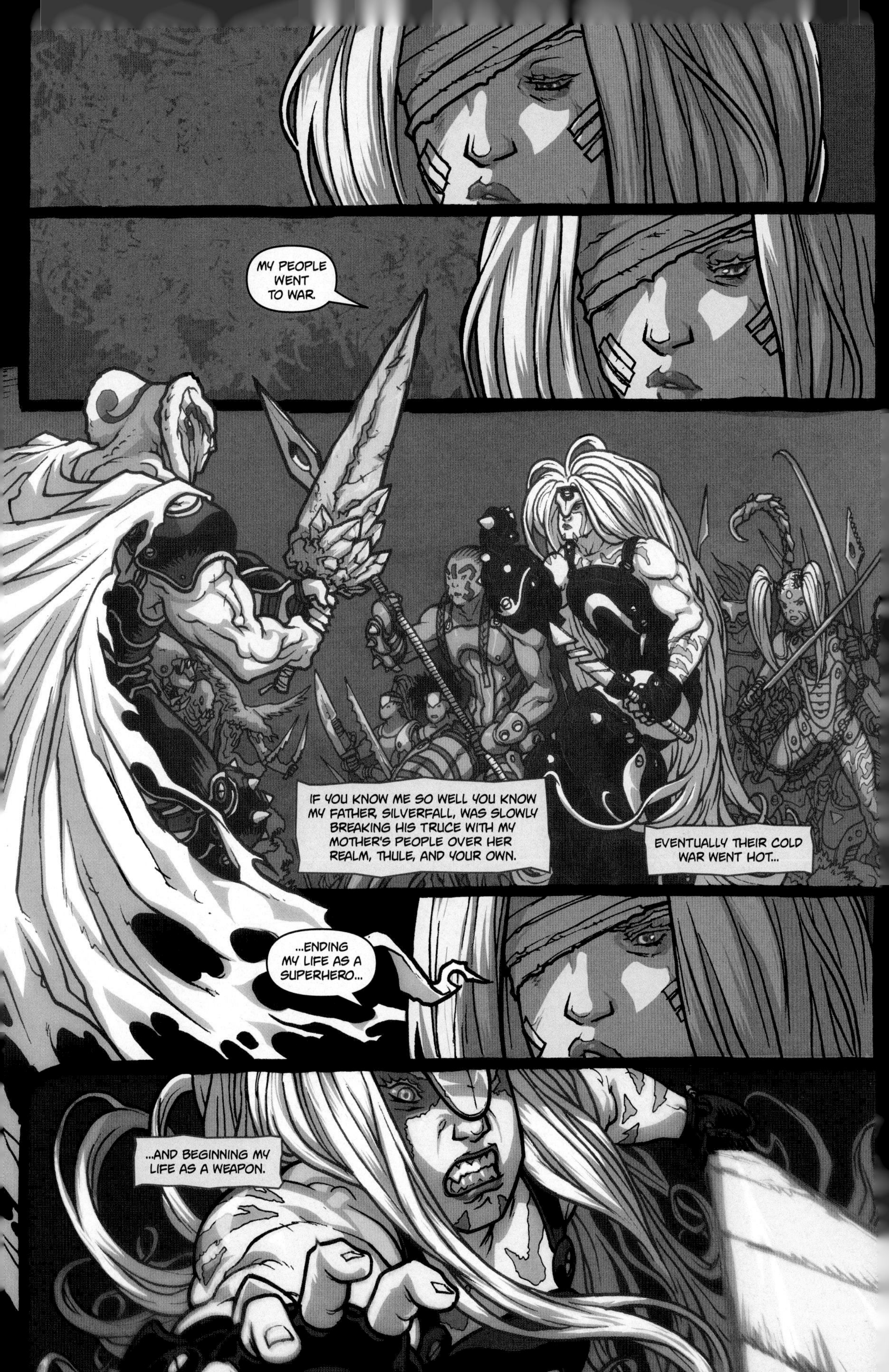
MY PEOPLE WENT TO WAR.
IF YOU KNOW ME SO WELL YOU KNOW MY FATHER, SILVERFALL, WAS SLOWLY BREAKING HIS TRUCE WITH MY MOTHER'S PEOPLE OVER HER REALM, THULE, AND YOUR OWN.
EVENTUALLY THEIR COLD WAR WENT HOT...
...ENDING MY LIFE AS A SUPERHERO...
...AND BEGINNING MY LIFE AS A WEAPON.

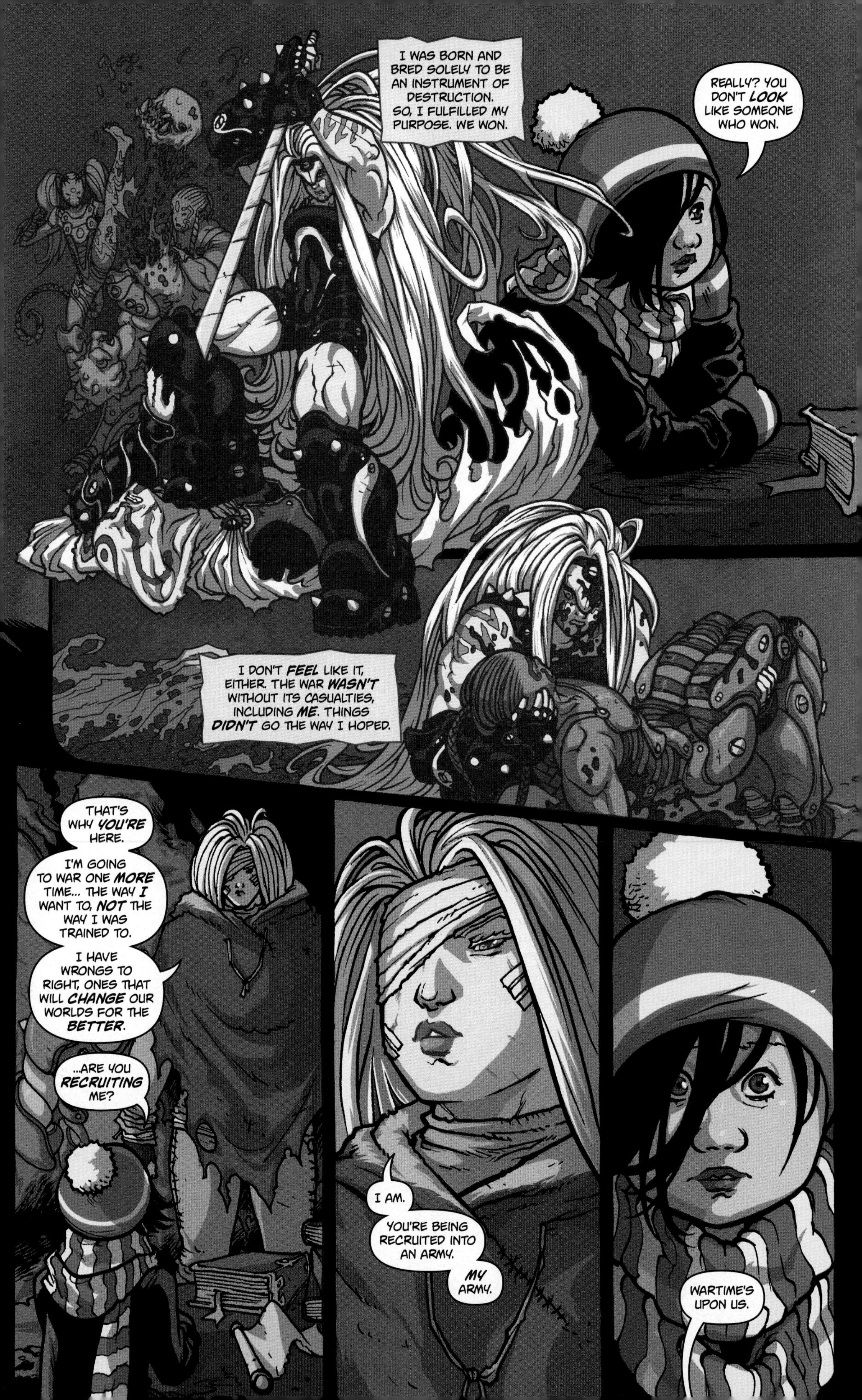
I WAS BORN AND BRED SOLELY TO BE AN INSTRUMENT OF DESTRUCTION. SO, I FULFILLED MY PURPOSE. WE WON.
REALLY? YOU DON'T LOOK LIKE SOMEONE WHO WON.
I DON'T FEEL LIKE IT, EITHER. THE WAR WASN'T WITHOUT ITS CASUALTIES, INCLUDING ME. THINGS DIDN'T GO THE WAY I HOPED.
THAT'S WHY YOU'RE HERE.
I'M GOING TO WAR ONE MORE TIME... THE WAY I WANT TO, NOT THE WAY I WAS TRAINED TO.
I HAVE WRONGS TO RIGHT, ONES THAT WILL CHANGE OUR WORLDS FOR THE BETTER.
...ARE YOU RECRUITING ME?
I AM.
YOU'RE BEING RECRUITED INTO AN ARMY.
MY ARMY.
WARTIME'S UPON US.

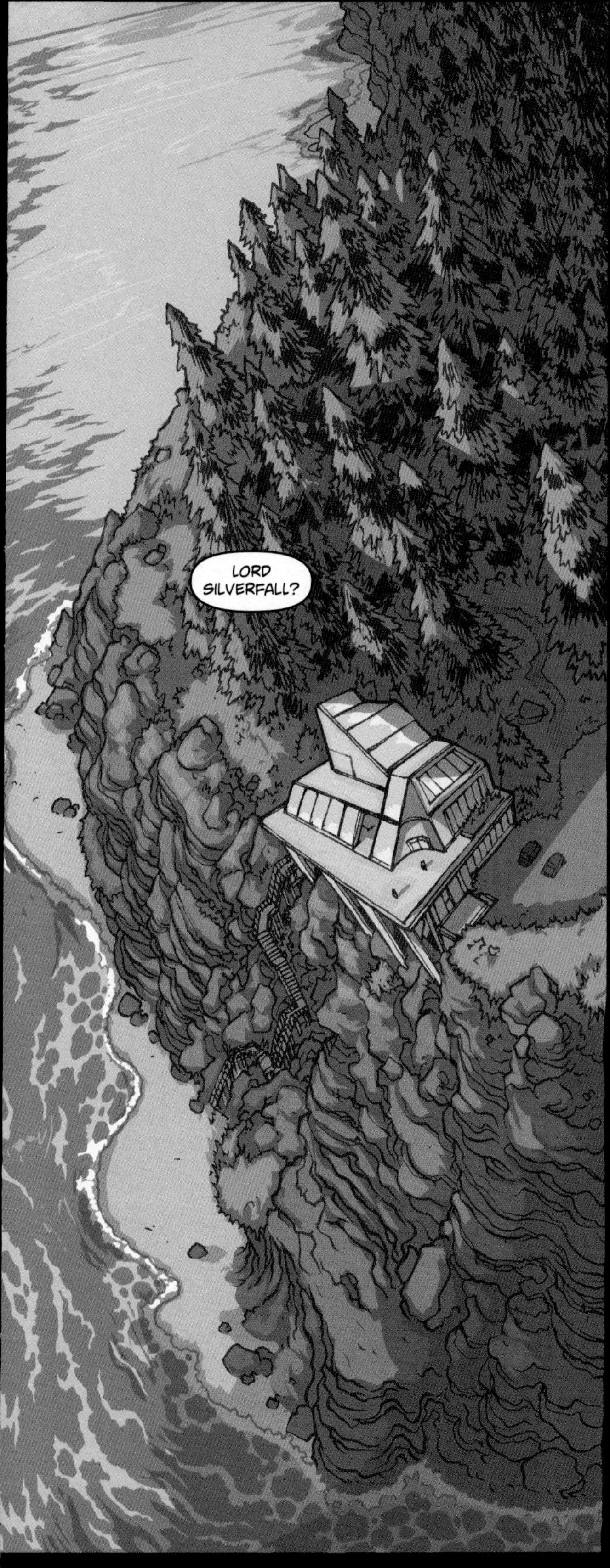
LORD SILVERFALL?

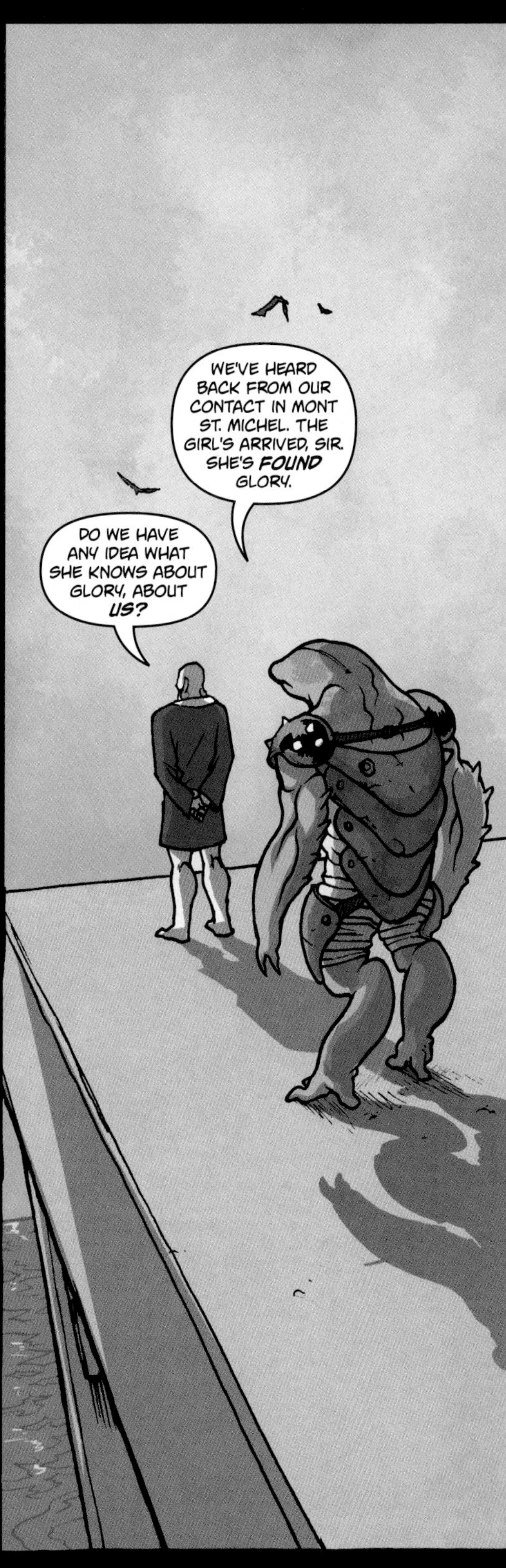
WE'VE HEARD BACK FROM OUR CONTACT IN MONT ST. MICHEL. THE GIRL'S ARRIVED, SIR. SHE'S FOUND GLORY.
DO WE HAVE ANY IDEA WHAT SHE KNOWS ABOUT GLORY, ABOUT US?

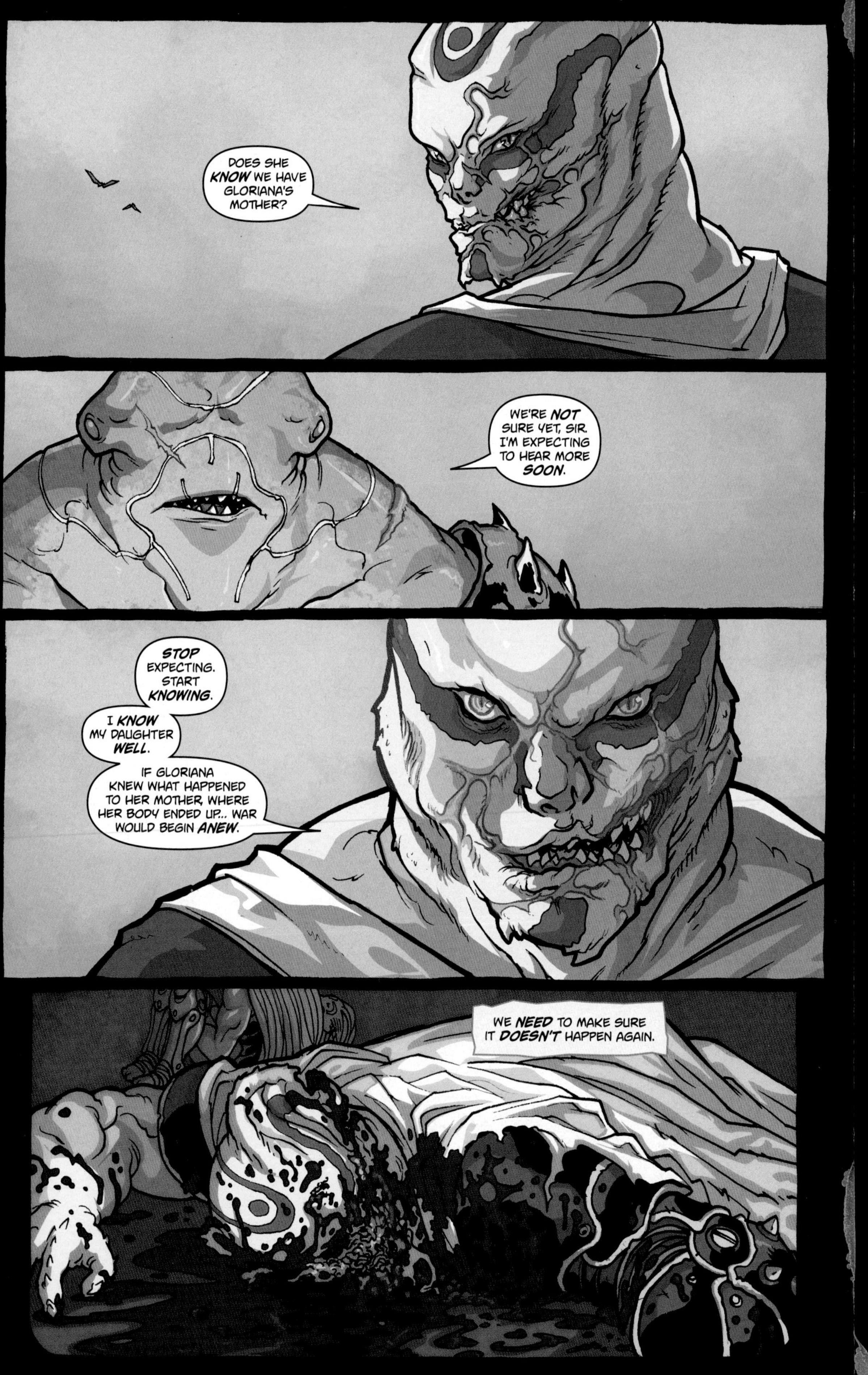
DOES SHE KNOW WE HAVE GLORIANA'S MOTHER?
WE'RE NOT SURE YET, SIR. I'M EXPECTING TO HEAR MORE SOON.
STOP EXPECTING. START KNOWING.
I KNOW MY DAUGHTER WELL.
IF GLORIANA KNEW WHAT HAPPENED TO HER MOTHER, WHERE HER BODY ENDED UP... WAR WOULD BEGIN ANEW.
WE NEED TO MAKE SURE IT DOESN'T HAPPEN AGAIN.

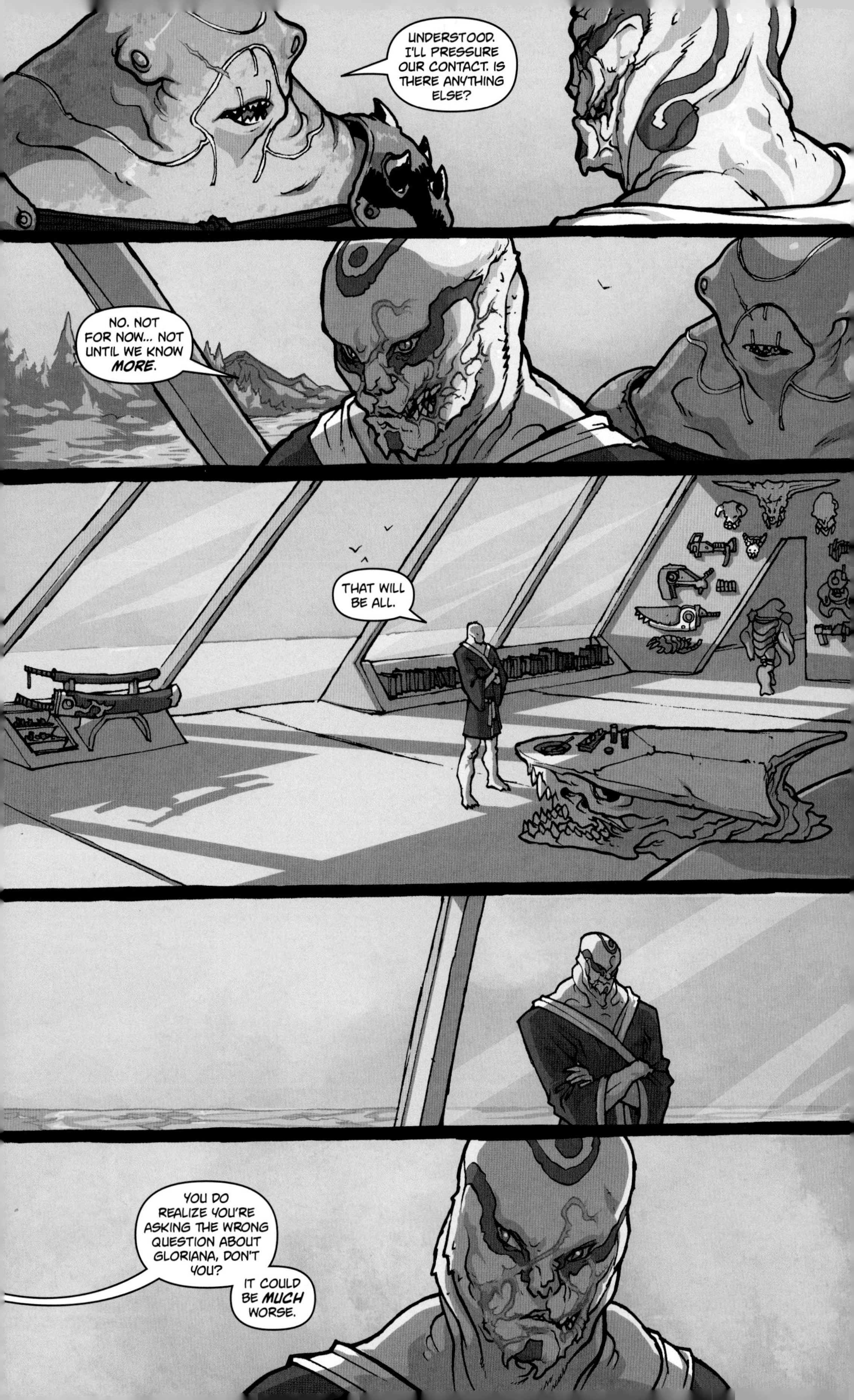
UNDERSTOOD. I'LL PRESSURE OUR CONTACT. IS THERE ANYTHING ELSE?
NO. NOT FOR NOW... NOT UNTIL WE KNOW MORE.
THAT WILL BE ALL.
YOU DO REALIZE YOU'RE ASKING THE WRONG QUESTION ABOUT GLORIANA, DON'T YOU?
IT COULD BE MUCH WORSE.

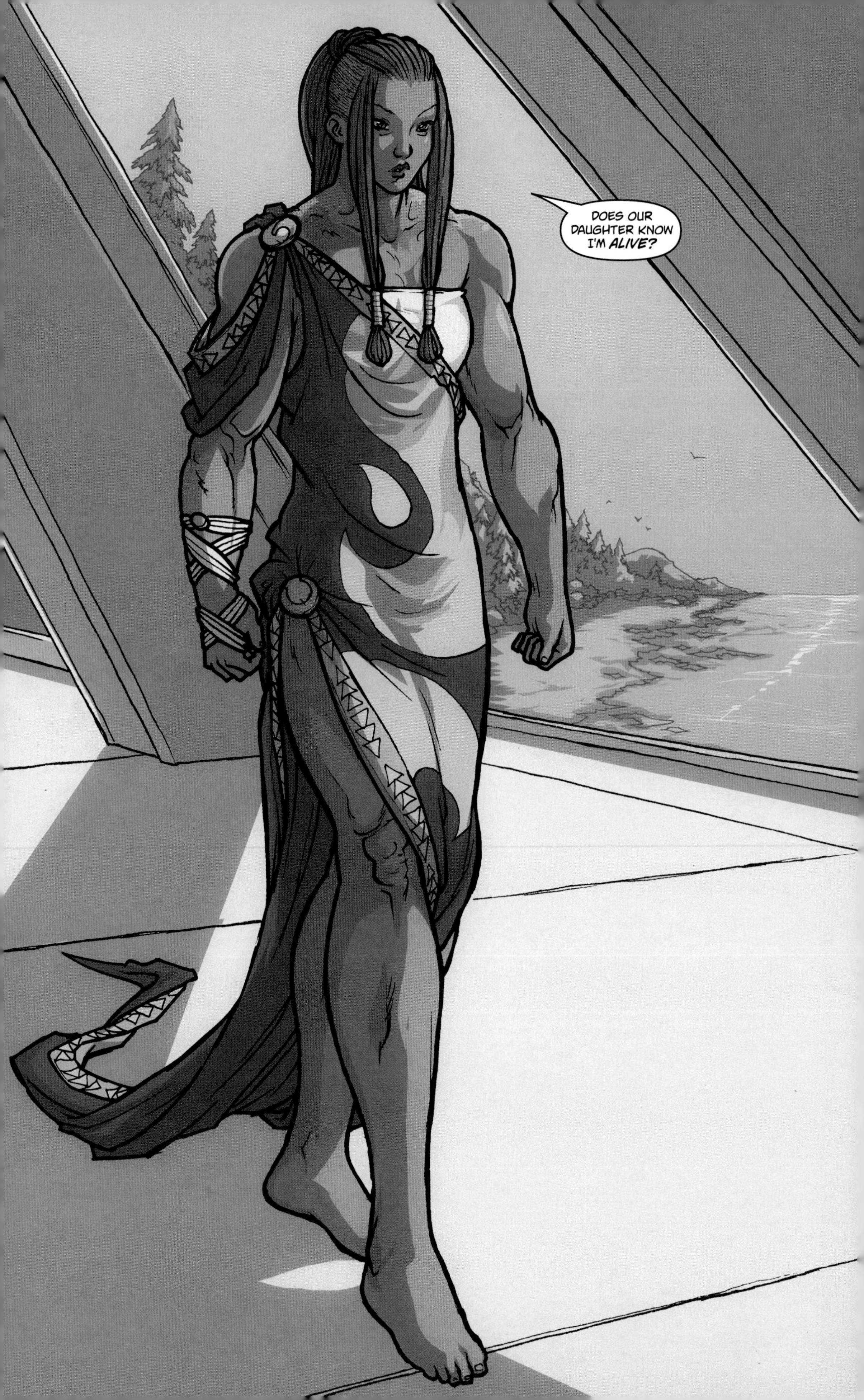
DOES OUR DAUGHTER KNOW I'M *ALIVE?*

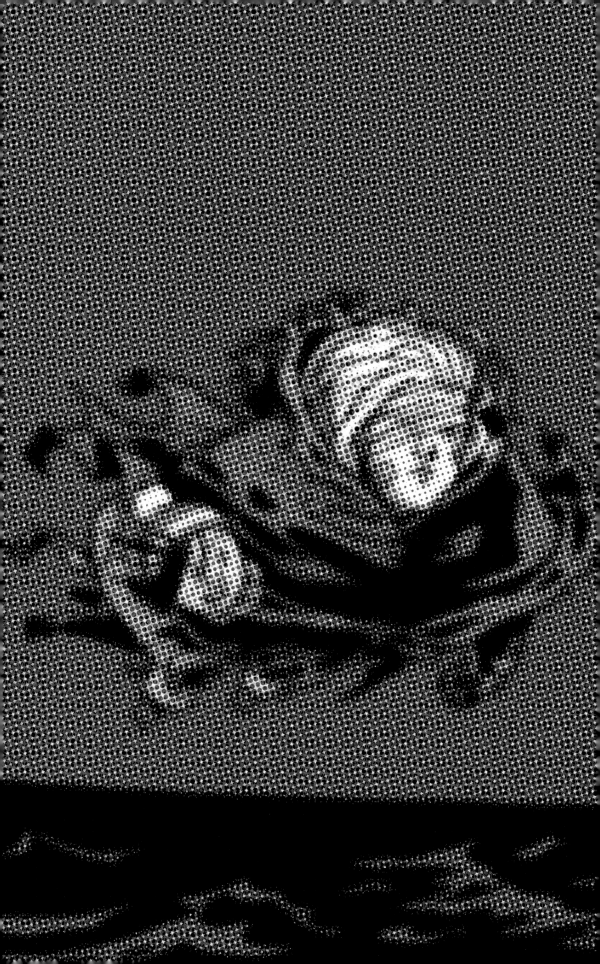

Chapter Three

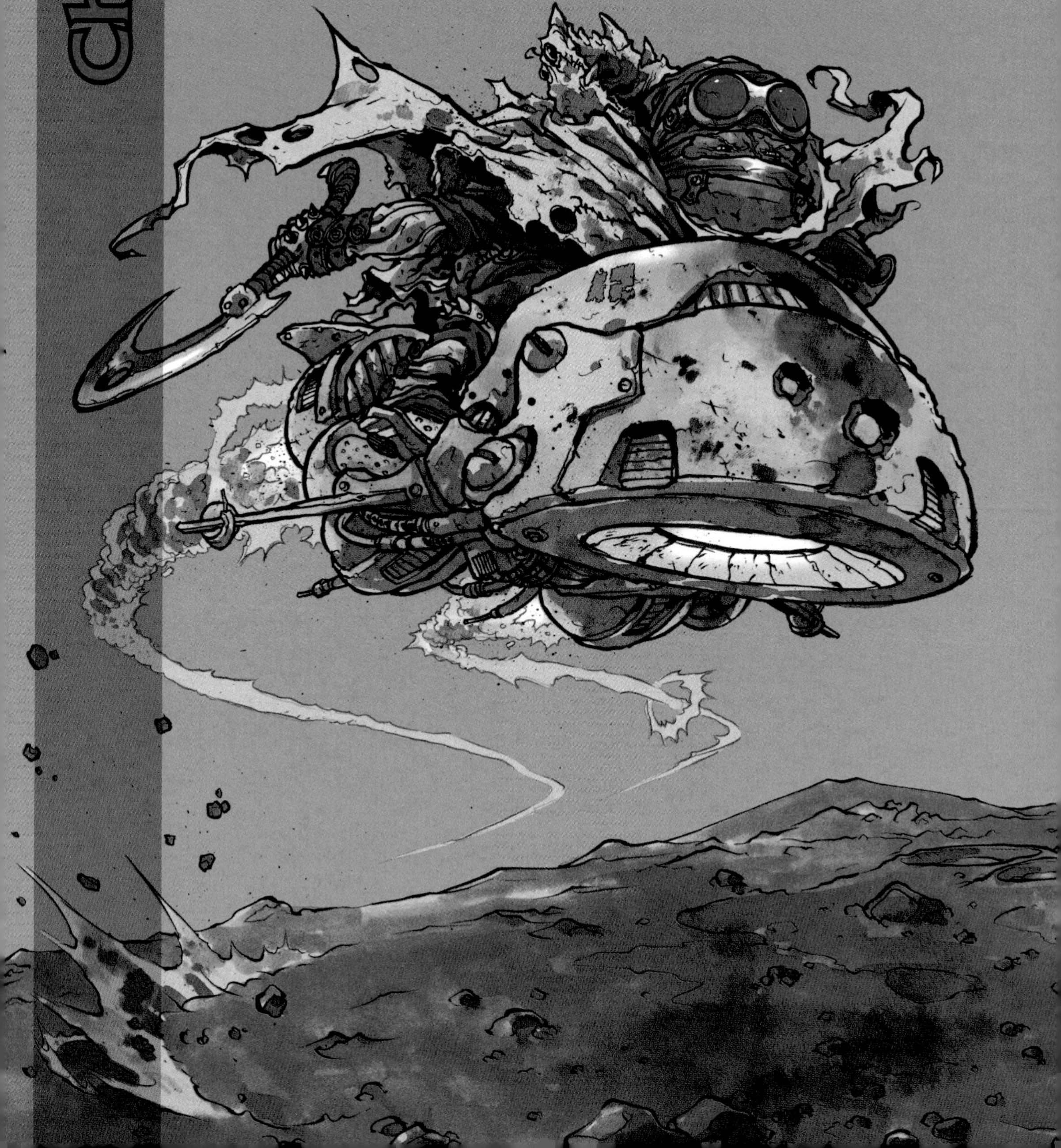

RILEY

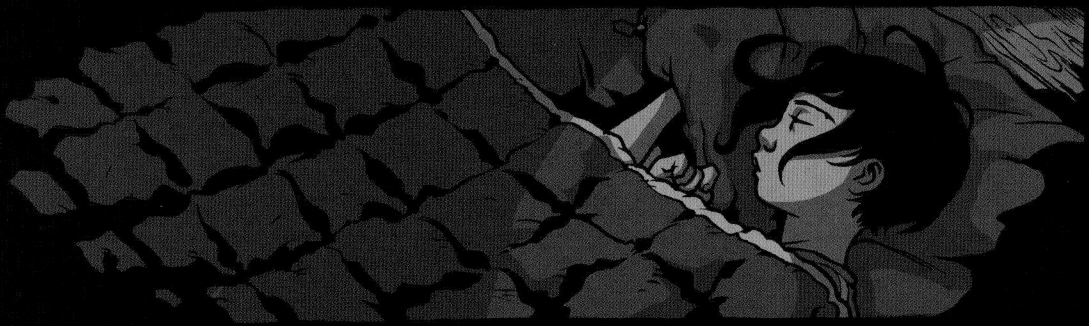

DREAMS

FIVE HUNDRED

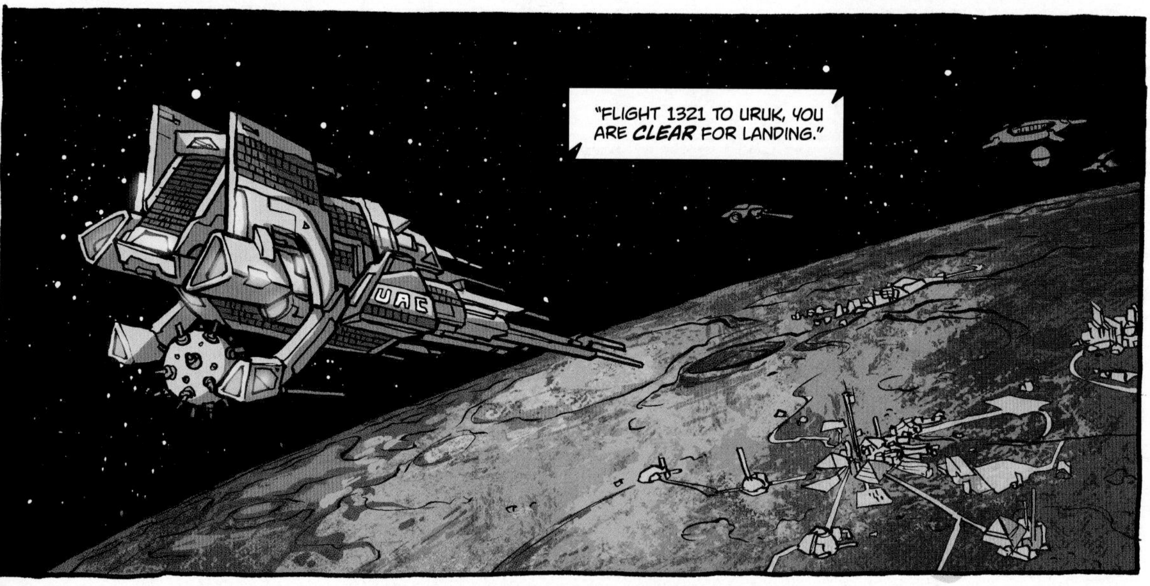
"FLIGHT 1321 TO URUK, YOU ARE *CLEAR* FOR LANDING."
UAC

YEARS

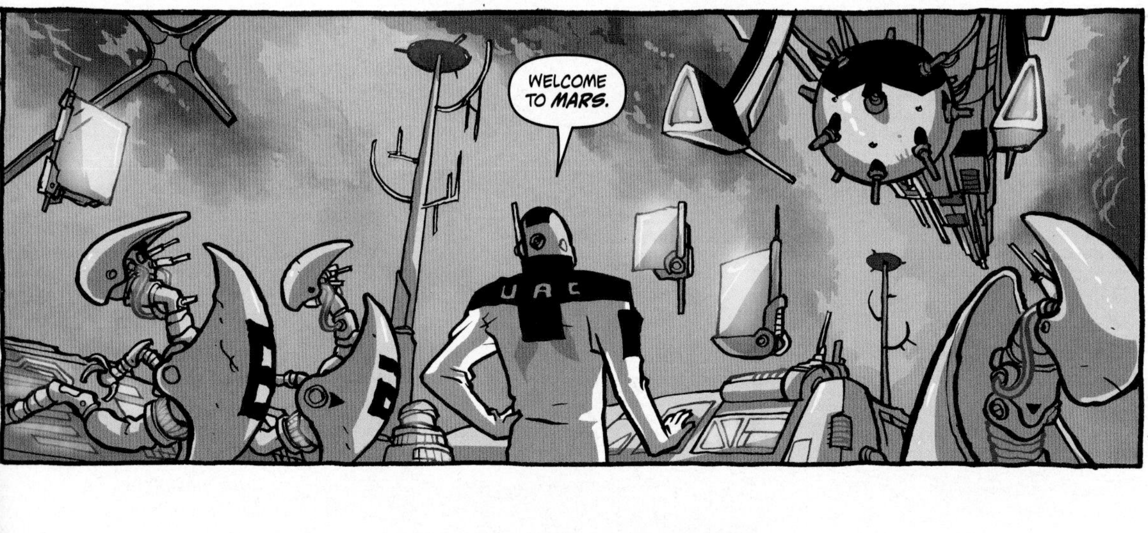
WELCOME TO *MARS*.
UAC

LATER

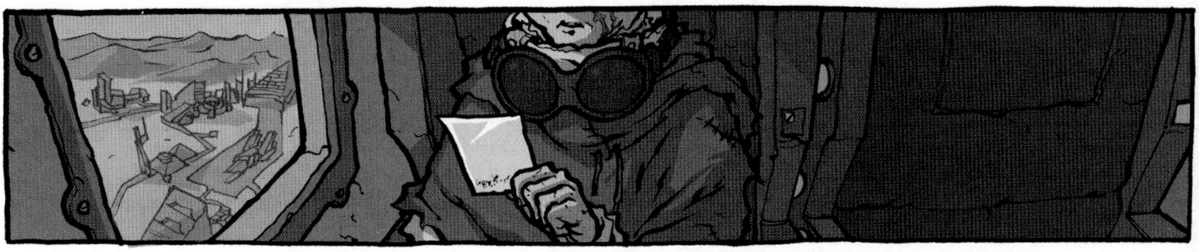

IMAGE COMICS PRESENTS

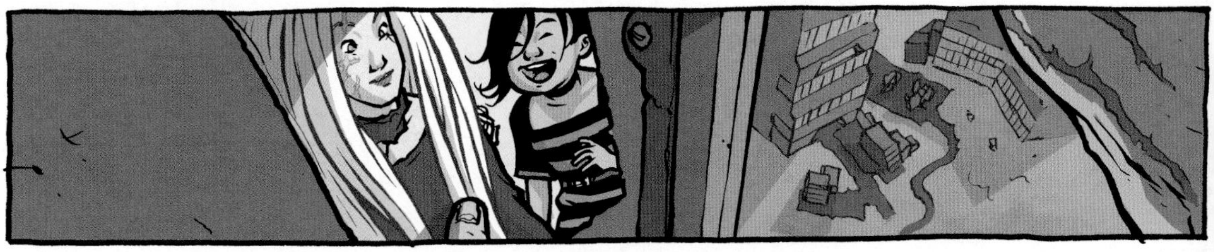

JOE KEATINGE
WRITER

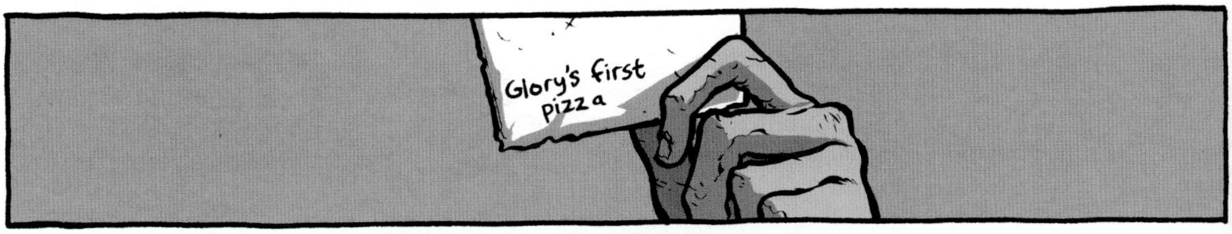
Glory's first pizza

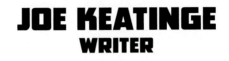

ROSS CAMPBELL
ARTIST

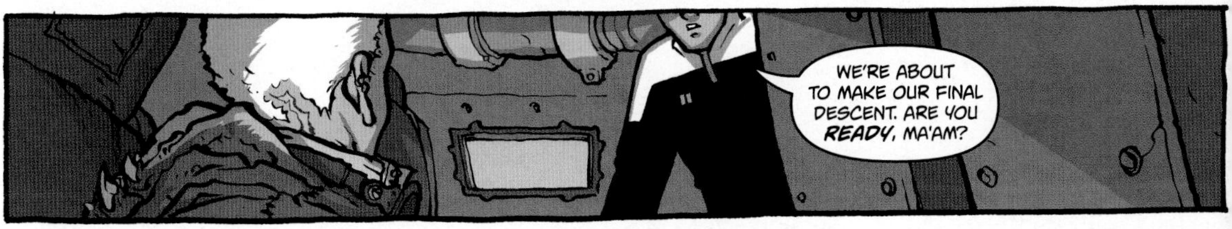
WE'RE ABOUT TO MAKE OUR FINAL DESCENT. ARE YOU *READY*, MA'AM?

MS,SHATIA HAMILTON
COLORIST

DOUGLAS E. SHERWOOD
LETTERER

ERIC STEPHENSON
EDITOR

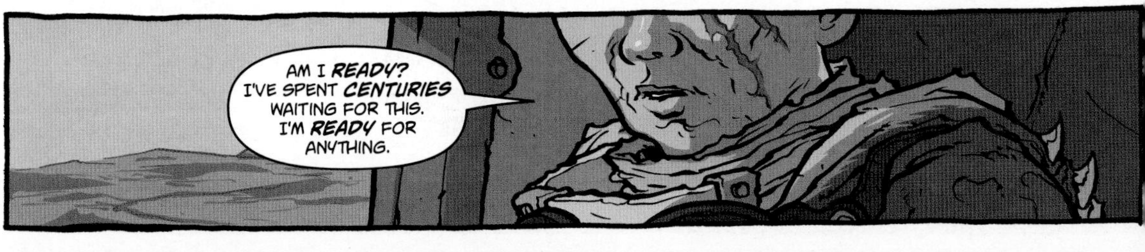
AM I *READY*? I'VE SPENT *CENTURIES* WAITING FOR THIS. I'M *READY* FOR ANYTHING.

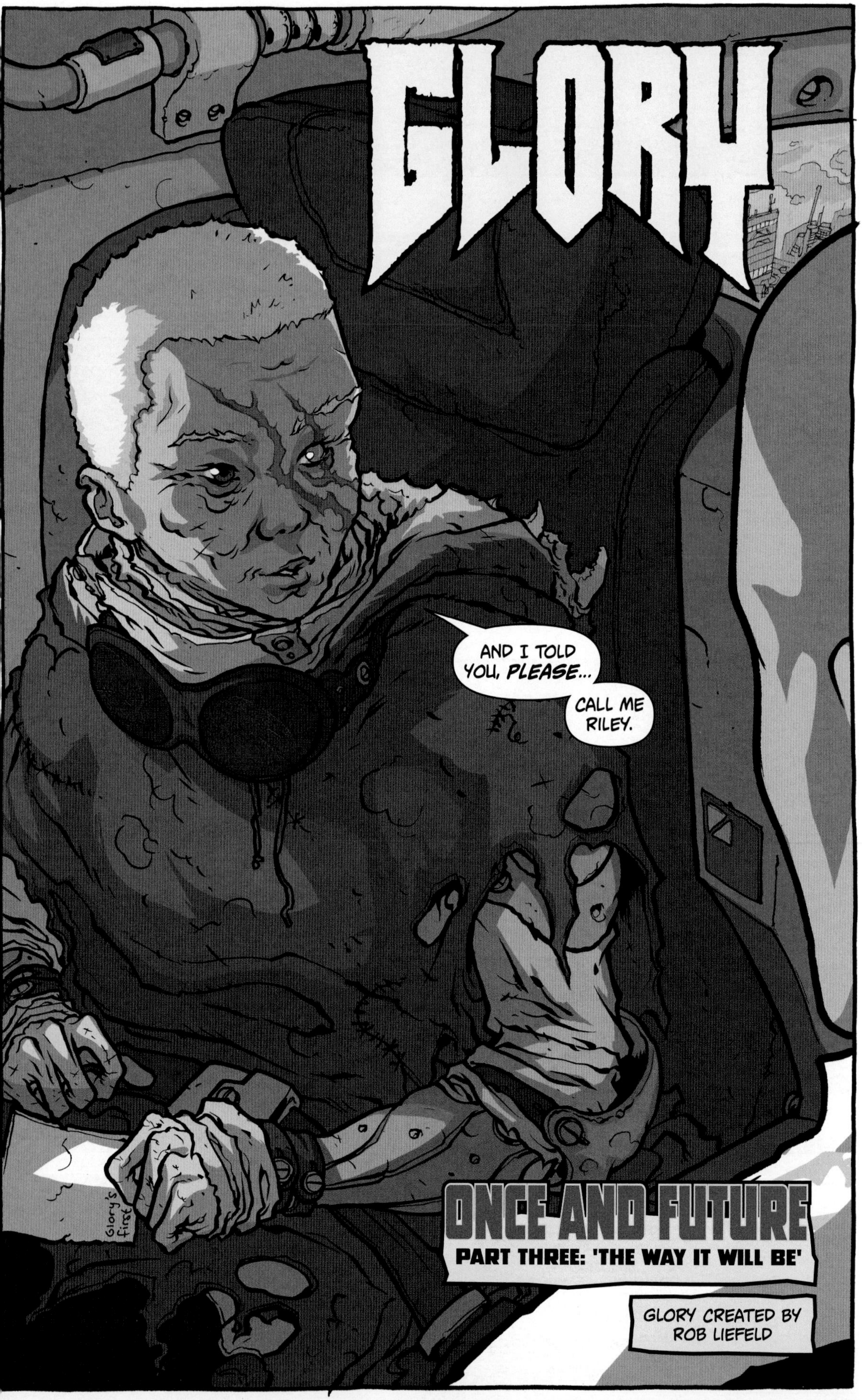
GLORY
AND I TOLD YOU, PLEASE...
CALL ME RILEY.
Glory's first
ONCE AND FUTURE
PART THREE: 'THE WAY IT WILL BE'
GLORY CREATED BY ROB LIEFELD

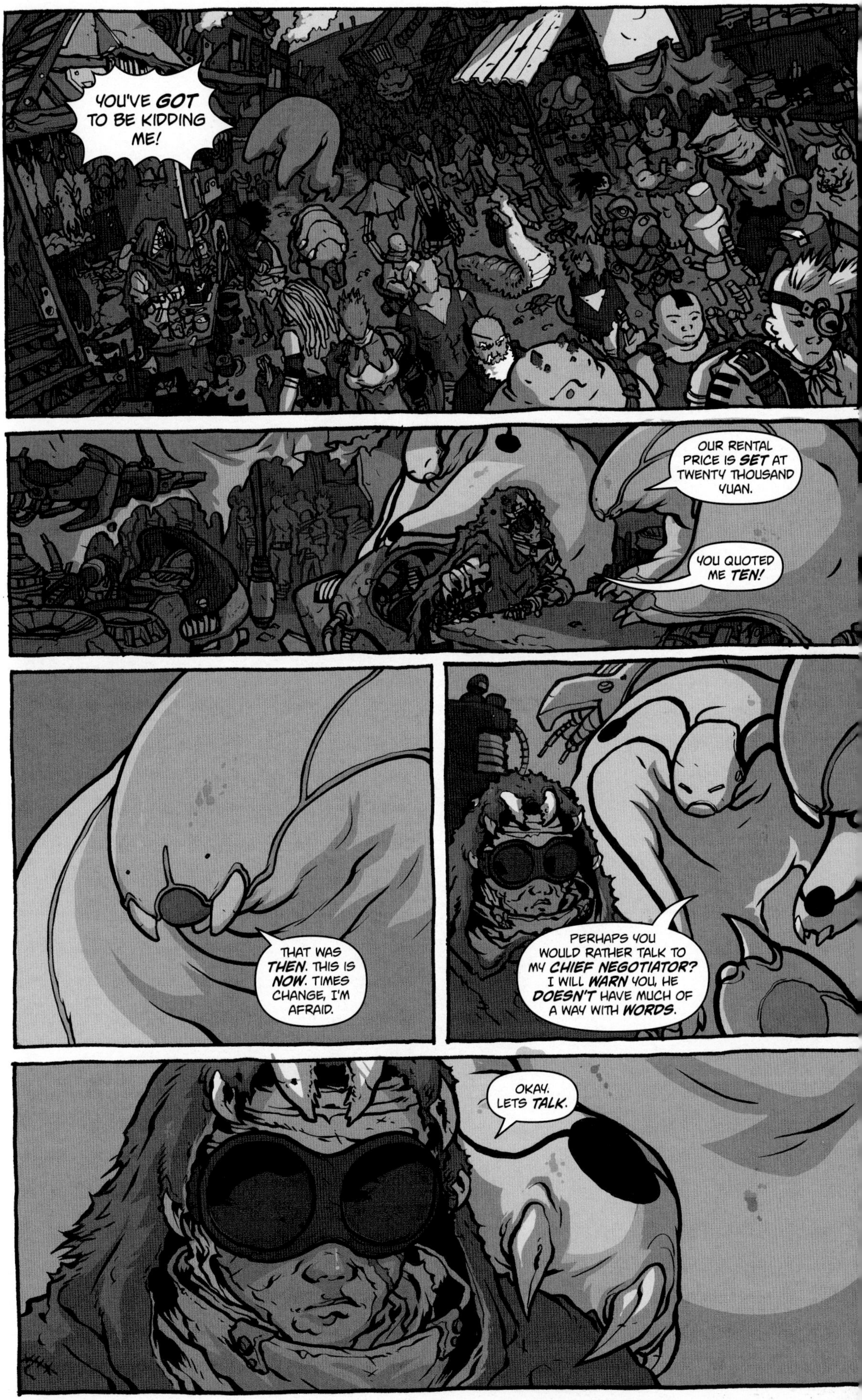
YOU'VE GOT TO BE KIDDING ME!
OUR RENTAL PRICE IS SET AT TWENTY THOUSAND YUAN.
YOU QUOTED ME TEN!
THAT WAS THEN. THIS IS NOW. TIMES CHANGE, I'M AFRAID.
PERHAPS YOU WOULD RATHER TALK TO MY CHIEF NEGOTIATOR? I WILL WARN YOU, HE DOESN'T HAVE MUCH OF A WAY WITH WORDS.
OKAY. LETS TALK.

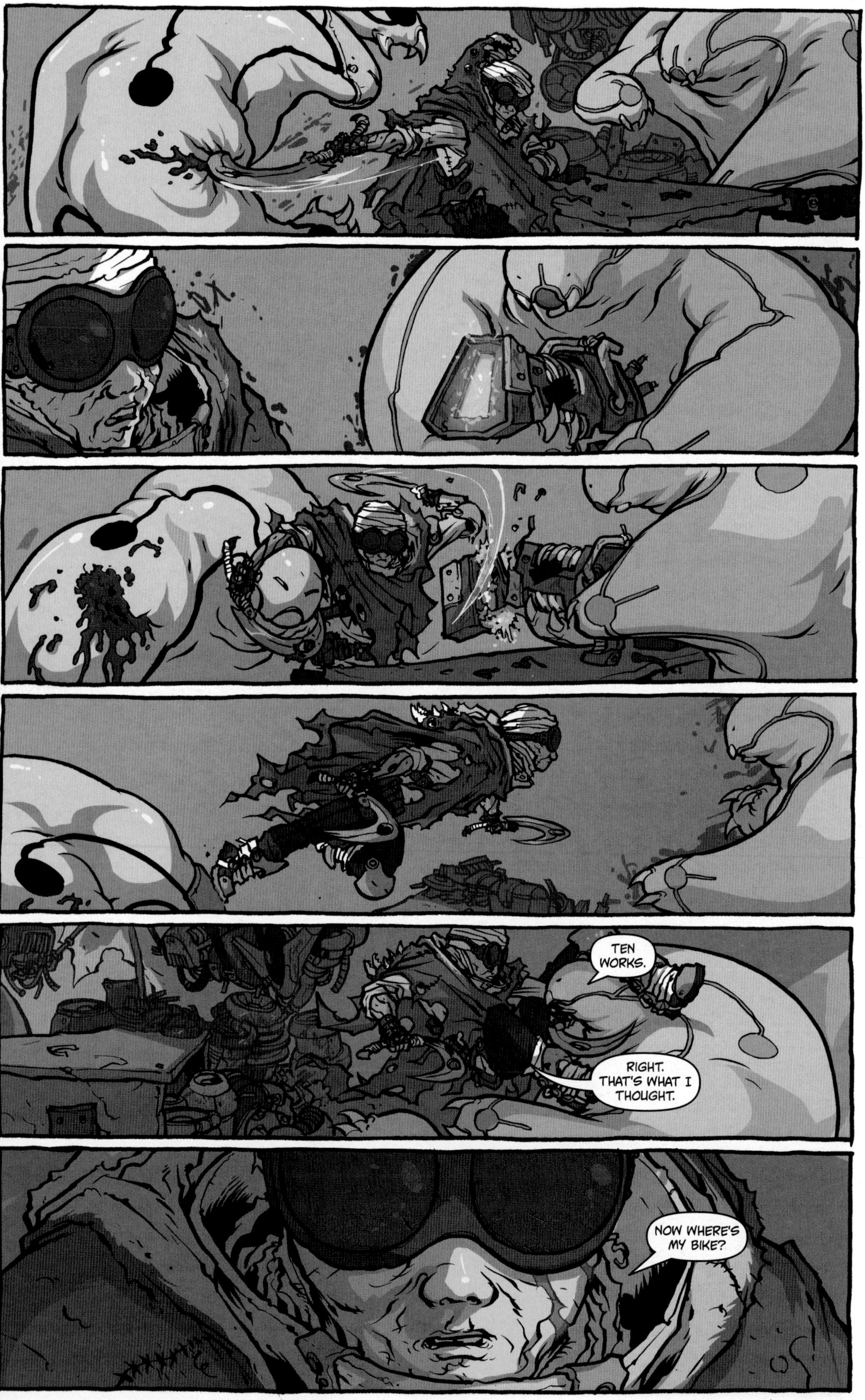
TEN WORKS.
RIGHT. THAT'S WHAT I THOUGHT.
NOW WHERE'S MY BIKE?

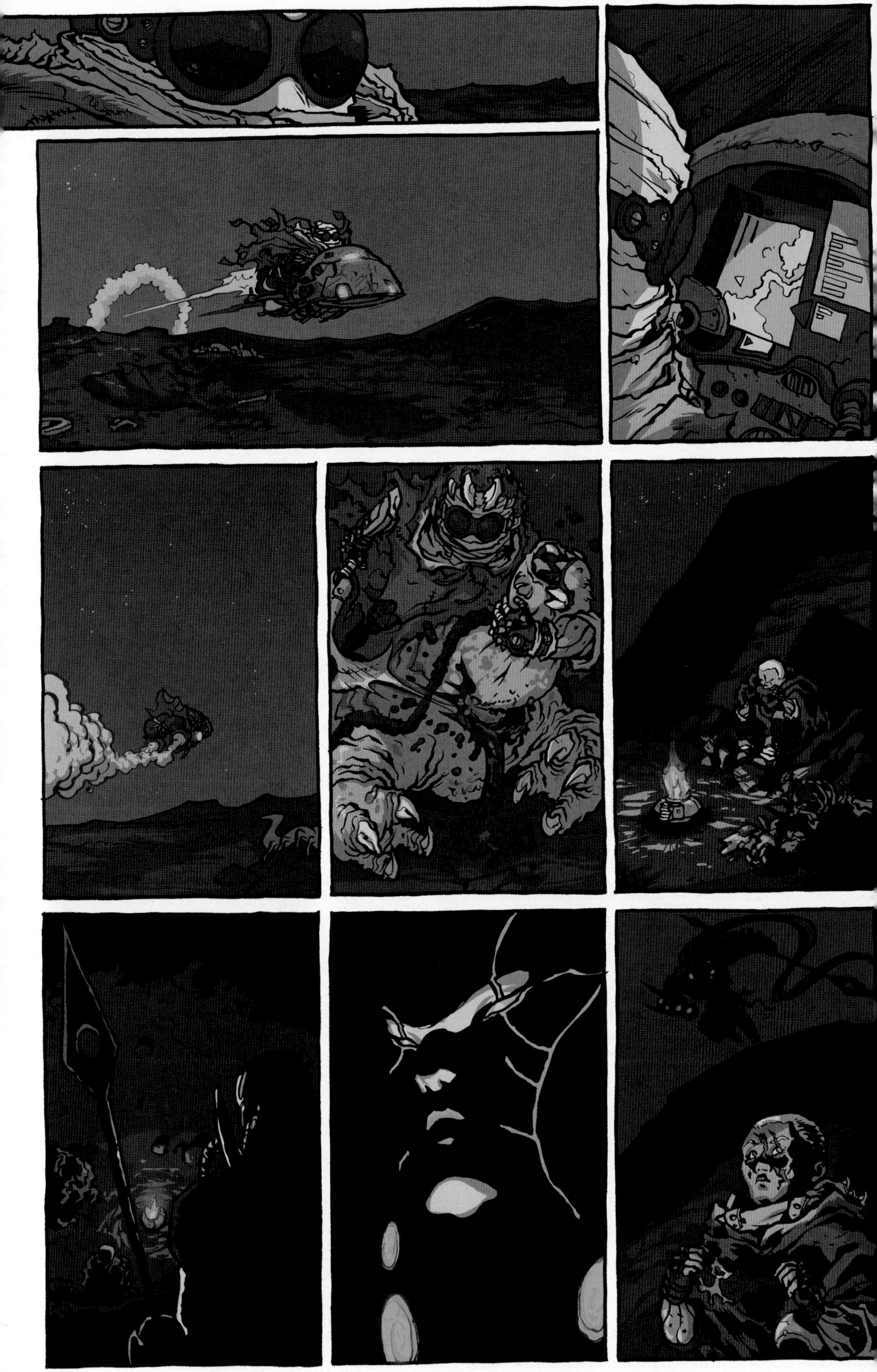

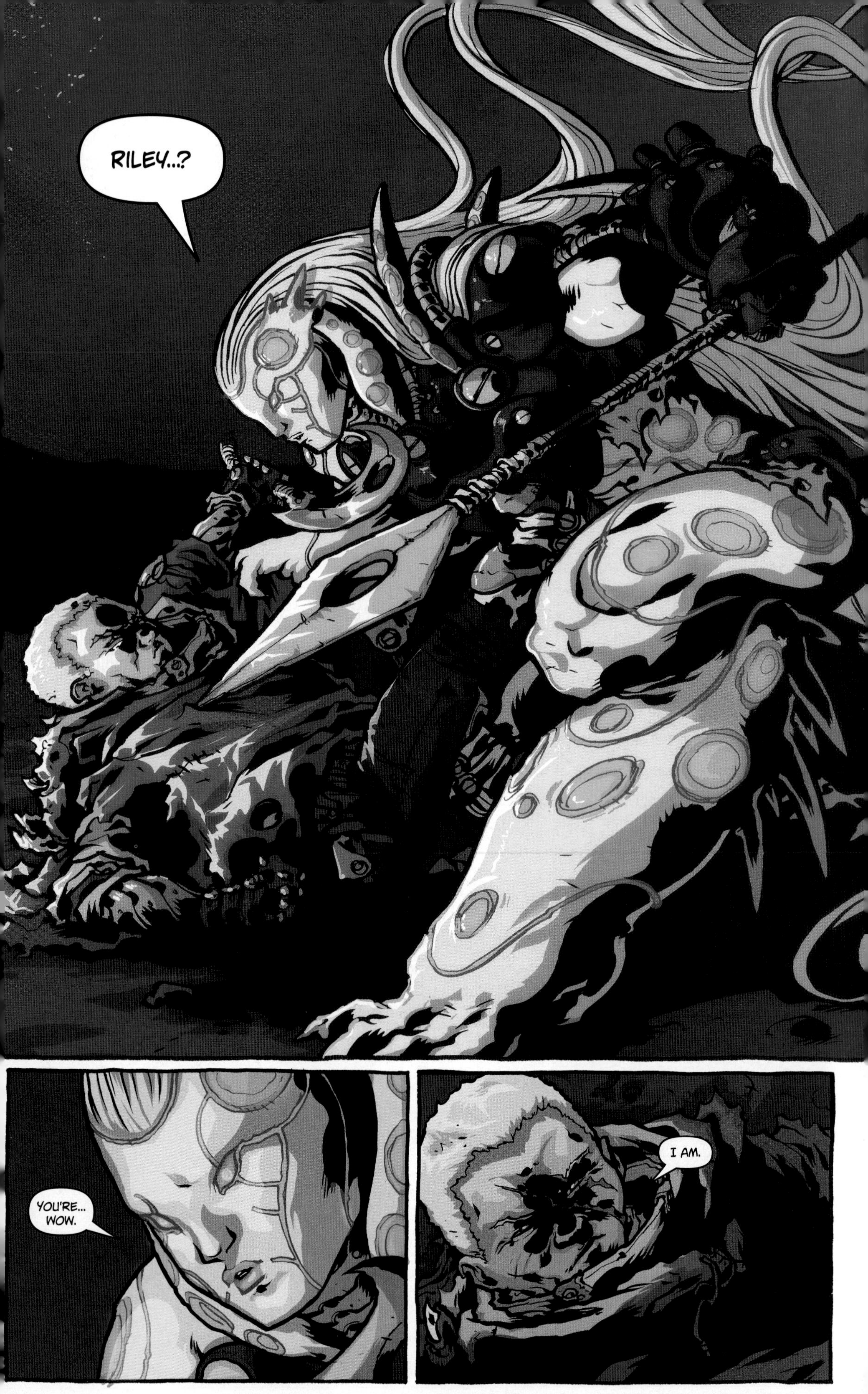
RILEY...?
YOU'RE... WOW.
I AM.

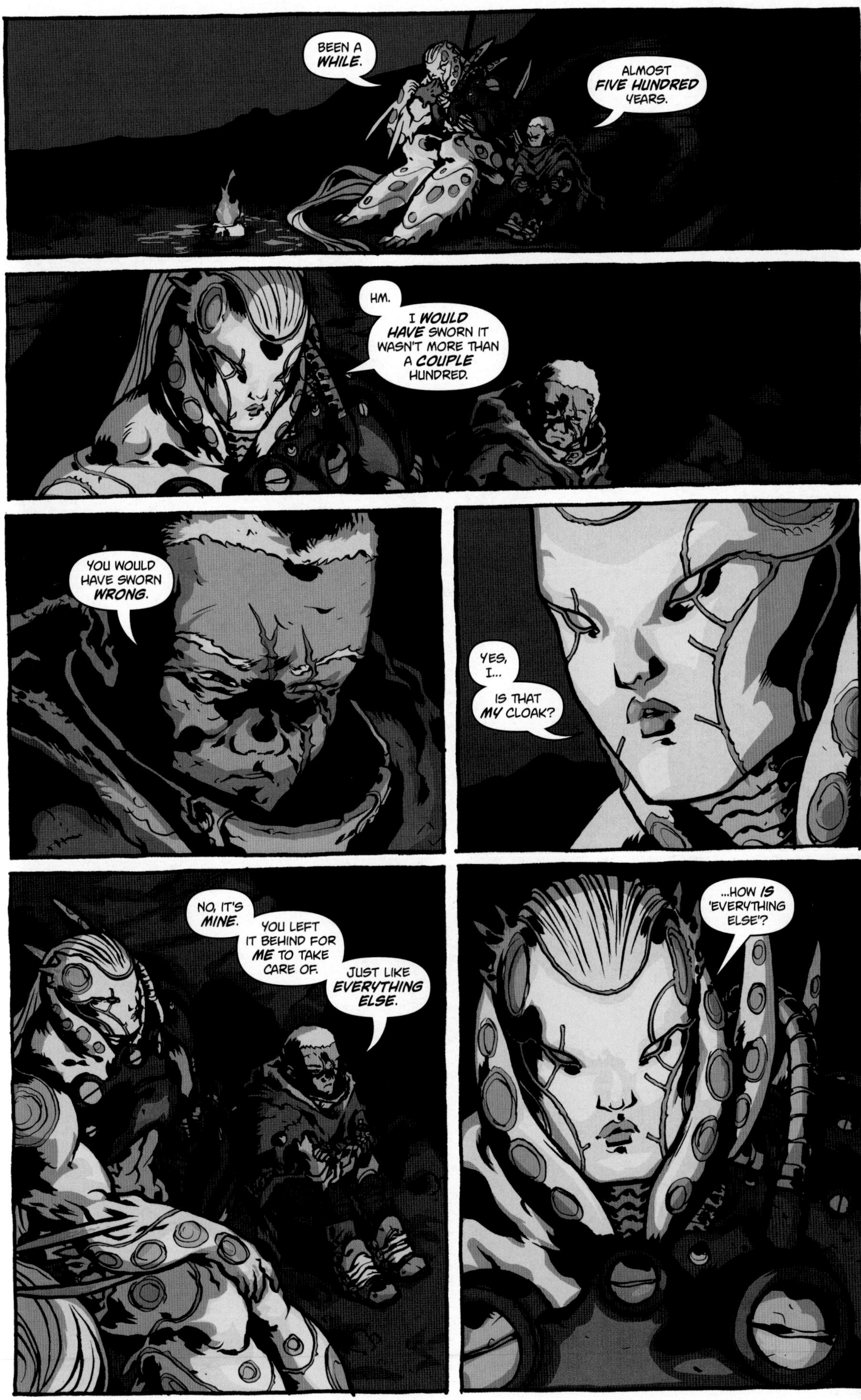

BEEN A WHILE.
ALMOST FIVE HUNDRED YEARS.
HM.
I WOULD HAVE SWORN IT WASN'T MORE THAN A COUPLE HUNDRED.
YOU WOULD HAVE SWORN WRONG.
YES, I...
IS THAT MY CLOAK?
NO, IT'S MINE.
YOU LEFT IT BEHIND FOR ME TO TAKE CARE OF.
JUST LIKE EVERYTHING ELSE.
...HOW IS 'EVERYTHING ELSE'?

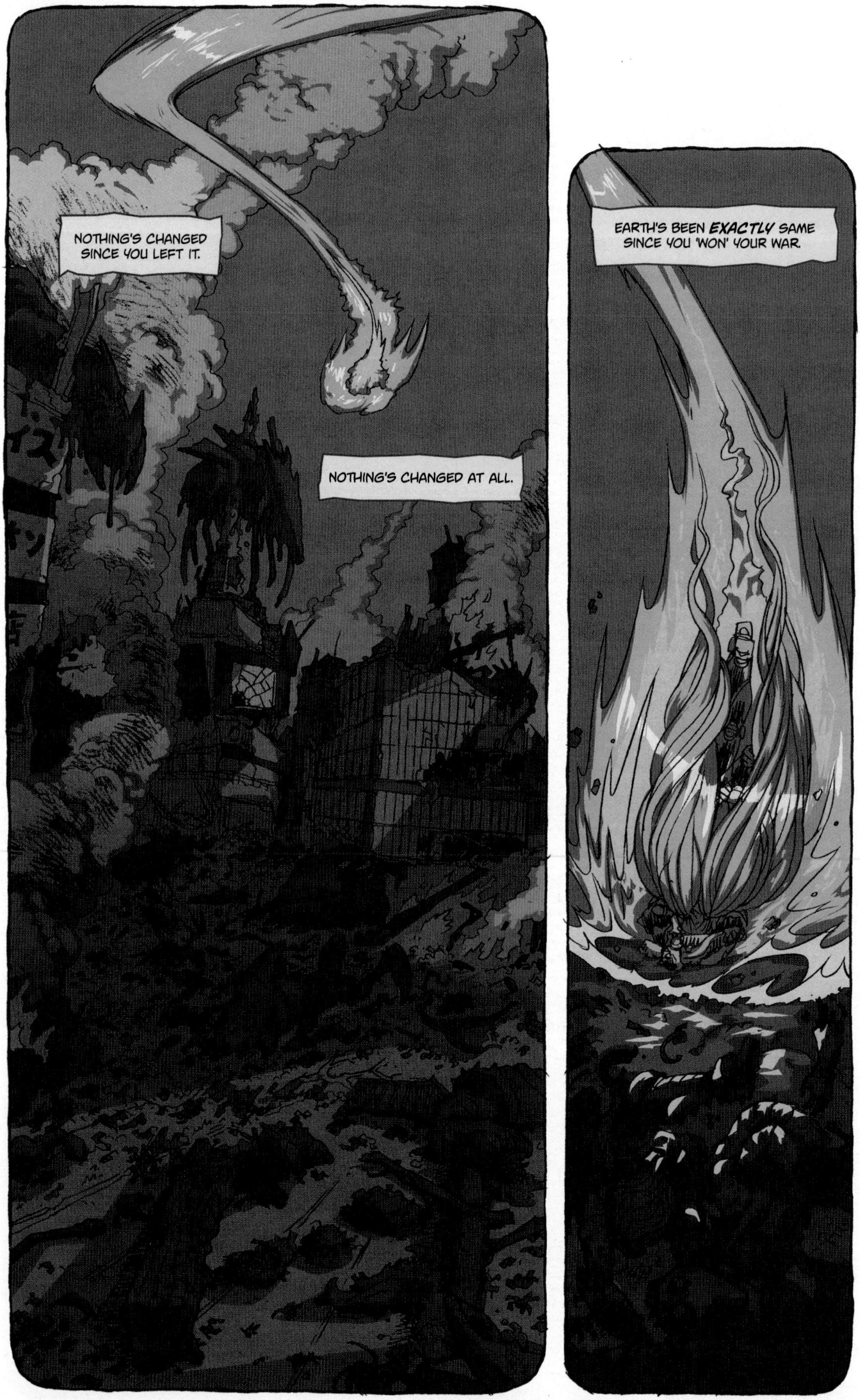
NOTHING'S CHANGED SINCE YOU LEFT IT.
NOTHING'S CHANGED AT ALL.
EARTH'S BEEN EXACTLY SAME SINCE YOU 'WON' YOUR WAR.

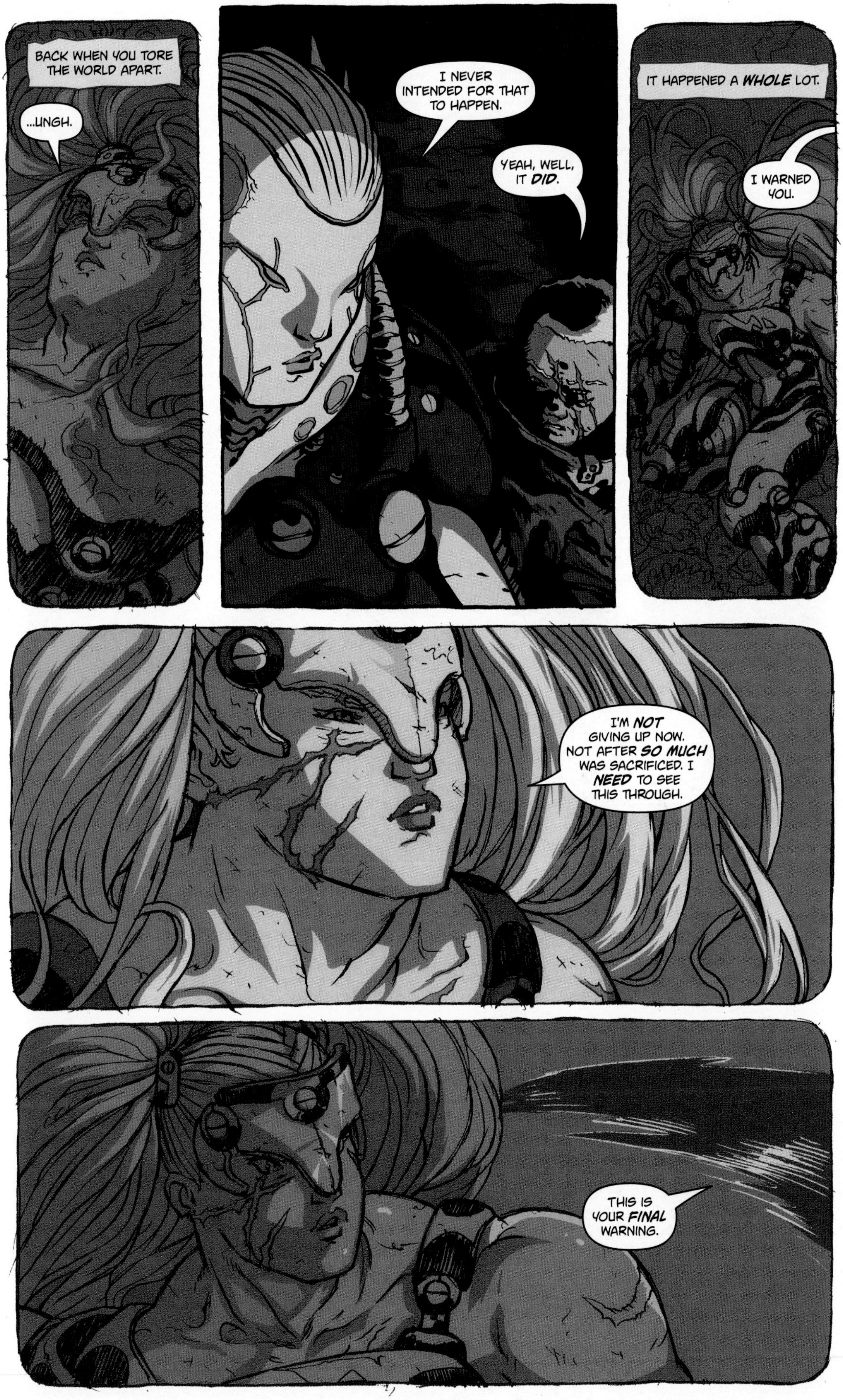
BACK WHEN YOU TORE THE WORLD APART.
...UNGH.
I NEVER INTENDED FOR THAT TO HAPPEN.
YEAH, WELL, IT DID.
IT HAPPENED A WHOLE LOT.
I WARNED YOU.
I'M NOT GIVING UP NOW. NOT AFTER SO MUCH WAS SACRIFICED. I NEED TO SEE THIS THROUGH.
THIS IS YOUR FINAL WARNING.

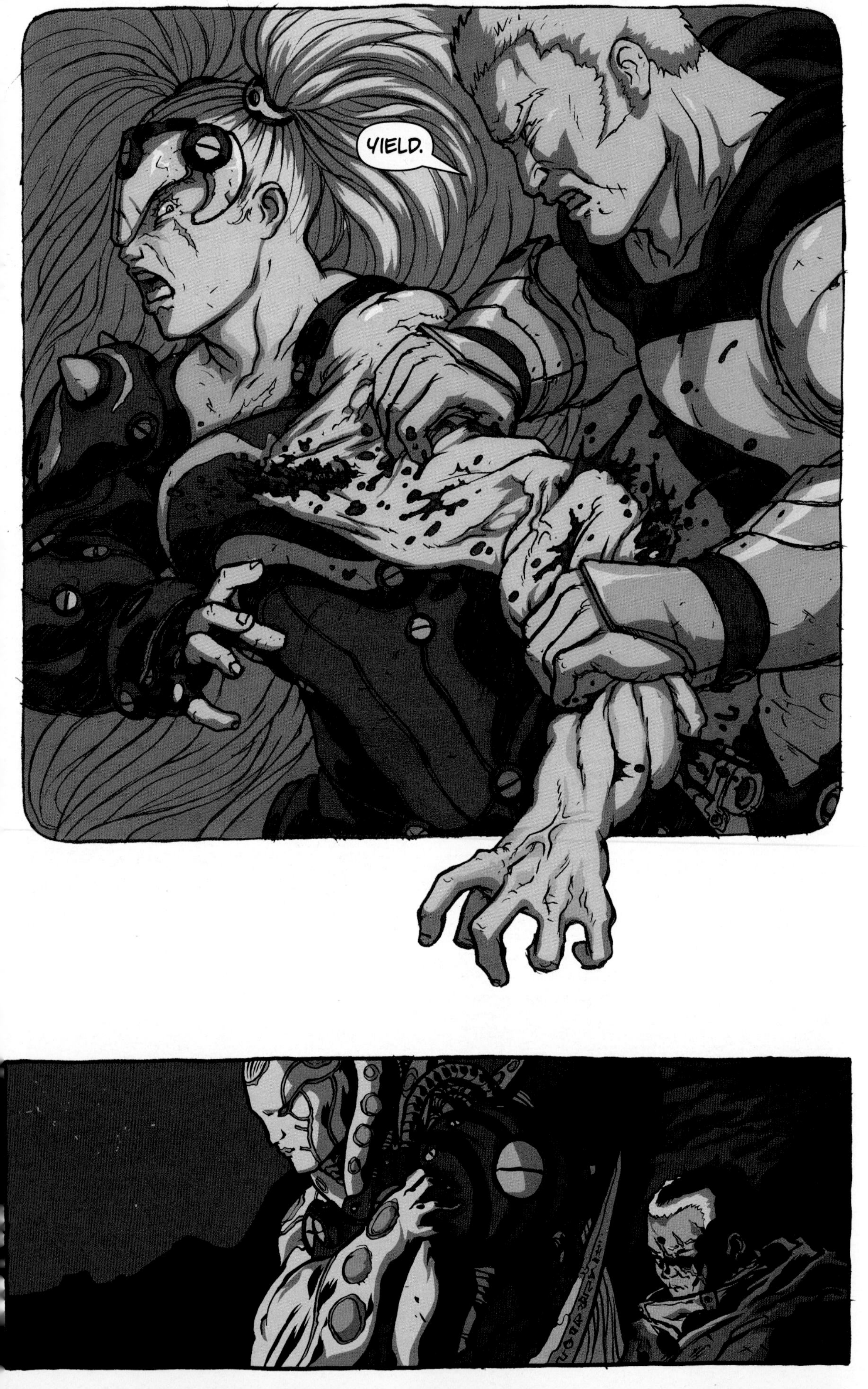
YIELD.

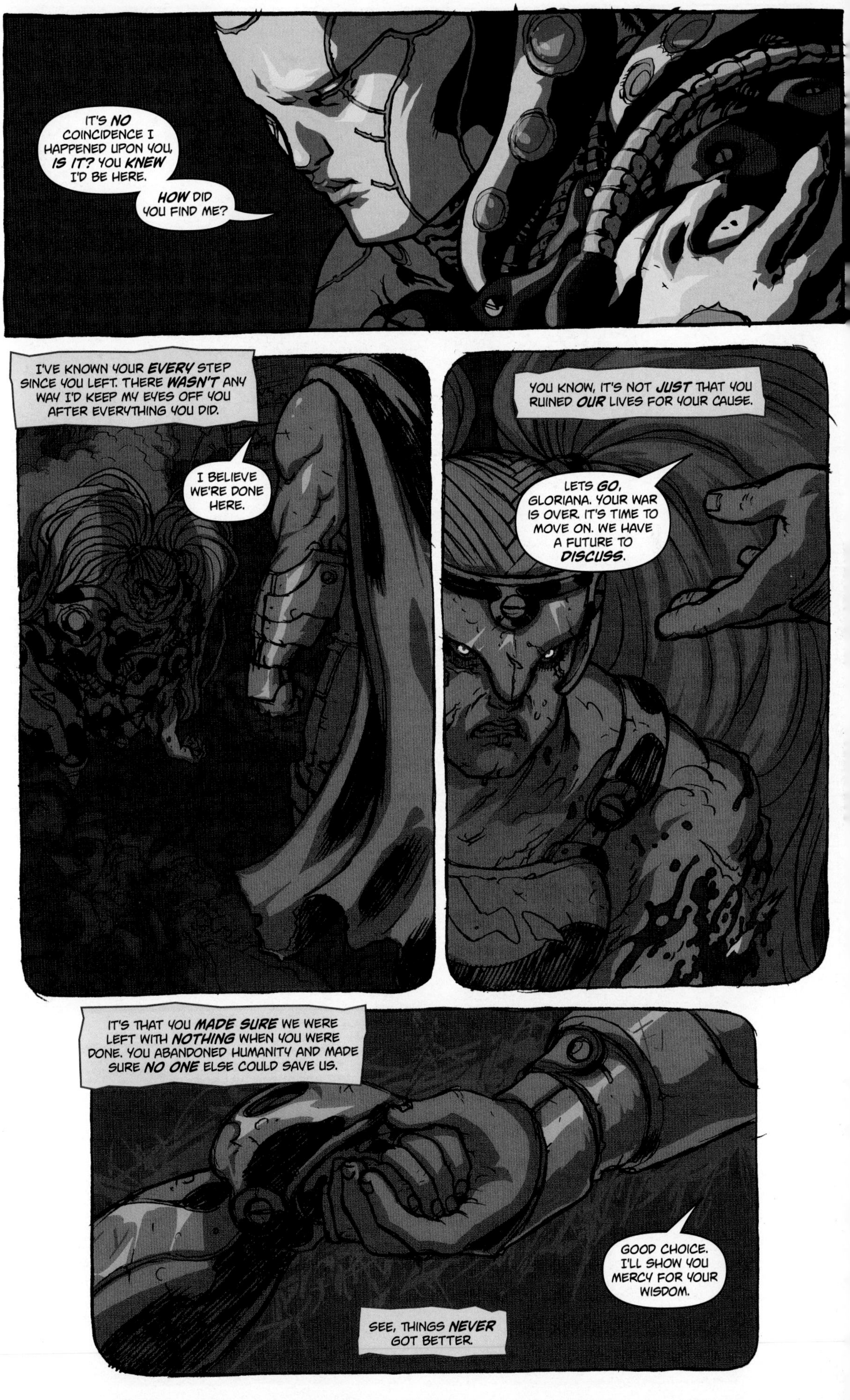

IT'S NO COINCIDENCE I HAPPENED UPON YOU, IS IT? YOU KNEW I'D BE HERE.
HOW DID YOU FIND ME?
I'VE KNOWN YOUR EVERY STEP SINCE YOU LEFT. THERE WASN'T ANY WAY I'D KEEP MY EYES OFF YOU AFTER EVERYTHING YOU DID.
I BELIEVE WE'RE DONE HERE.
YOU KNOW, IT'S NOT JUST THAT YOU RUINED OUR LIVES FOR YOUR CAUSE.
LETS GO, GLORIANA. YOUR WAR IS OVER. IT'S TIME TO MOVE ON. WE HAVE A FUTURE TO DISCUSS.
IT'S THAT YOU MADE SURE WE WERE LEFT WITH NOTHING WHEN YOU WERE DONE. YOU ABANDONED HUMANITY AND MADE SURE NO ONE ELSE COULD SAVE US.
GOOD CHOICE. I'LL SHOW YOU MERCY FOR YOUR WISDOM.
SEE, THINGS NEVER GOT BETTER.

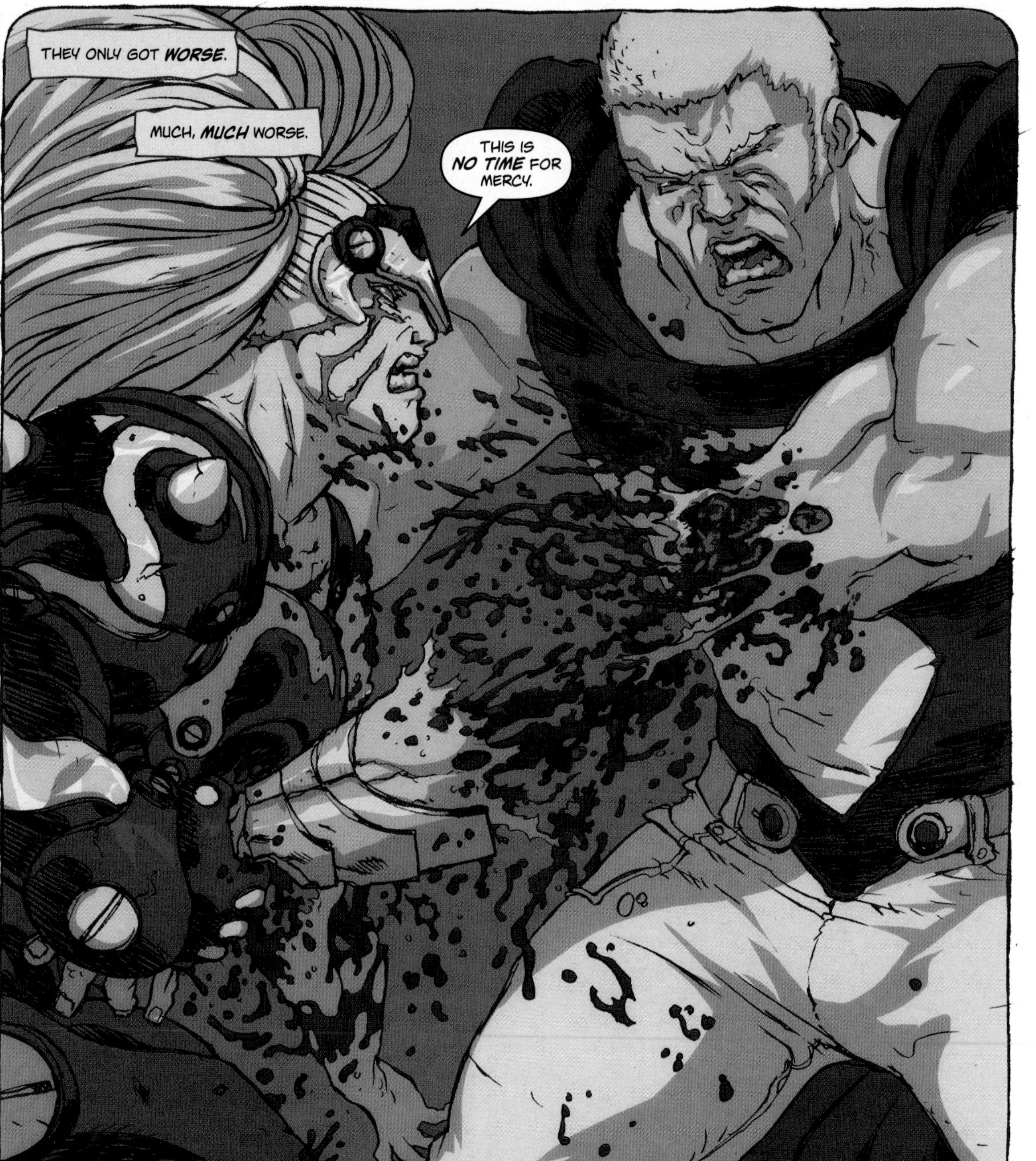
THEY ONLY GOT WORSE.
MUCH, MUCH WORSE.
THIS IS NO TIME FOR MERCY.

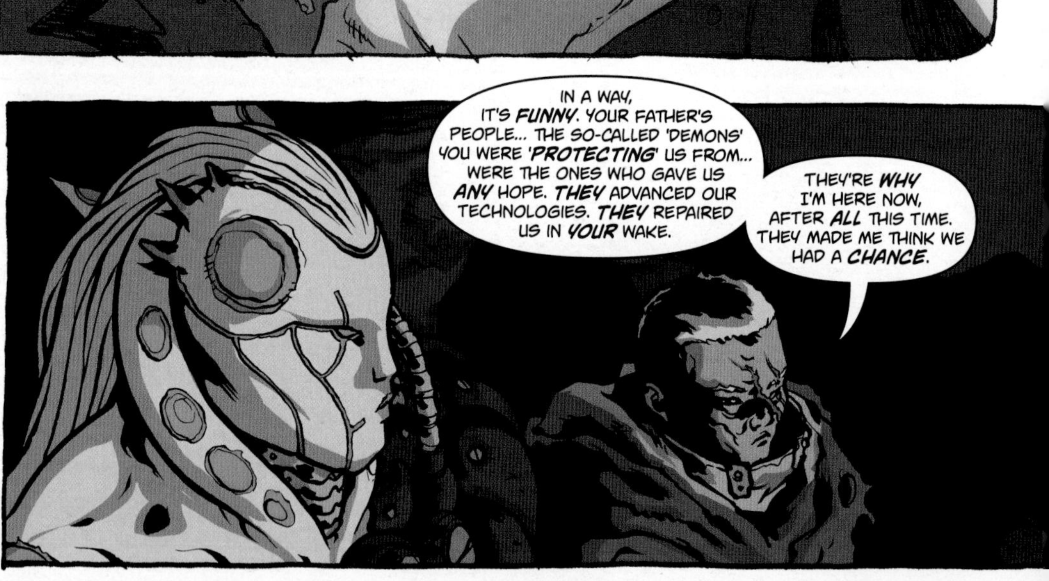
IN A WAY, IT'S FUNNY. YOUR FATHER'S PEOPLE... THE SO-CALLED 'DEMONS' YOU WERE 'PROTECTING' US FROM... WERE THE ONES WHO GAVE US ANY HOPE. THEY ADVANCED OUR TECHNOLOGIES. THEY REPAIRED US IN YOUR WAKE.
THEY'RE WHY I'M HERE NOW, AFTER ALL THIS TIME. THEY MADE ME THINK WE HAD A CHANCE.

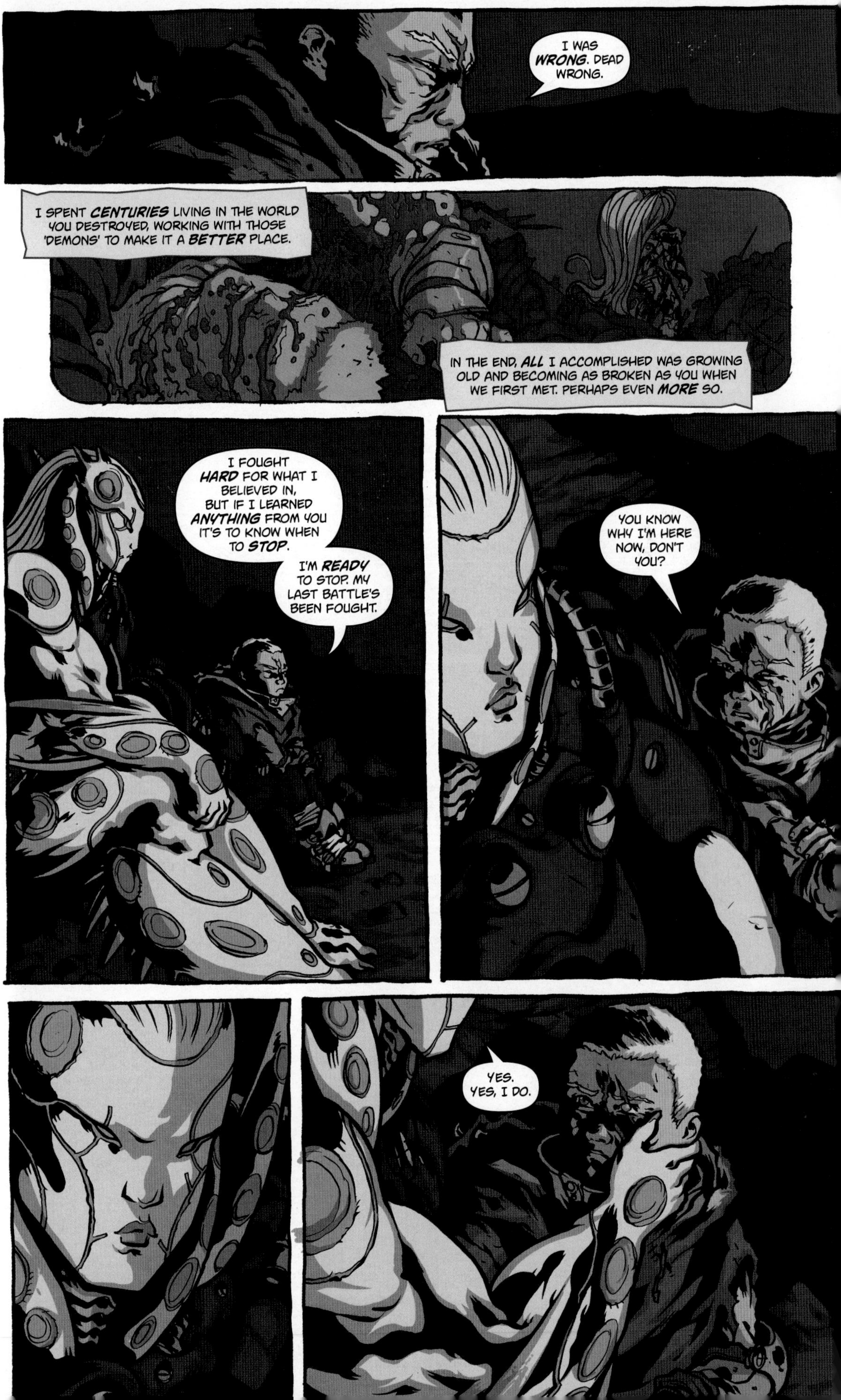
I WAS WRONG. DEAD WRONG.
I SPENT CENTURIES LIVING IN THE WORLD YOU DESTROYED, WORKING WITH THOSE 'DEMONS' TO MAKE IT A BETTER PLACE.
IN THE END, ALL I ACCOMPLISHED WAS GROWING OLD AND BECOMING AS BROKEN AS YOU WHEN WE FIRST MET. PERHAPS EVEN MORE SO.
I FOUGHT HARD FOR WHAT I BELIEVED IN, BUT IF I LEARNED ANYTHING FROM YOU IT'S TO KNOW WHEN TO STOP.
I'M READY TO STOP. MY LAST BATTLE'S BEEN FOUGHT.
YOU KNOW WHY I'M HERE NOW, DON'T YOU?
YES. YES, I DO.

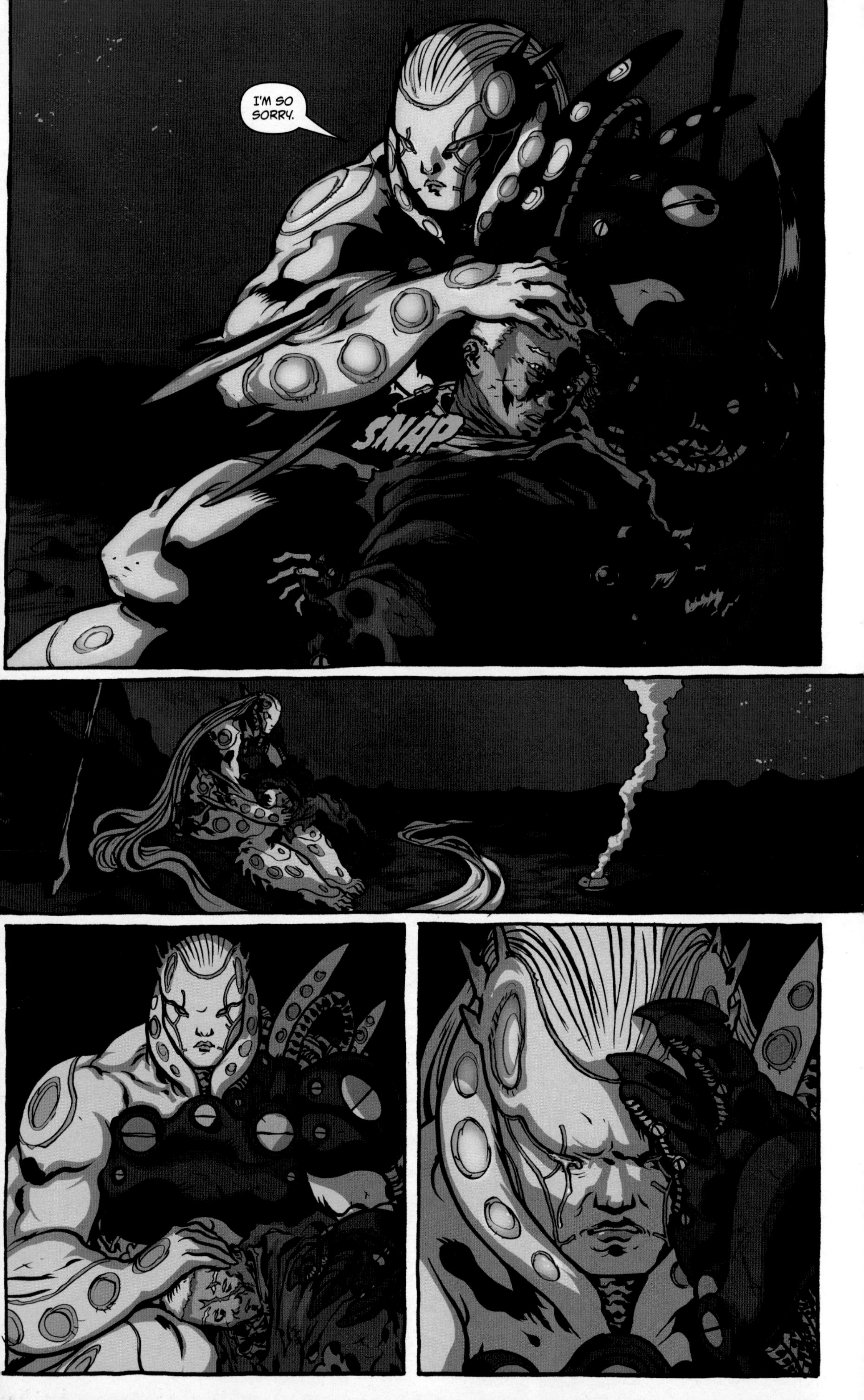
I'M SO SORRY.
SNAP

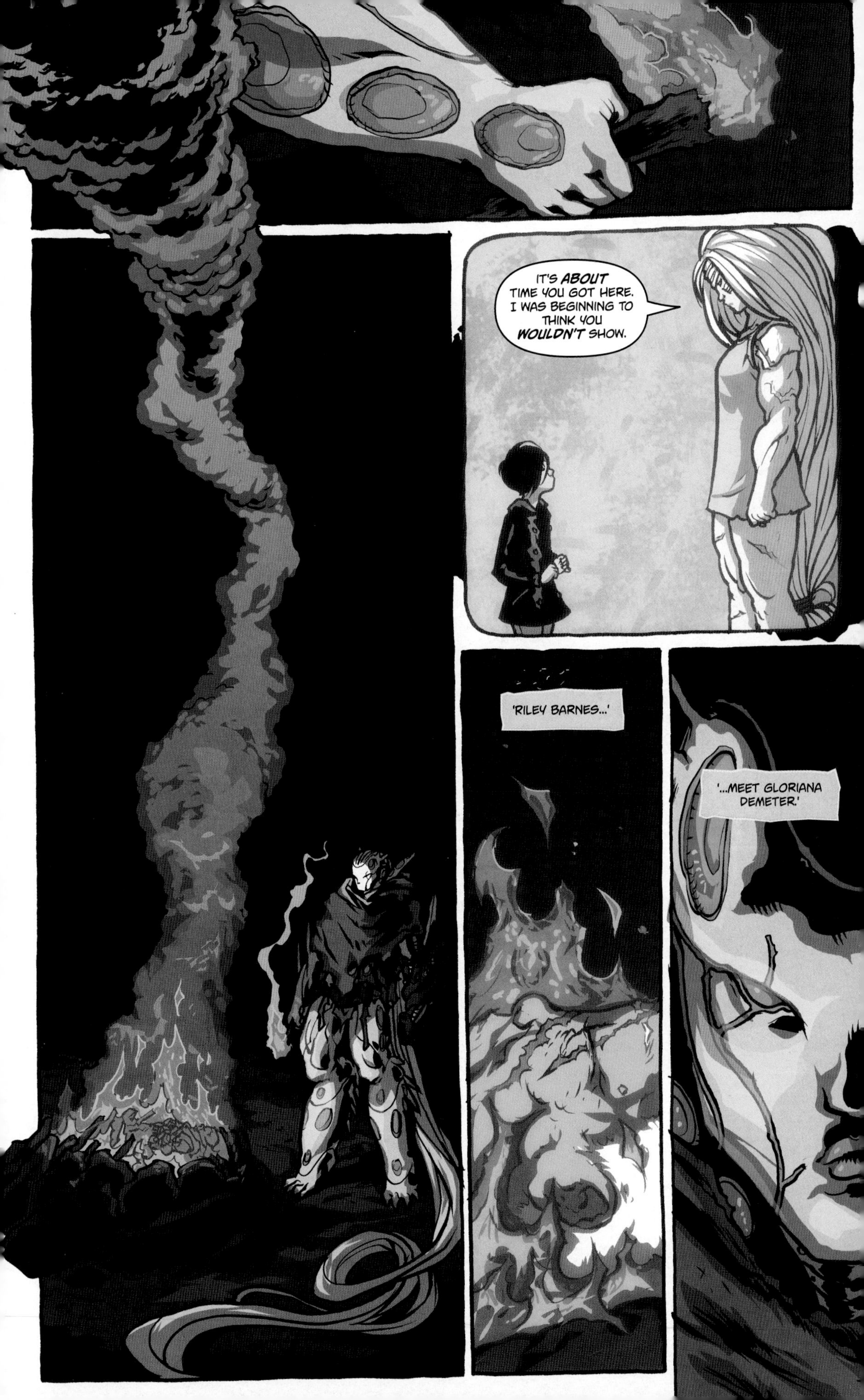
IT'S ABOUT TIME YOU GOT HERE. I WAS BEGINNING TO THINK YOU WOULDN'T SHOW.
'RILEY BARNES...'
'...MEET GLORIANA DEMETER.'

RILEY

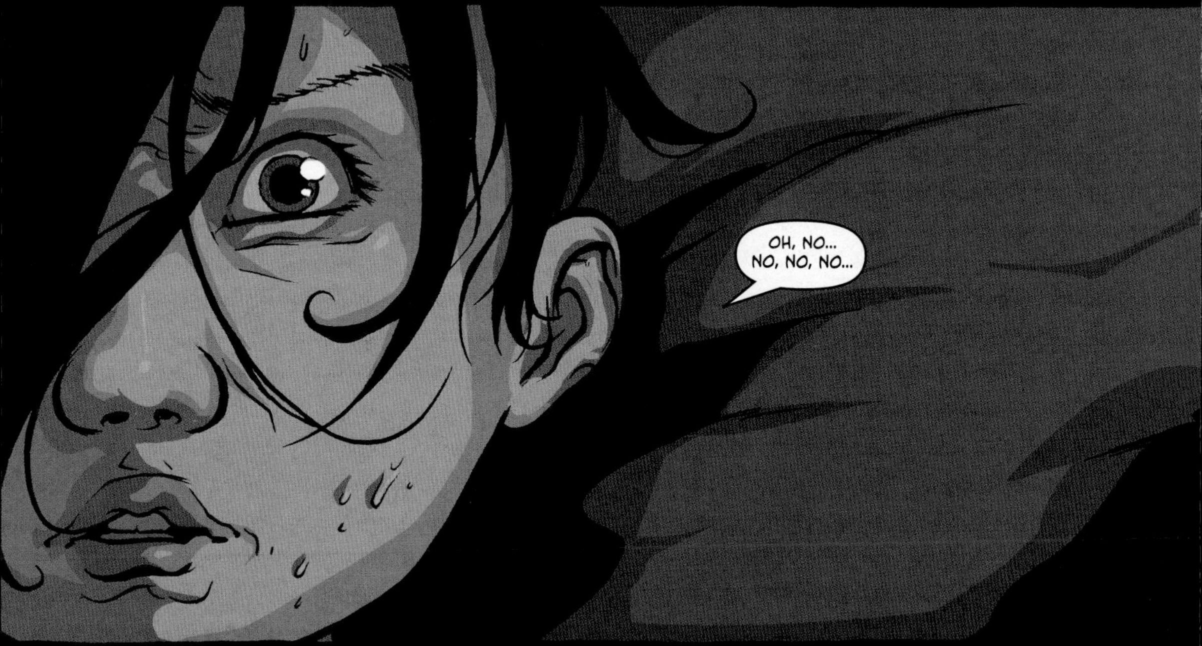
OH, NO...
NO, NO, NO...

AWAKENS

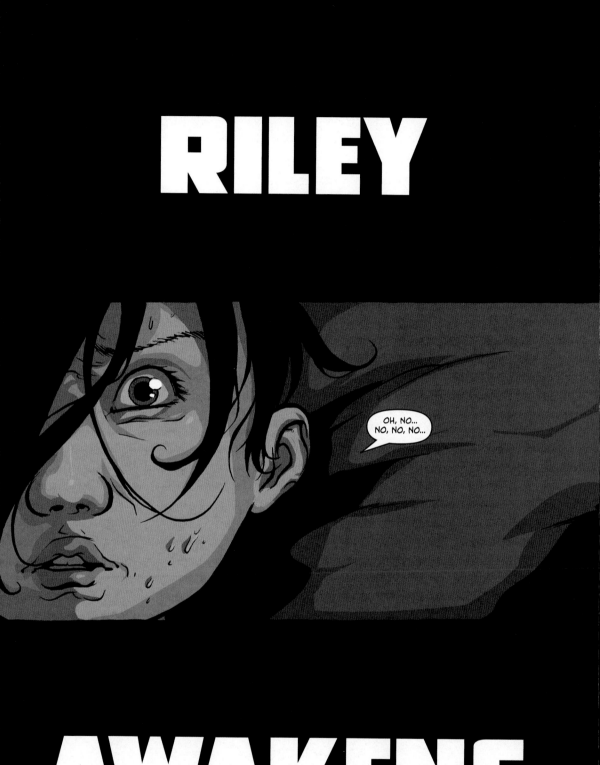

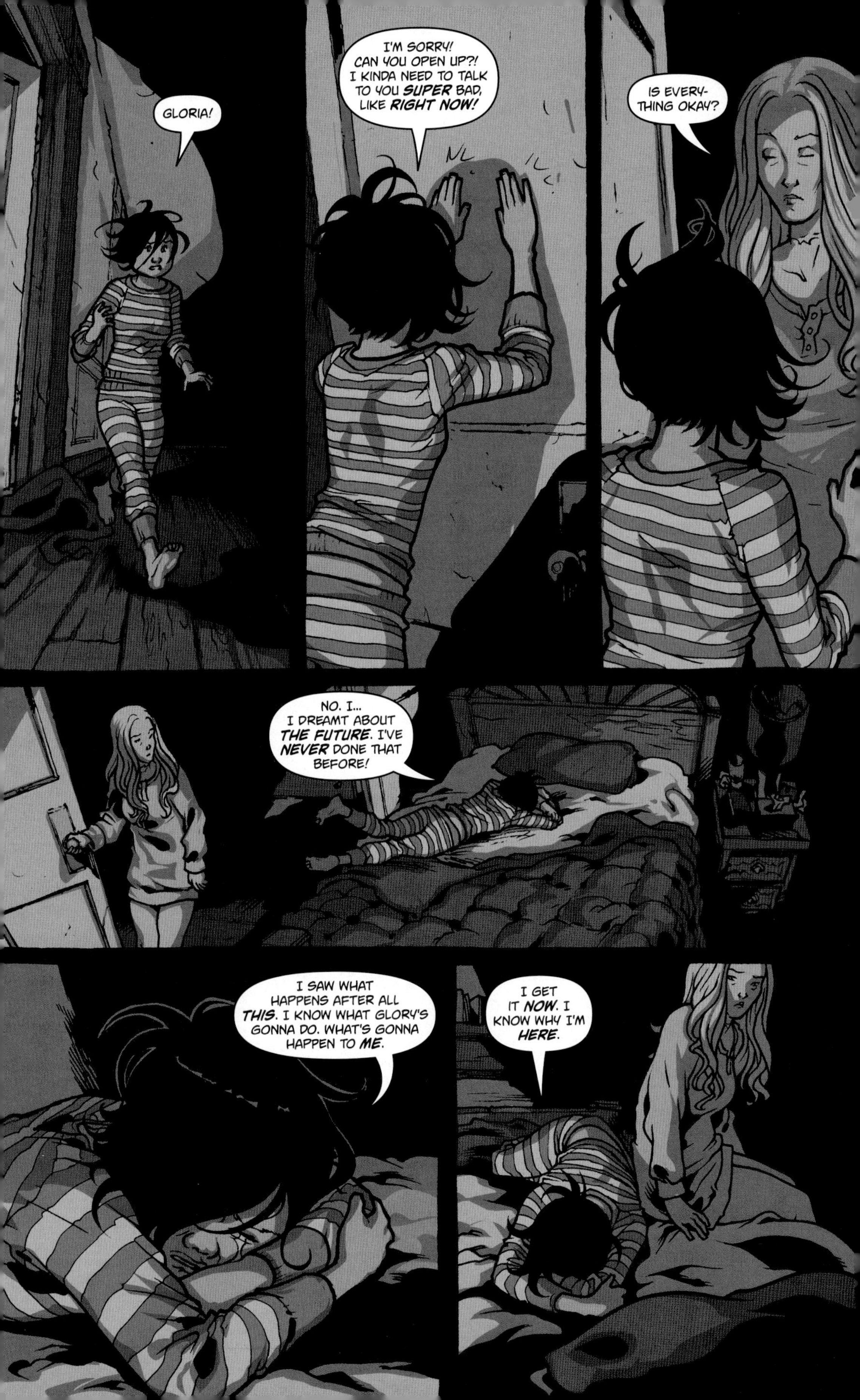
GLORIA!
I'M SORRY! CAN YOU OPEN UP?! I KINDA NEED TO TALK TO YOU SUPER BAD, LIKE RIGHT NOW!
IS EVERY-THING OKAY?
NO. I... I DREAMT ABOUT THE FUTURE. I'VE NEVER DONE THAT BEFORE!
I SAW WHAT HAPPENS AFTER ALL THIS. I KNOW WHAT GLORY'S GONNA DO. WHAT'S GONNA HAPPEN TO ME.
I GET IT NOW. I KNOW WHY I'M HERE.

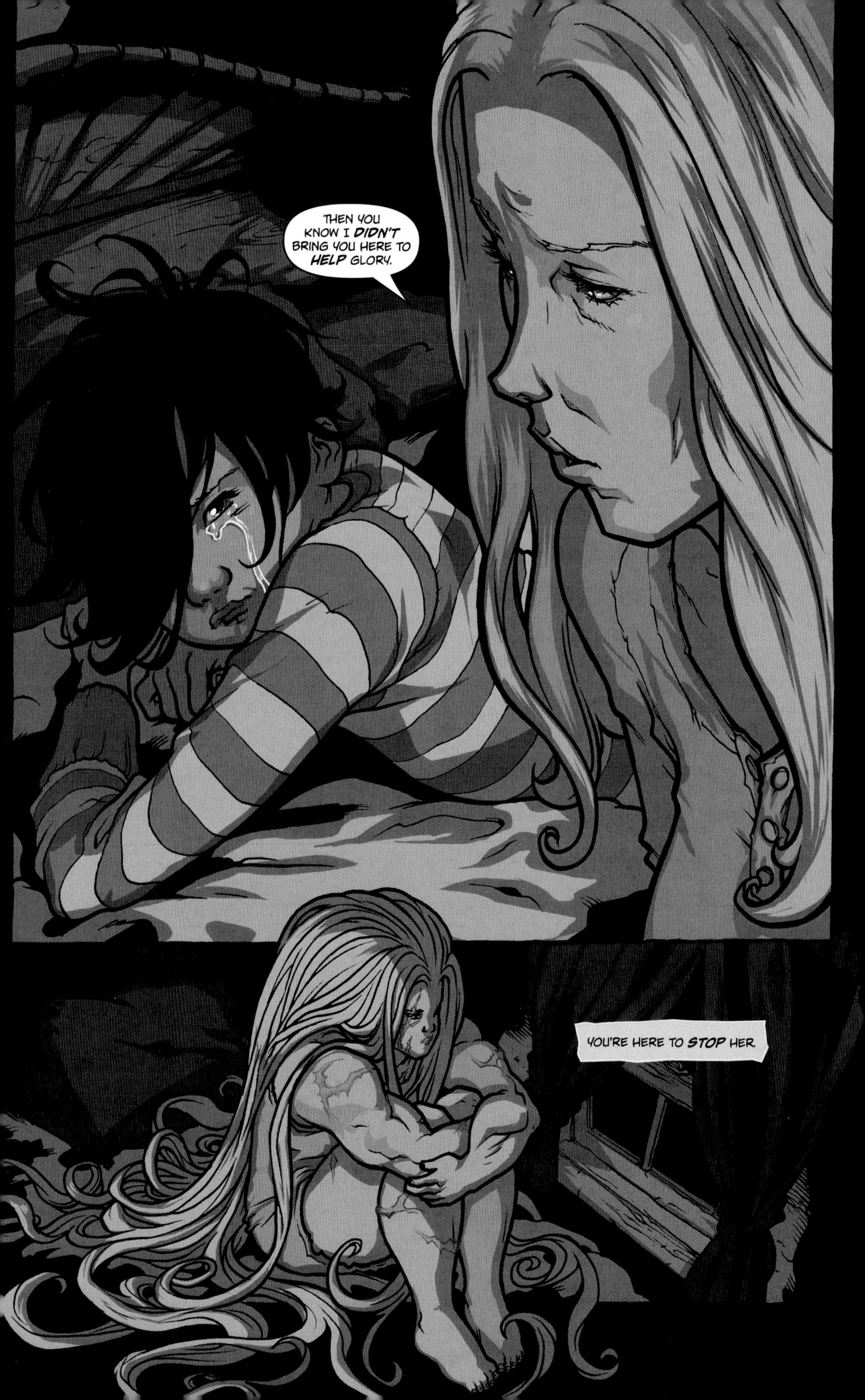
THEN YOU KNOW I *DIDN'T* BRING YOU HERE TO *HELP* GLORY.
YOU'RE HERE TO *STOP* HER.

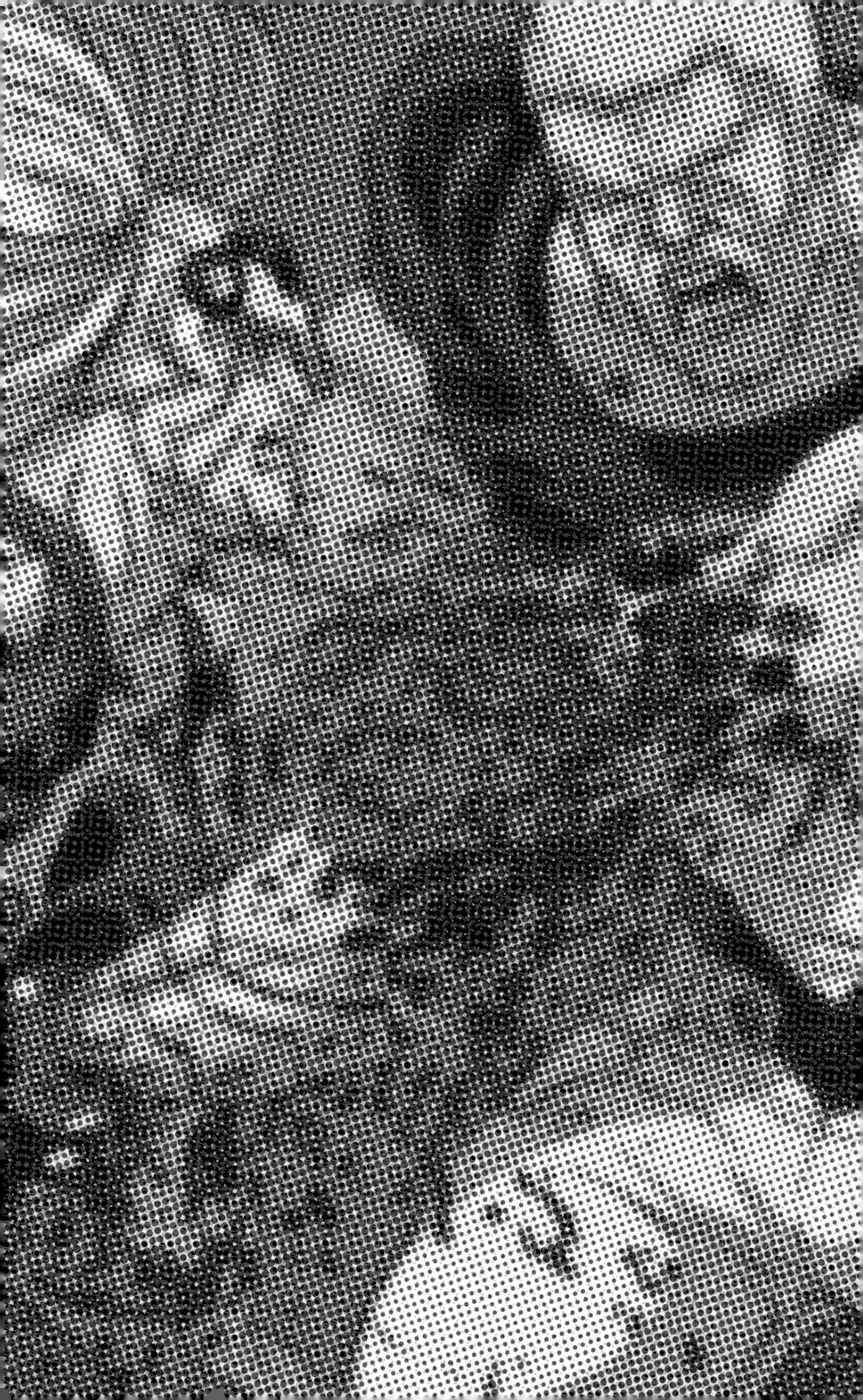

Chapter Four

Cover by Ulises Farinas

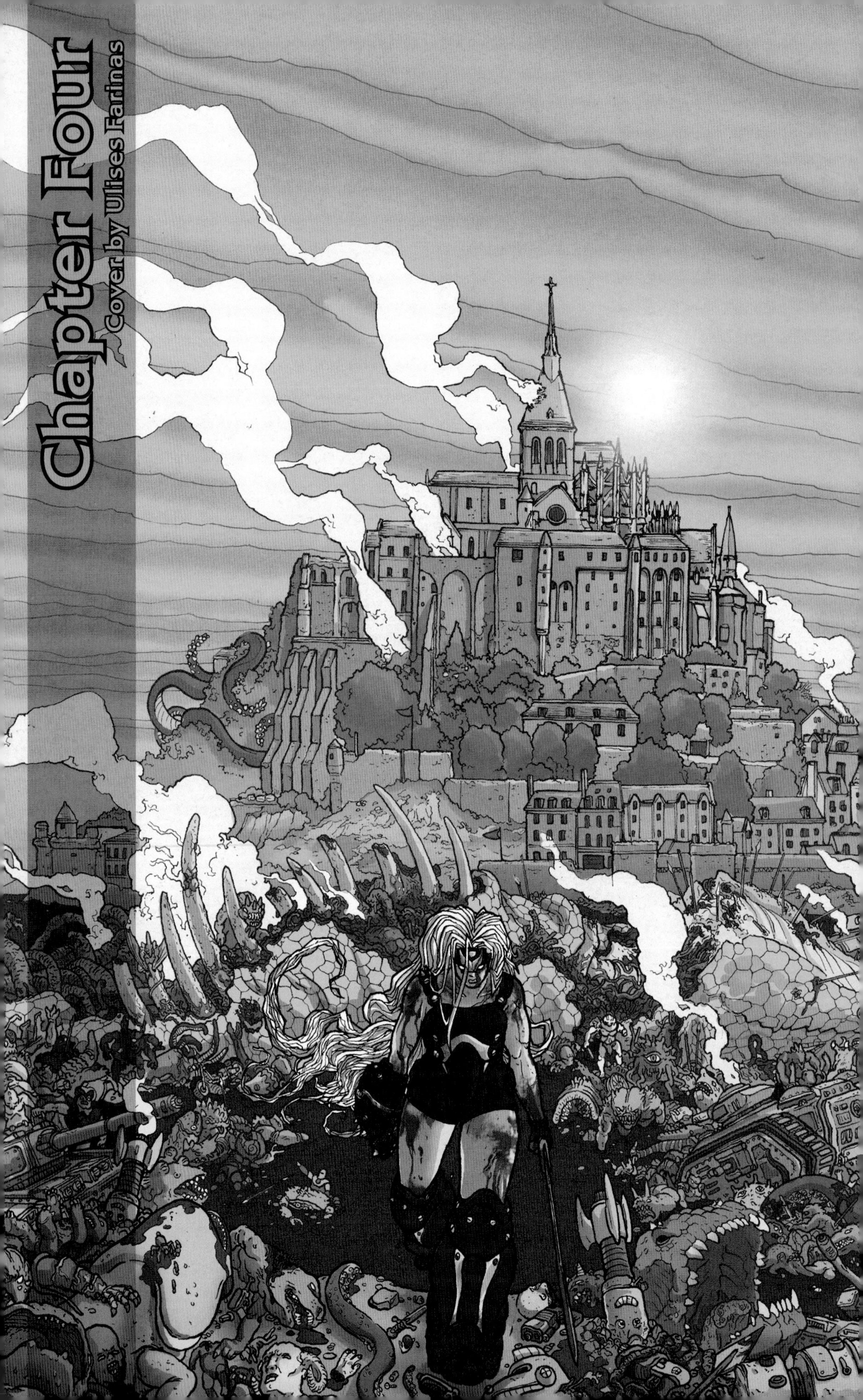

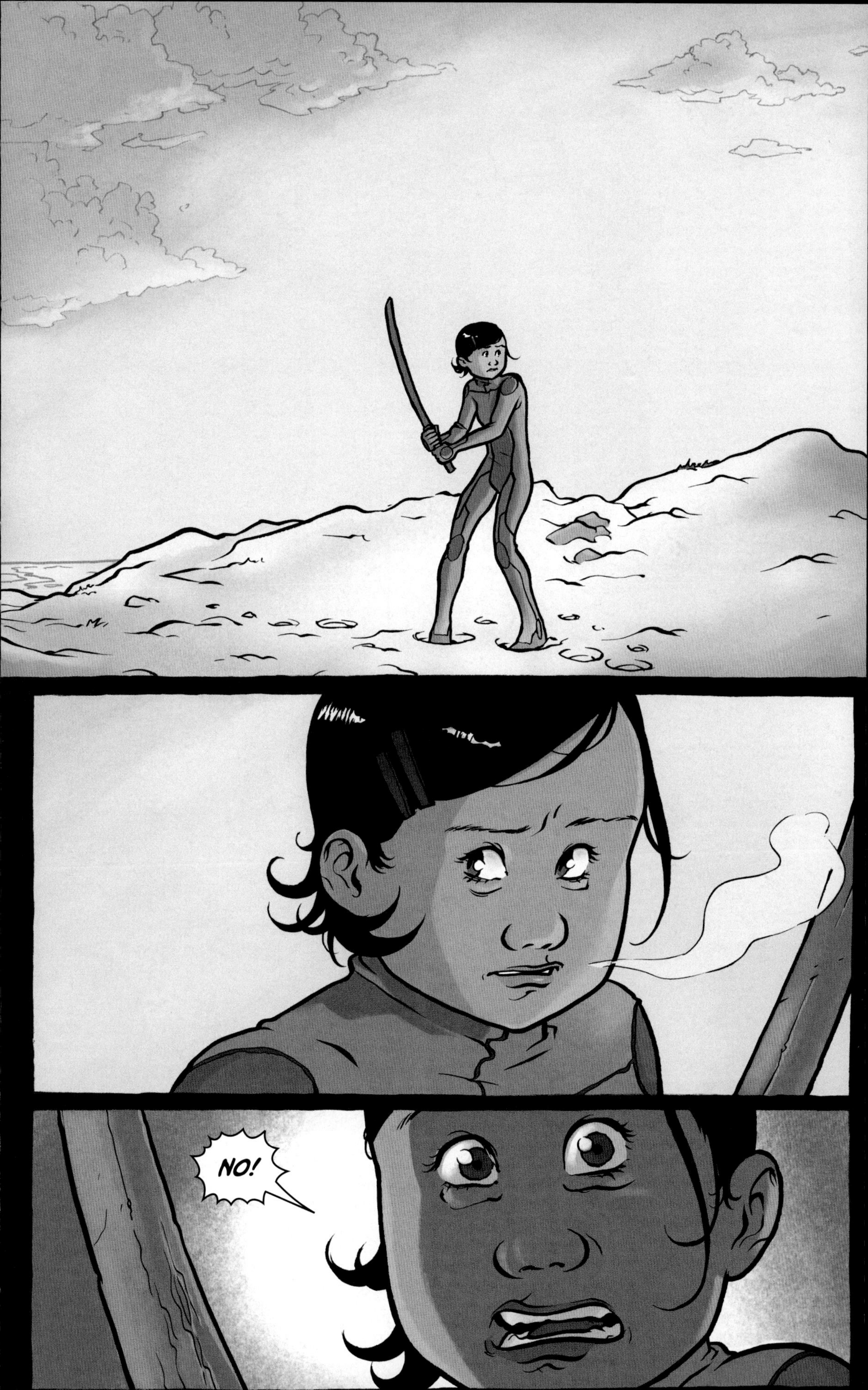
NO!

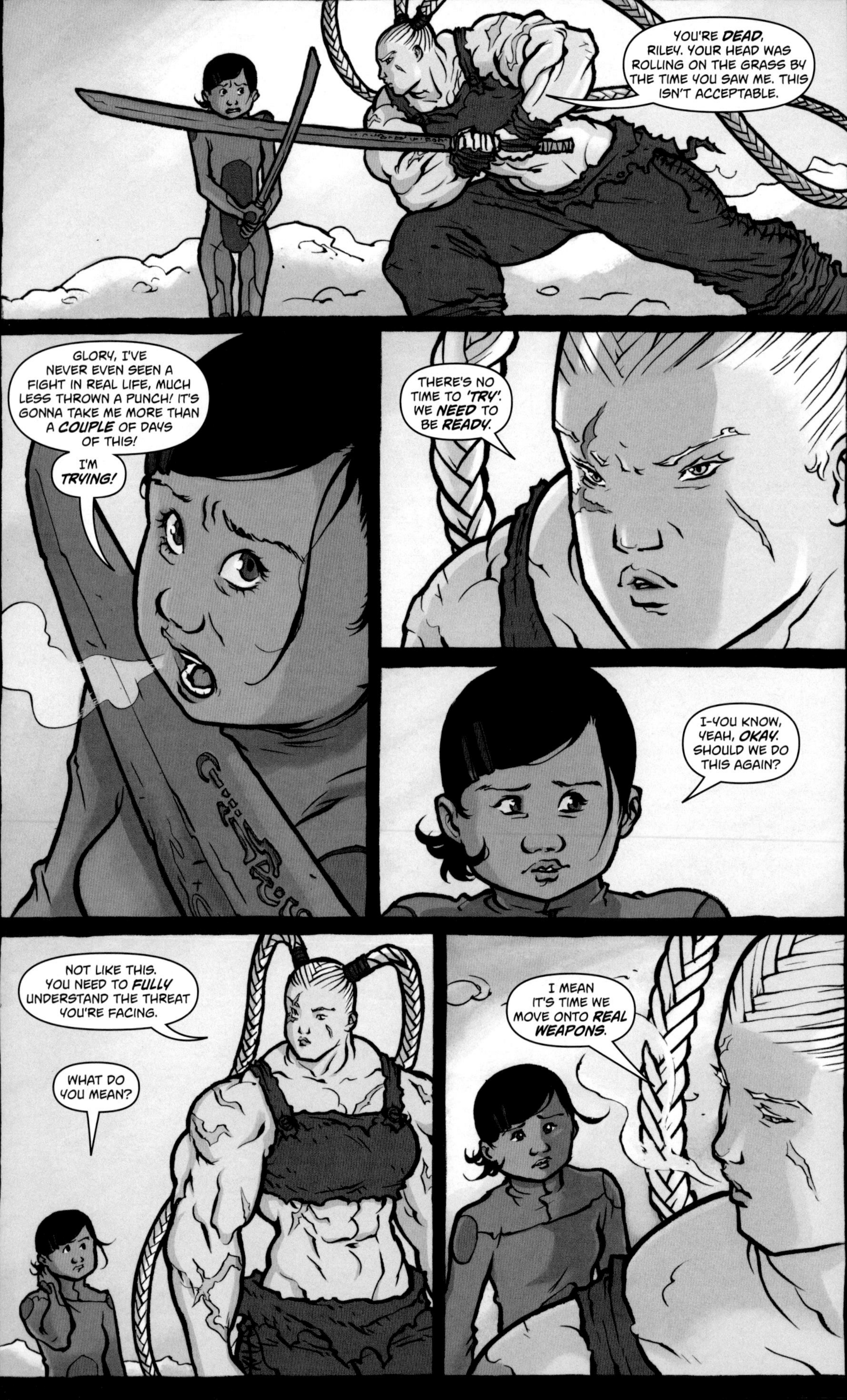

YOU'RE DEAD, RILEY. YOUR HEAD WAS ROLLING ON THE GRASS BY THE TIME YOU SAW ME. THIS ISN'T ACCEPTABLE.
GLORY, I'VE NEVER EVEN SEEN A FIGHT IN REAL LIFE, MUCH LESS THROWN A PUNCH! IT'S GONNA TAKE ME MORE THAN A COUPLE OF DAYS OF THIS!
I'M TRYING!
THERE'S NO TIME TO 'TRY'. WE NEED TO BE READY.
I-YOU KNOW, YEAH, OKAY. SHOULD WE DO THIS AGAIN?
NOT LIKE THIS. YOU NEED TO FULLY UNDERSTAND THE THREAT YOU'RE FACING.
WHAT DO YOU MEAN?
I MEAN IT'S TIME WE MOVE ONTO REAL WEAPONS.

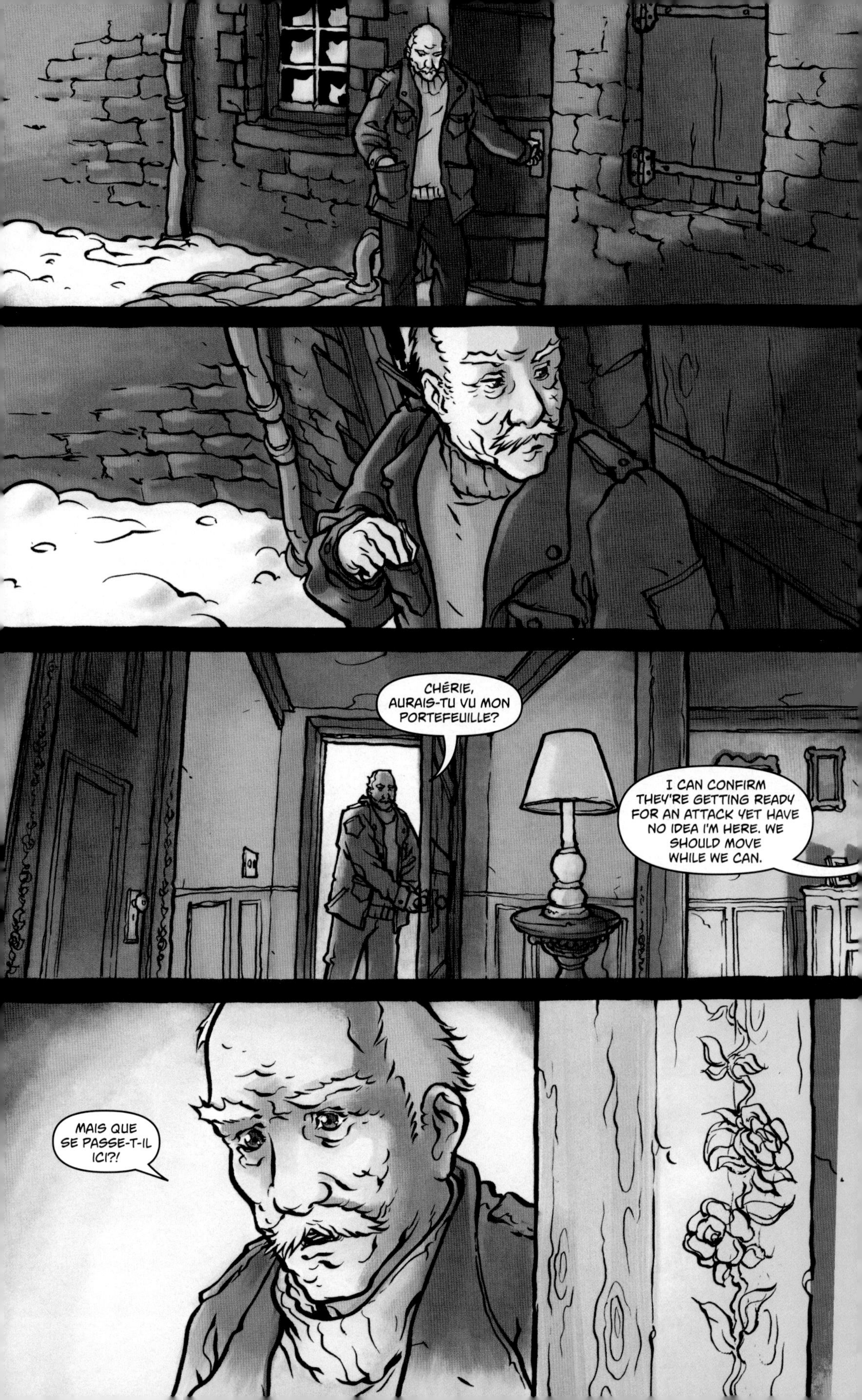

CHÉRIE, AURAIS-TU VU MON PORTEFEUILLE?
I CAN CONFIRM THEY'RE GETTING READY FOR AN ATTACK YET HAVE NO IDEA I'M HERE. WE SHOULD MOVE WHILE WE CAN.
MAIS QUE SE PASSE-T-IL ICI?!

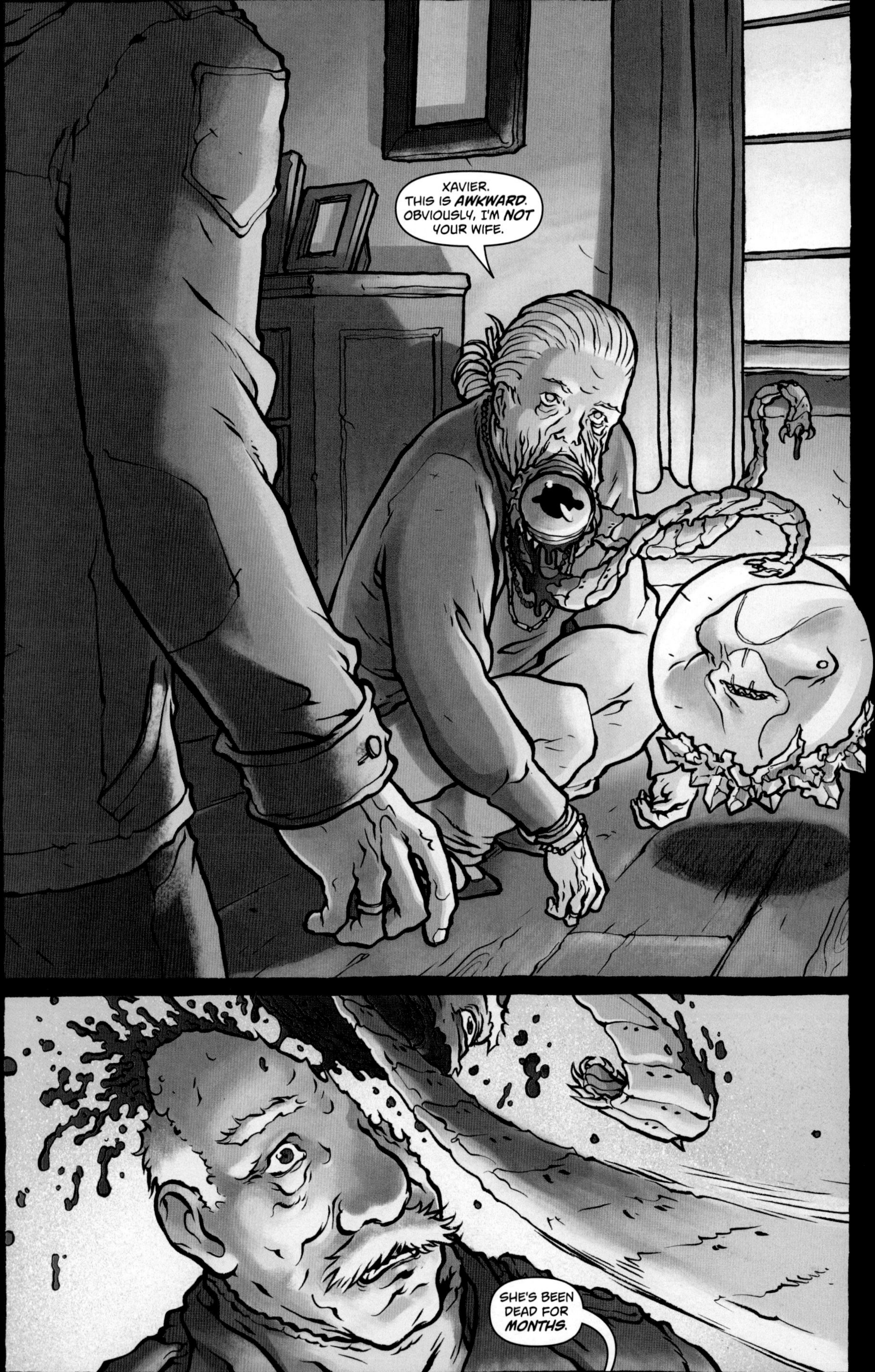
XAVIER. THIS IS *AWKWARD*. OBVIOUSLY, I'M *NOT* YOUR WIFE.
SHE'S BEEN DEAD FOR *MONTHS*.

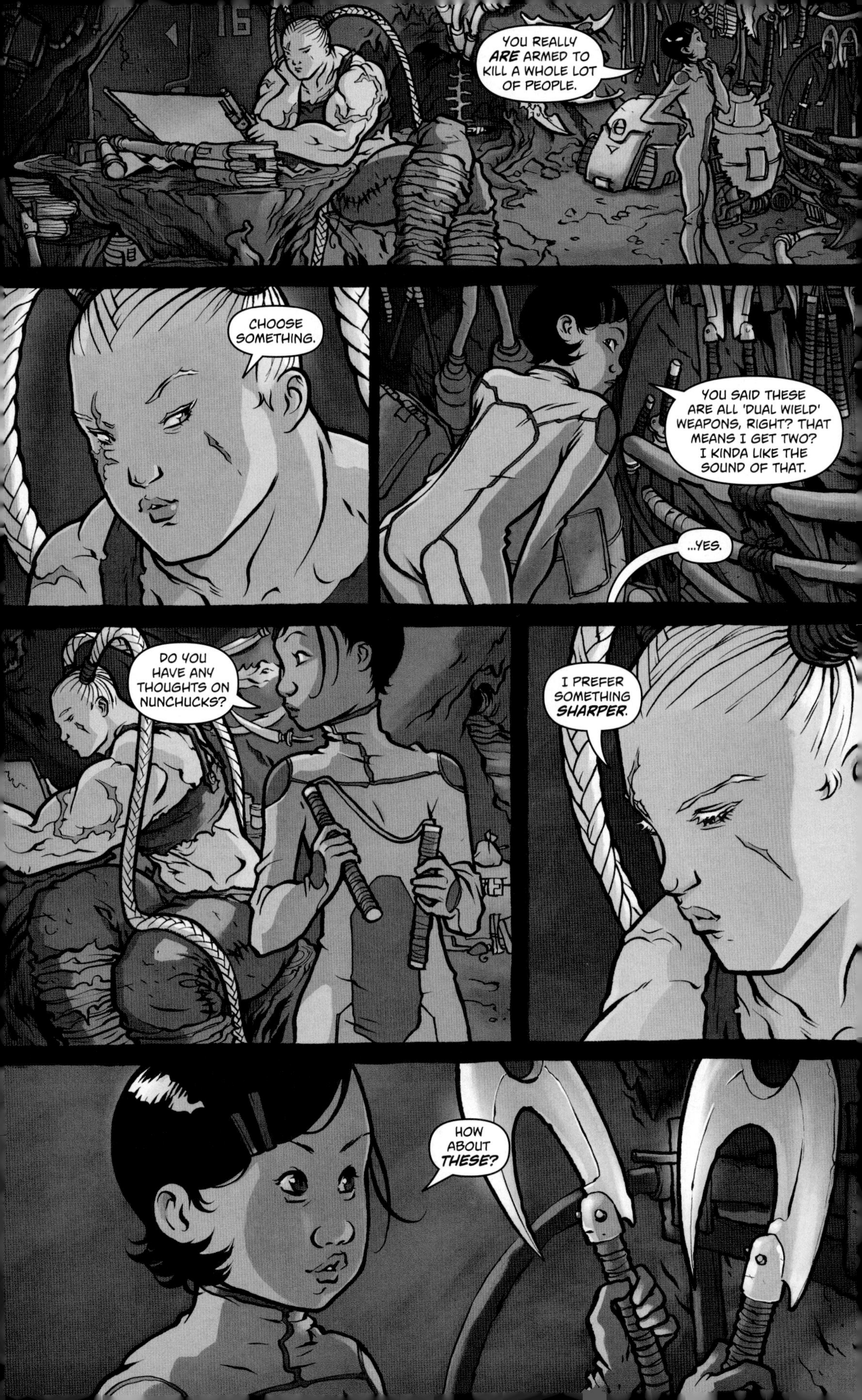
YOU REALLY ARE ARMED TO KILL A WHOLE LOT OF PEOPLE.
CHOOSE SOMETHING.
YOU SAID THESE ARE ALL 'DUAL WIELD' WEAPONS, RIGHT? THAT MEANS I GET TWO? I KINDA LIKE THE SOUND OF THAT.
...YES.
DO YOU HAVE ANY THOUGHTS ON NUNCHUCKS?
I PREFER SOMETHING SHARPER.
HOW ABOUT THESE?

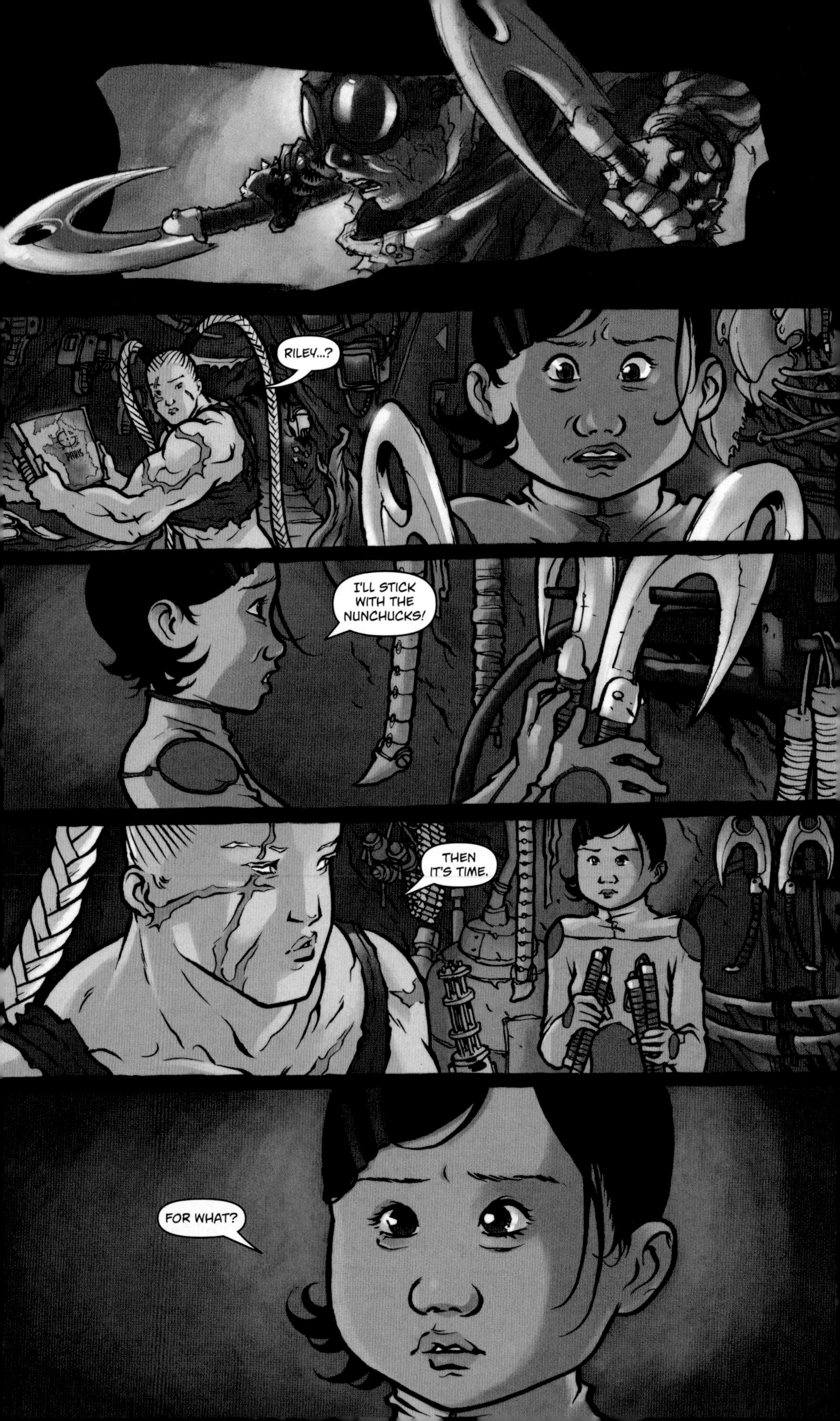
RILEY...?
I'LL STICK WITH THE NUNCHUCKS!
THEN IT'S TIME.
FOR WHAT?

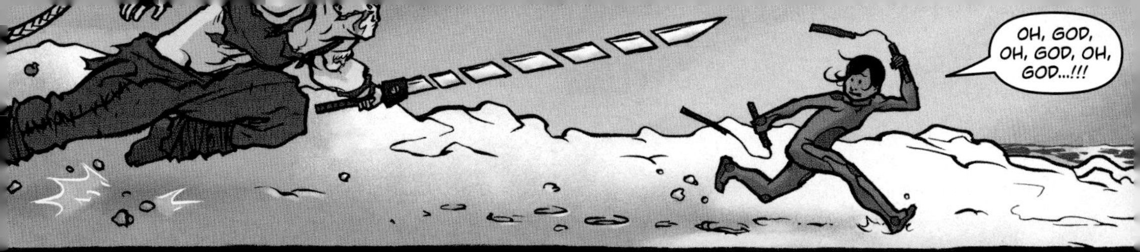
OH, GOD, OH, GOD, OH, GOD...!!!

IMAGE COMICS PRESENTS

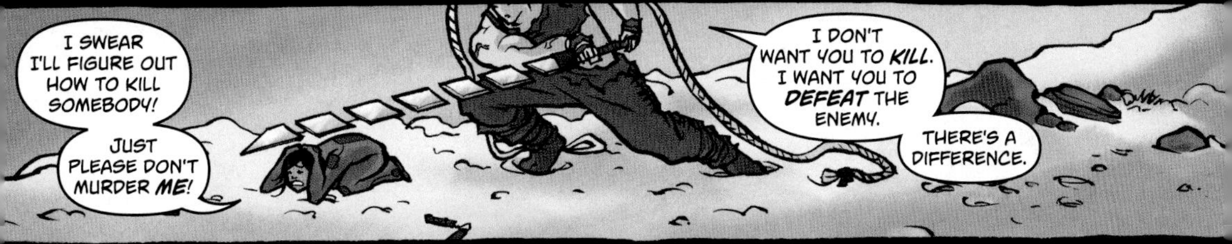
I SWEAR I'LL FIGURE OUT HOW TO KILL SOMEBODY!
JUST PLEASE DON'T MURDER ME!
I DON'T WANT YOU TO KILL. I WANT YOU TO DEFEAT THE ENEMY.
THERE'S A DIFFERENCE.

JOE KEATINGE
WRITER

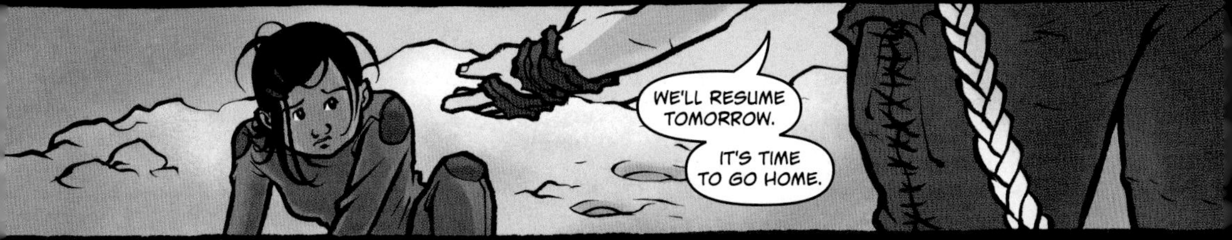
WE'LL RESUME TOMORROW.
IT'S TIME TO GO HOME.

ROSS CAMPBELL
ARTIST

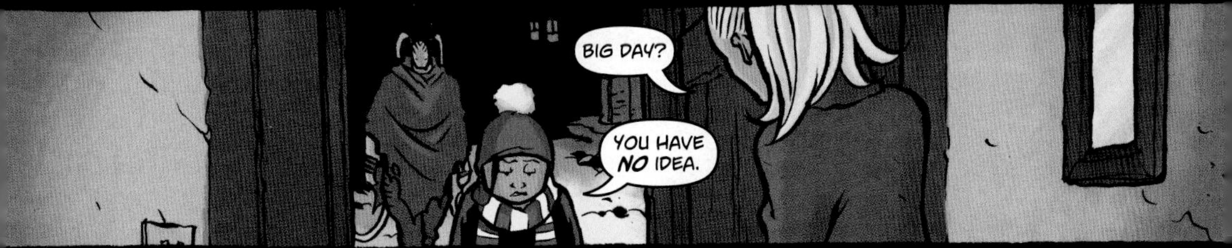
BIG DAY?
YOU HAVE NO IDEA.

JOSEPH BERGIN III	DOUGLAS E. SHERWOOD	ERIC STEPHENSON	ULISES FARINAS
COLORIST	LETTERER	EDITOR	COVER ART

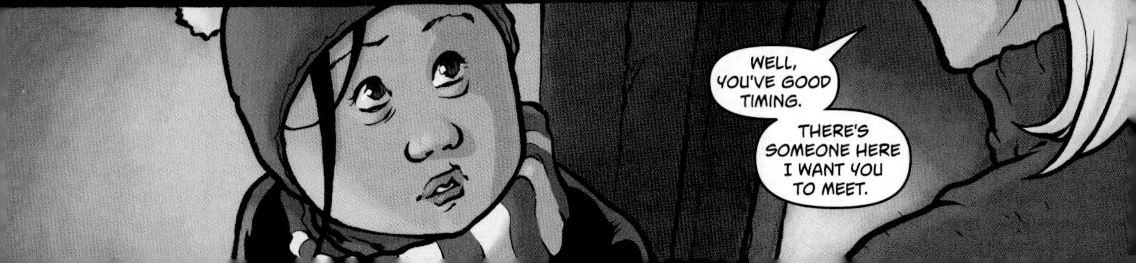
WELL, YOU'VE GOOD TIMING.
THERE'S SOMEONE HERE I WANT YOU TO MEET.

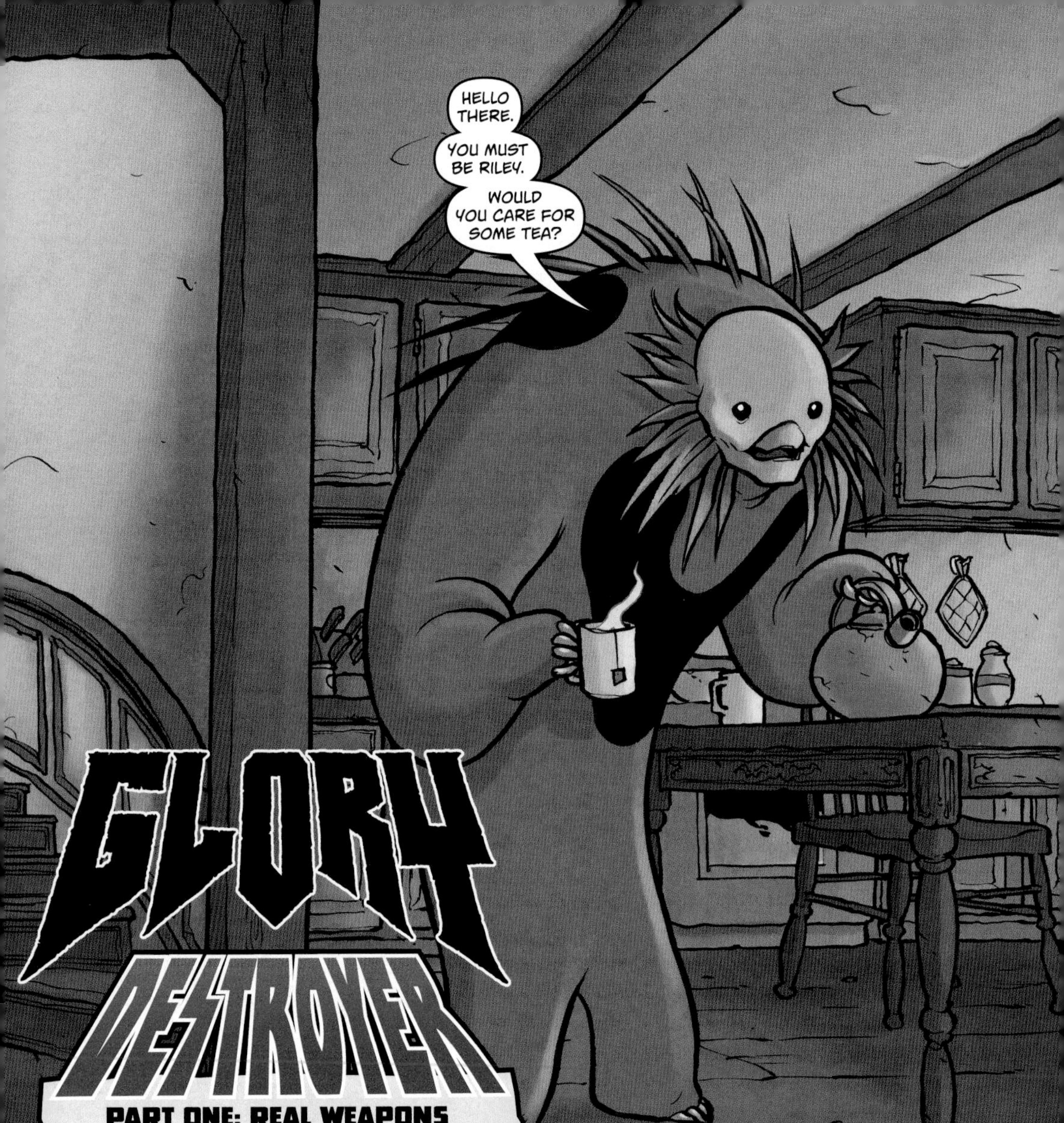
HELLO THERE.
YOU MUST BE RILEY.
WOULD YOU CARE FOR SOME TEA?
GLORY
DESTROYER
PART ONE: REAL WEAPONS
GLORY CREATED BY ROB LIEFELD

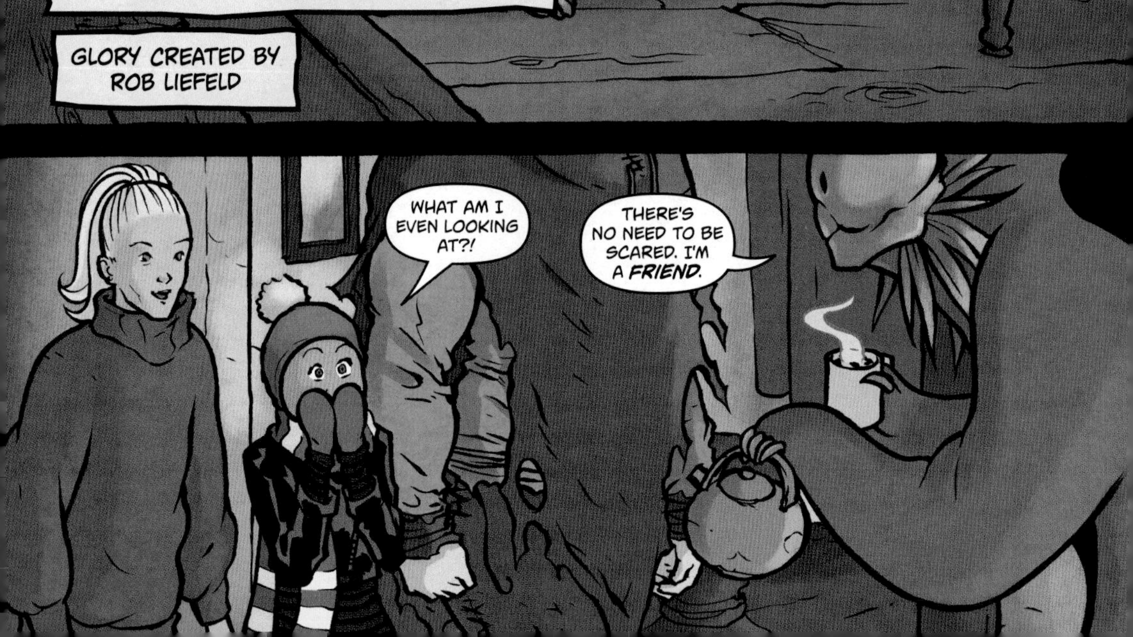
WHAT AM I EVEN LOOKING AT?!
THERE'S NO NEED TO BE SCARED. I'M A FRIEND.

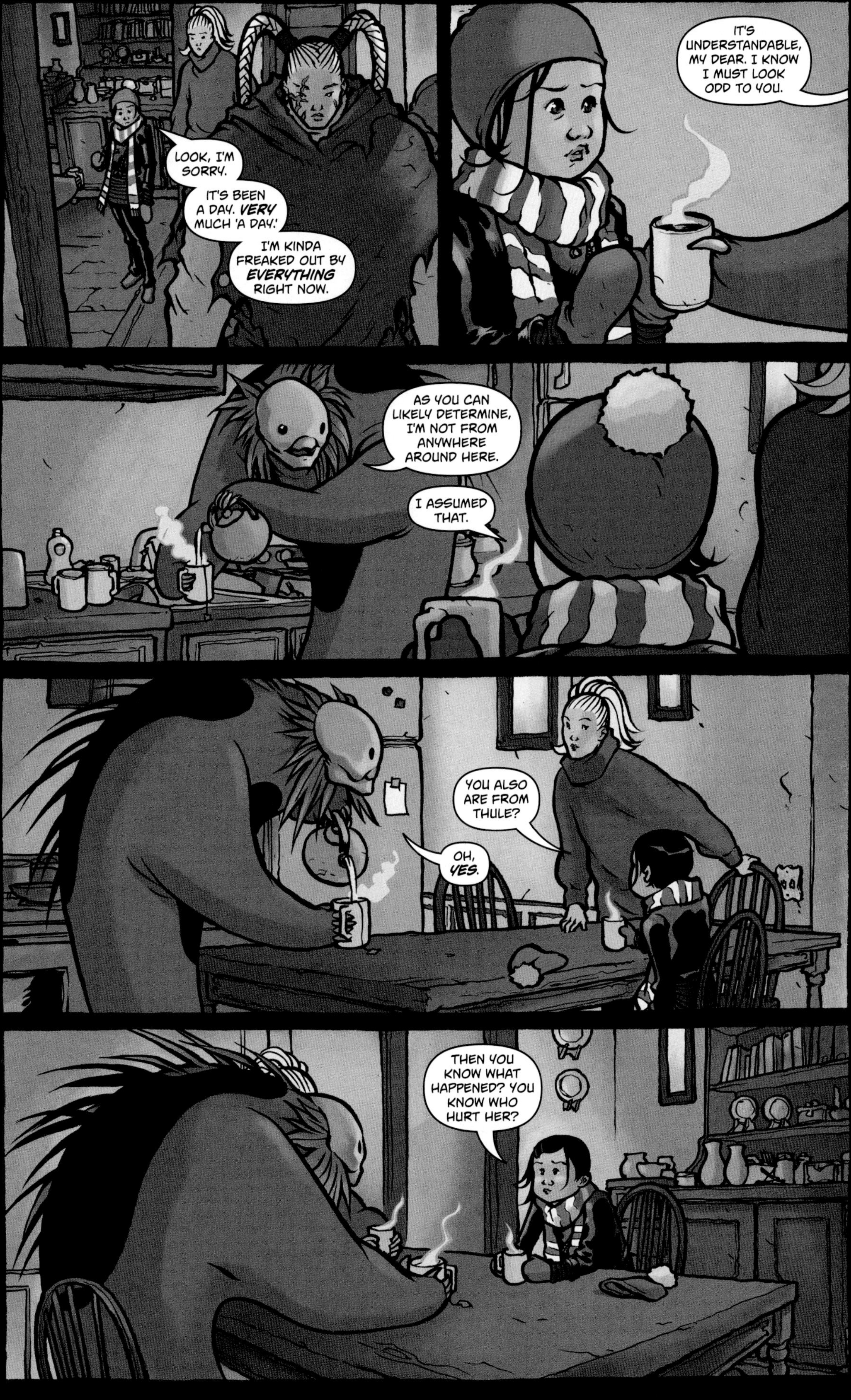
LOOK, I'M SORRY.
IT'S BEEN A DAY. *VERY* MUCH 'A DAY.'
I'M KINDA FREAKED OUT BY ***EVERYTHING*** RIGHT NOW.
IT'S UNDERSTANDABLE, MY DEAR. I KNOW I MUST LOOK ODD TO YOU.
AS YOU CAN LIKELY DETERMINE, I'M NOT FROM ANYWHERE AROUND HERE.
I ASSUMED THAT.
YOU ALSO ARE FROM THULE?
OH, ***YES***.
THEN YOU KNOW WHAT HAPPENED? YOU KNOW WHO HURT HER?

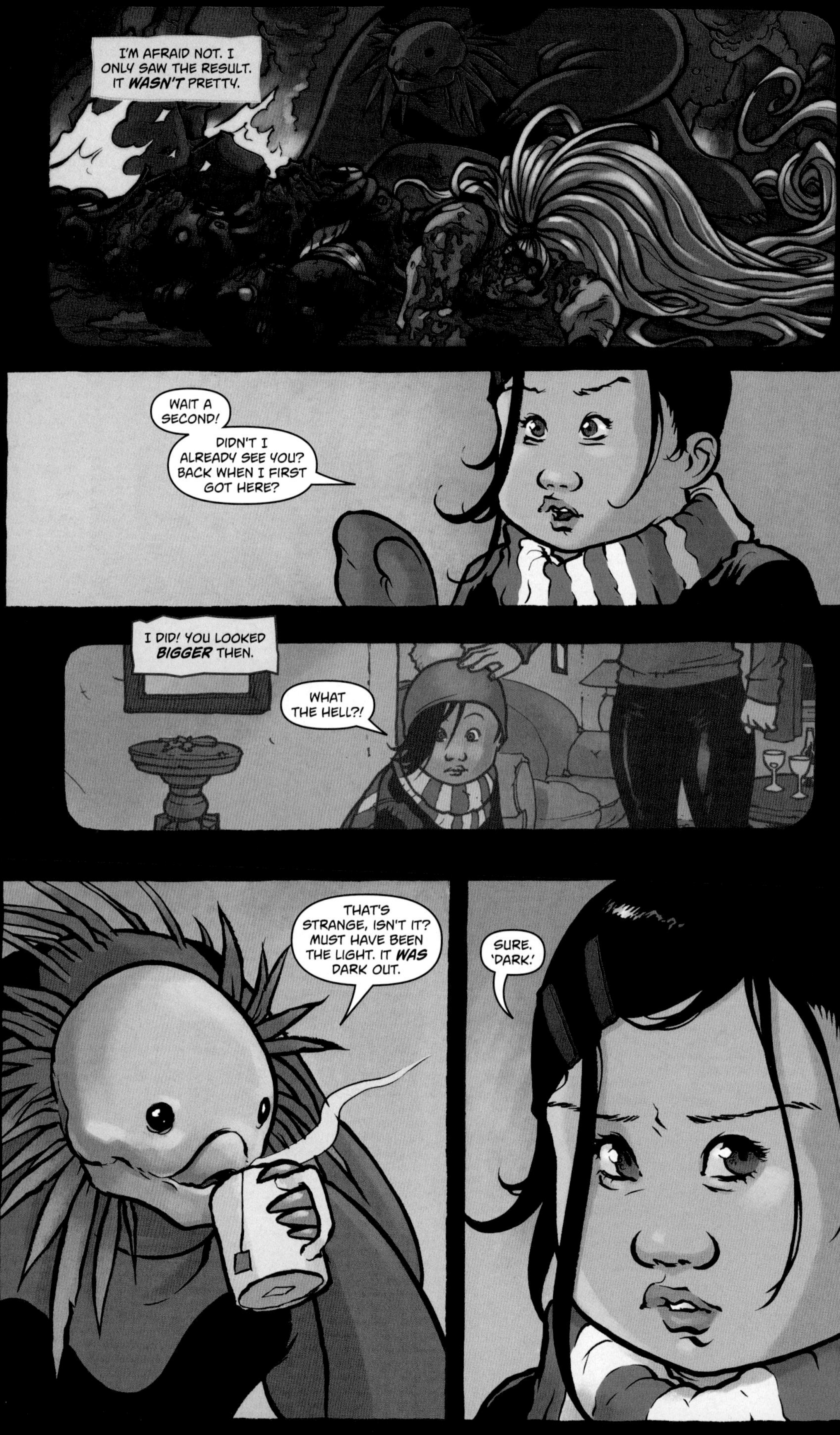
I'M AFRAID NOT. I ONLY SAW THE RESULT. IT *WASN'T* PRETTY.
WAIT A SECOND!
DIDN'T I ALREADY SEE YOU? BACK WHEN I FIRST GOT HERE?
I DID! YOU LOOKED *BIGGER* THEN.
WHAT THE HELL?!
THAT'S STRANGE, ISN'T IT? MUST HAVE BEEN THE LIGHT. IT *WAS* DARK OUT.
SURE. 'DARK.'

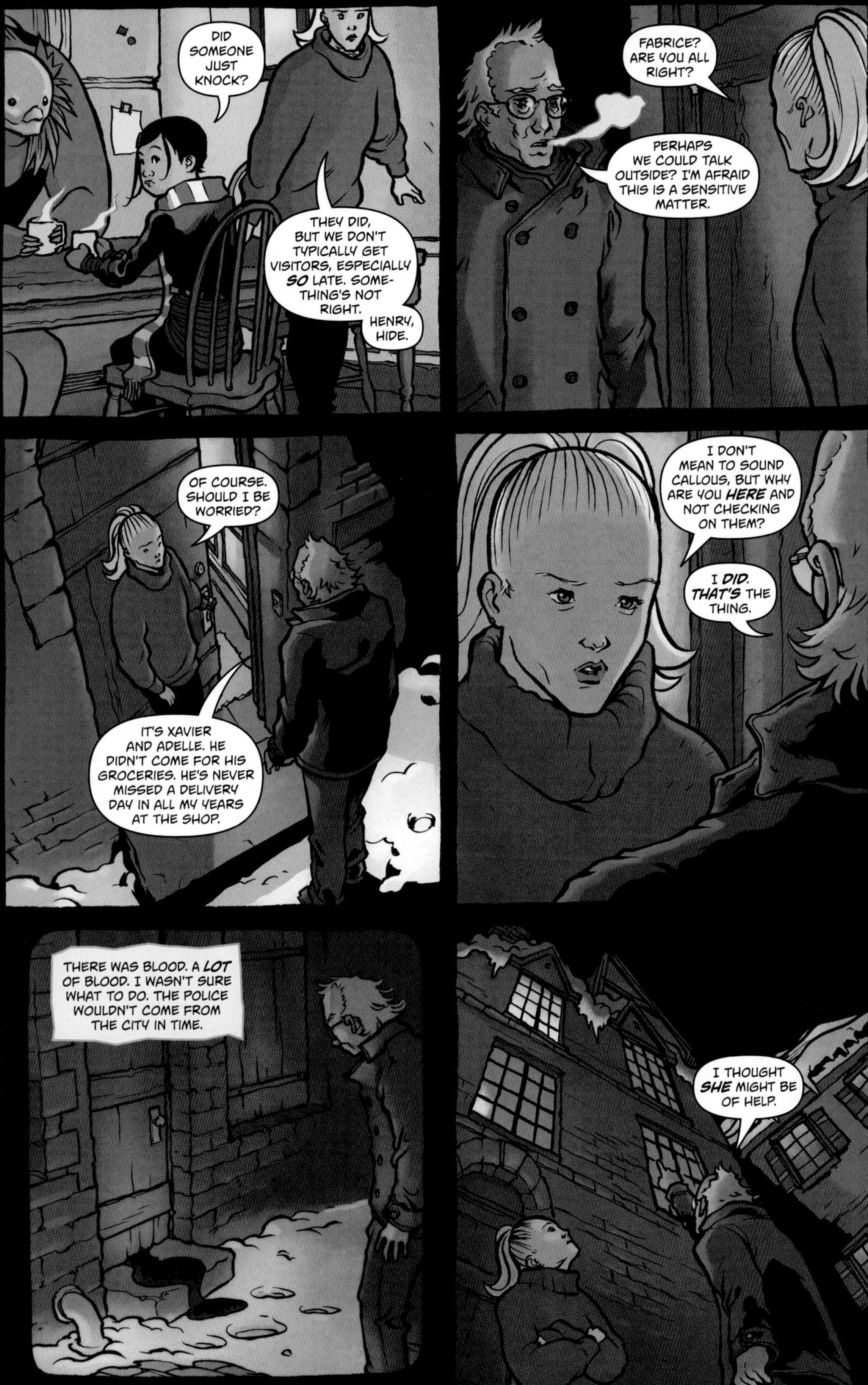
DID SOMEONE JUST KNOCK?
THEY DID, BUT WE DON'T TYPICALLY GET VISITORS, ESPECIALLY SO LATE. SOMETHING'S NOT RIGHT.
HENRY, HIDE.
FABRICE? ARE YOU ALL RIGHT?
PERHAPS WE COULD TALK OUTSIDE? I'M AFRAID THIS IS A SENSITIVE MATTER.
OF COURSE. SHOULD I BE WORRIED?
IT'S XAVIER AND ADELLE. HE DIDN'T COME FOR HIS GROCERIES. HE'S NEVER MISSED A DELIVERY DAY IN ALL MY YEARS AT THE SHOP.
I DON'T MEAN TO SOUND CALLOUS, BUT WHY ARE YOU HERE AND NOT CHECKING ON THEM?
I DID. THAT'S THE THING.
THERE WAS BLOOD. A LOT OF BLOOD. I WASN'T SURE WHAT TO DO. THE POLICE WOULDN'T COME FROM THE CITY IN TIME.
I THOUGHT SHE MIGHT BE OF HELP.

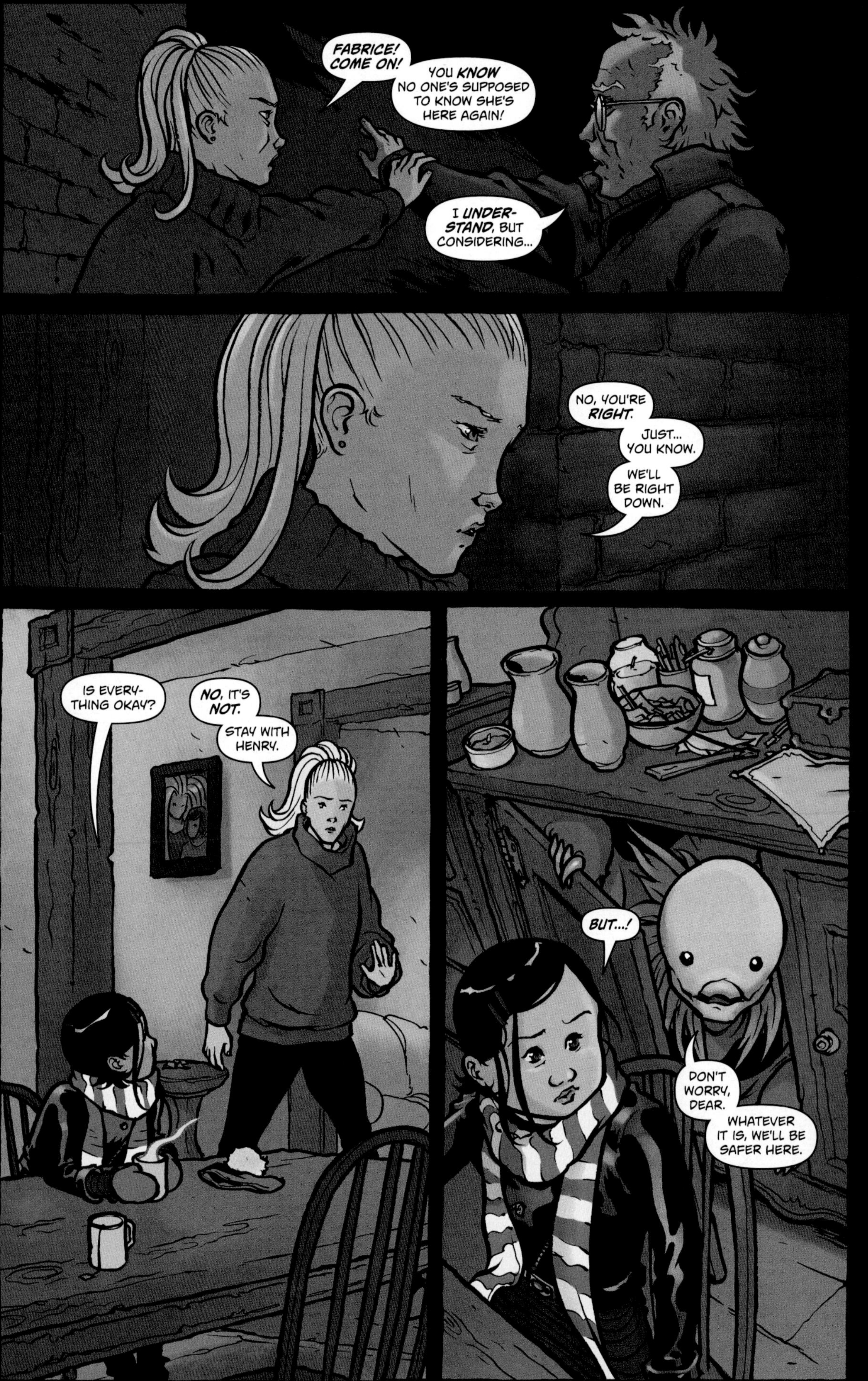
FABRICE! COME ON!
YOU KNOW NO ONE'S SUPPOSED TO KNOW SHE'S HERE AGAIN!
I UNDER-STAND, BUT CONSIDERING...
NO, YOU'RE RIGHT.
JUST... YOU KNOW.
WE'LL BE RIGHT DOWN.
IS EVERY-THING OKAY?
NO, IT'S NOT.
STAY WITH HENRY.
BUT...!
DON'T WORRY, DEAR.
WHATEVER IT IS, WE'LL BE SAFER HERE.

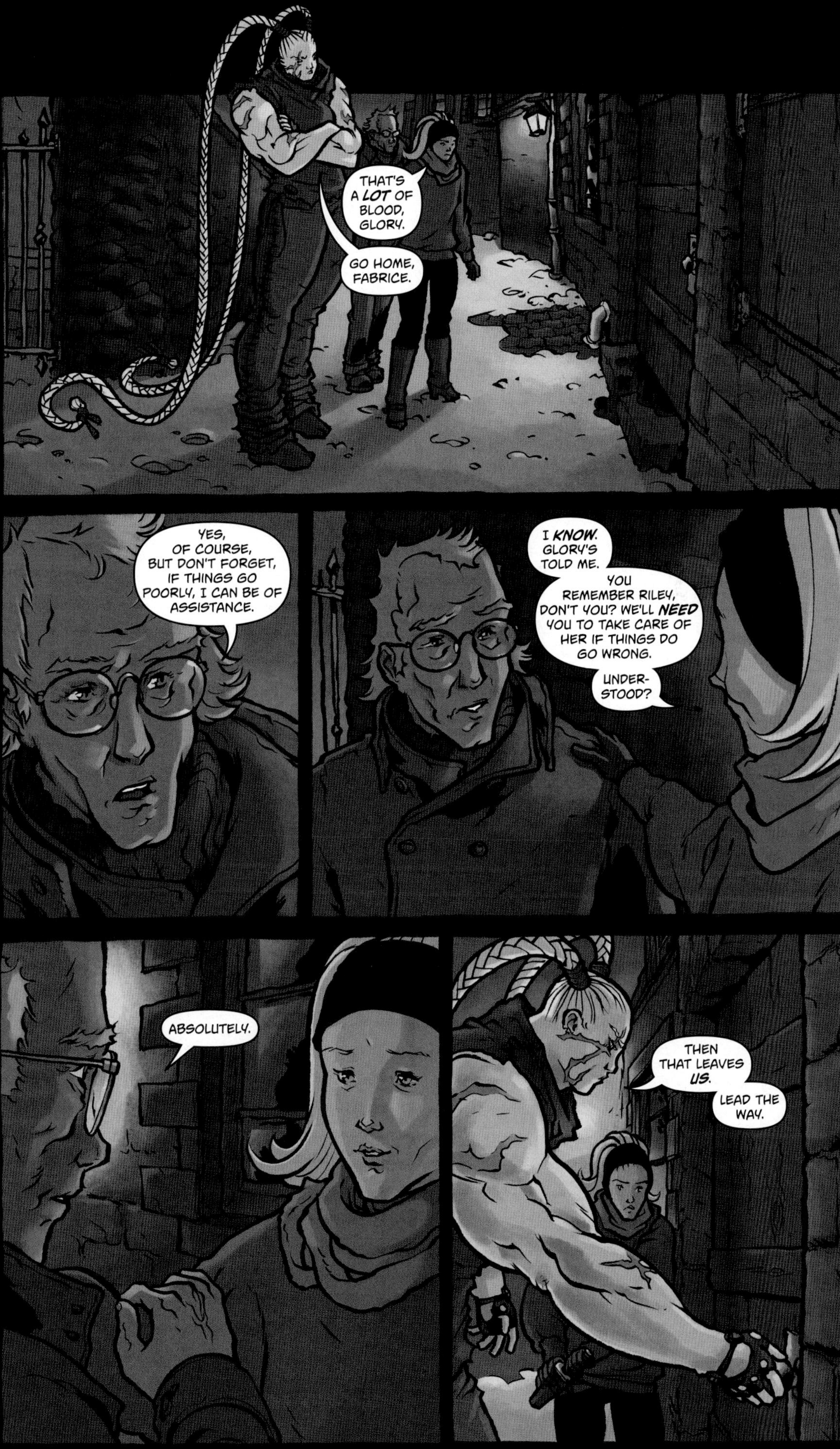
THAT'S A *LOT* OF BLOOD, GLORY.
GO HOME, FABRICE.
YES, OF COURSE, BUT DON'T FORGET, IF THINGS GO POORLY, I CAN BE OF ASSISTANCE.
I *KNOW*. GLORY'S TOLD ME.
YOU REMEMBER RILEY, DON'T YOU? WE'LL *NEED* YOU TO TAKE CARE OF HER IF THINGS DO GO WRONG.
UNDER-STOOD?
ABSOLUTELY.
THEN THAT LEAVES *US*.
LEAD THE WAY.

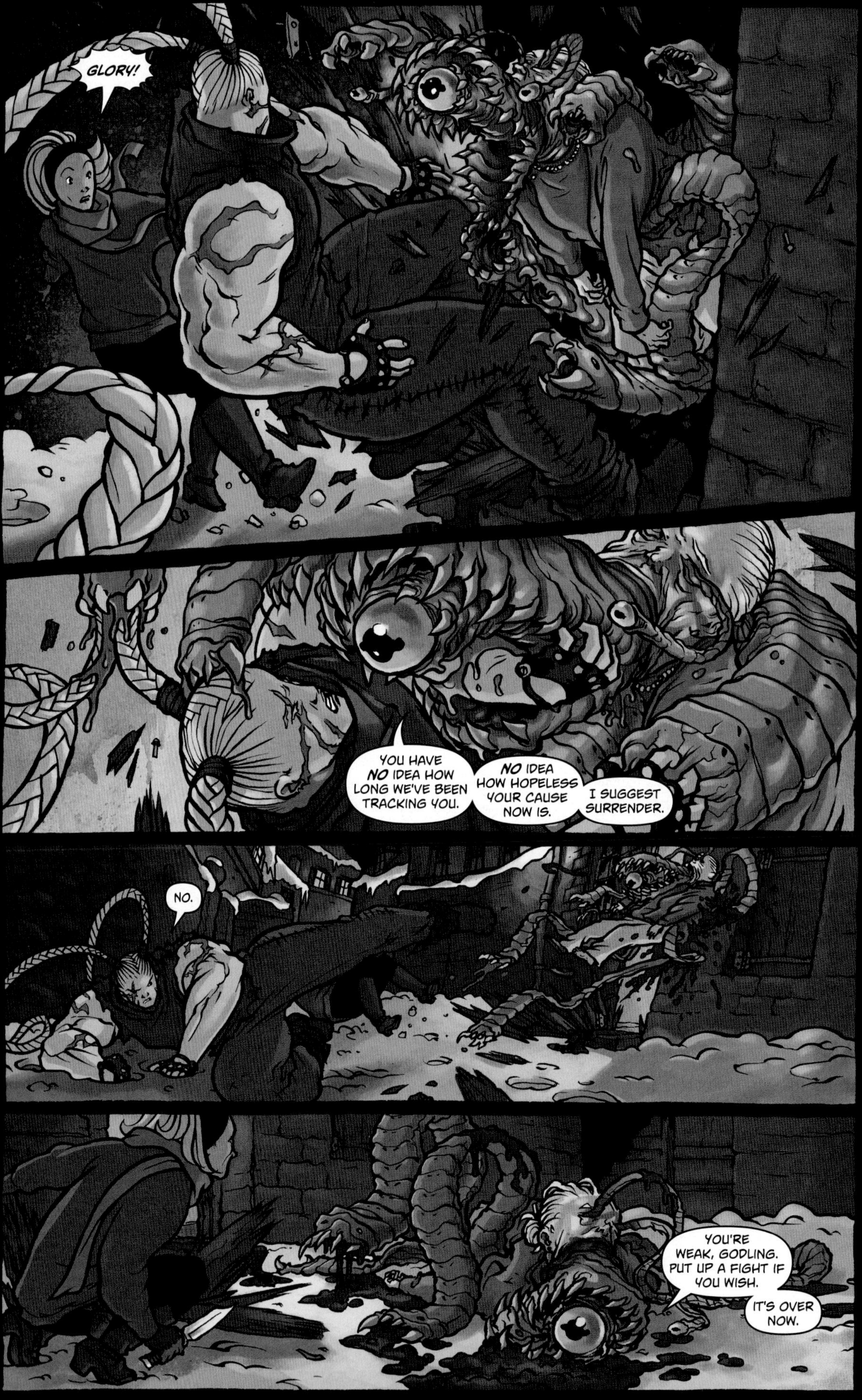

GLORY!
YOU HAVE NO IDEA HOW LONG WE'VE BEEN TRACKING YOU.
NO IDEA HOW HOPELESS YOUR CAUSE NOW IS.
I SUGGEST SURRENDER.
NO.
YOU'RE WEAK, GODLING. PUT UP A FIGHT IF YOU WISH.
IT'S OVER NOW.

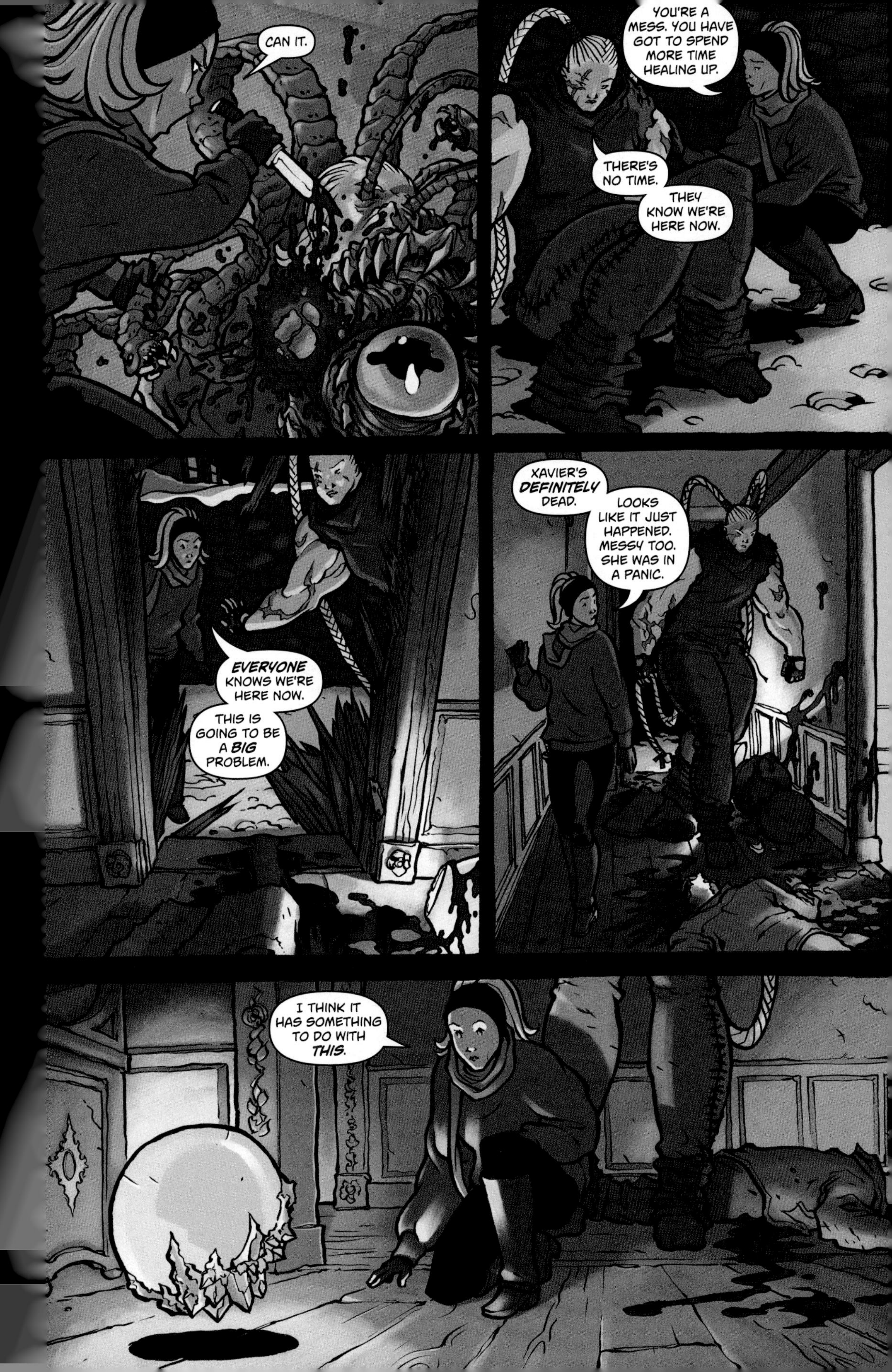
CAN IT.
YOU'RE A MESS. YOU HAVE GOT TO SPEND MORE TIME HEALING UP.
THERE'S NO TIME.
THEY KNOW WE'RE HERE NOW.
EVERYONE KNOWS WE'RE HERE NOW.
THIS IS GOING TO BE A BIG PROBLEM.
XAVIER'S DEFINITELY DEAD.
LOOKS LIKE IT JUST HAPPENED. MESSY TOO. SHE WAS IN A PANIC.
I THINK IT HAS SOMETHING TO DO WITH THIS.

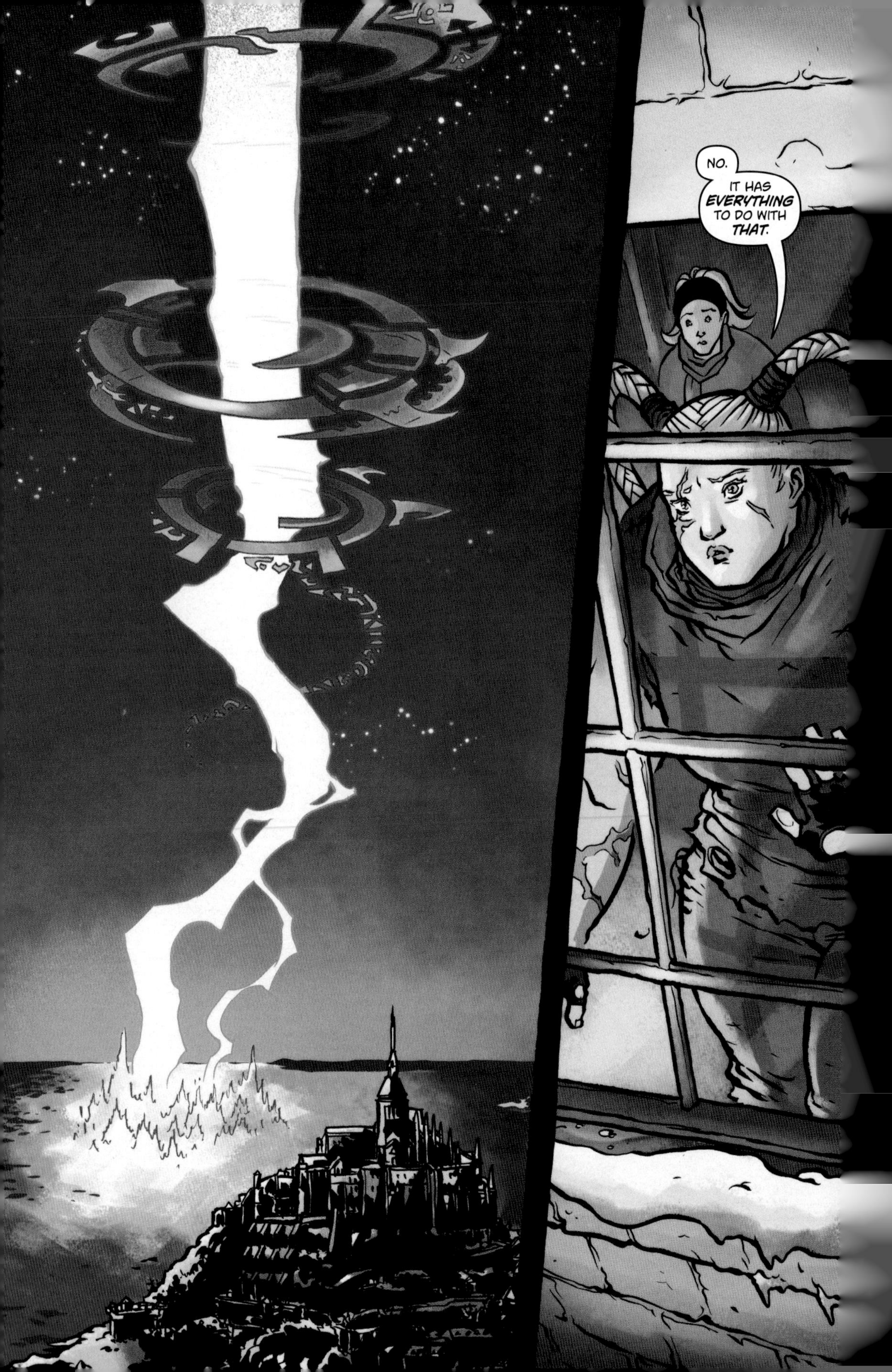
NO.
IT HAS *EVERYTHING* TO DO WITH *THAT*.

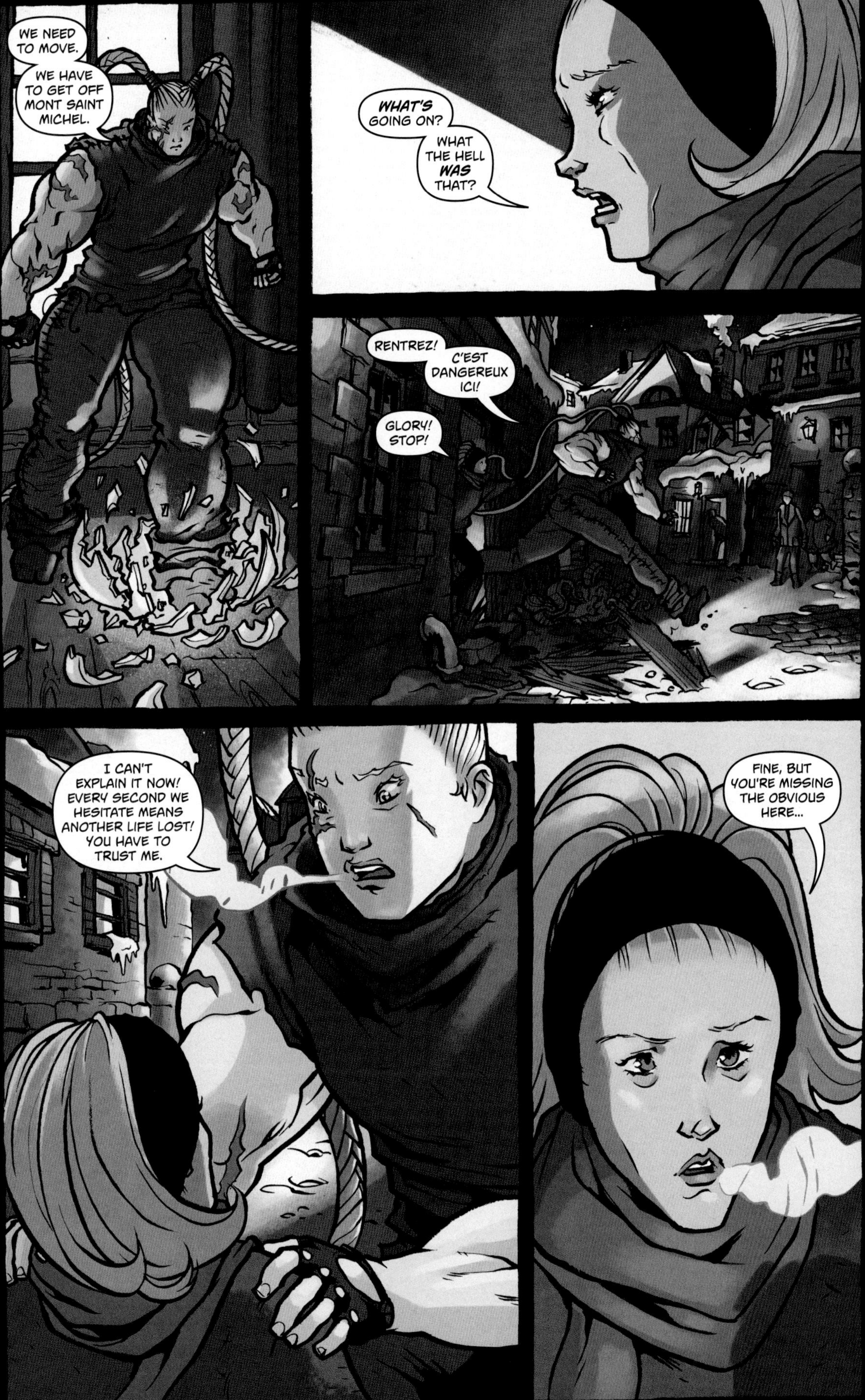
WE NEED TO MOVE.
WE HAVE TO GET OFF MONT SAINT MICHEL.
WHAT'S GOING ON?
WHAT THE HELL *WAS* THAT?
RENTREZ!
C'EST DANGEREUX ICI!
GLORY! STOP!
I CAN'T EXPLAIN IT NOW! EVERY SECOND WE HESITATE MEANS ANOTHER LIFE LOST! YOU HAVE TO TRUST ME.
FINE, BUT YOU'RE MISSING THE OBVIOUS HERE...

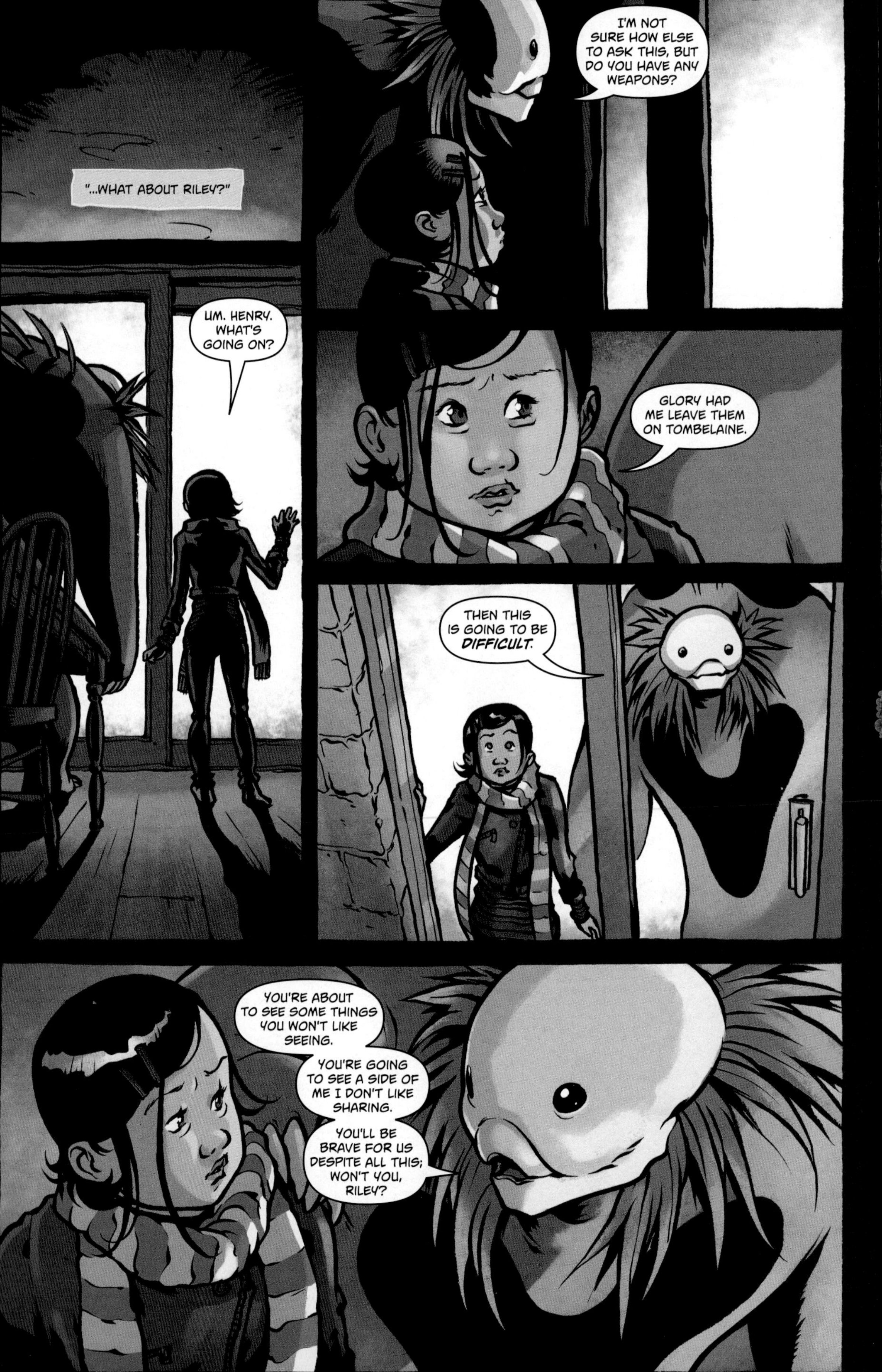
"...WHAT ABOUT RILEY?"
I'M NOT SURE HOW ELSE TO ASK THIS, BUT DO YOU HAVE ANY WEAPONS?
UM. HENRY. WHAT'S GOING ON?
GLORY HAD ME LEAVE THEM ON TOMBELAINE.
THEN THIS IS GOING TO BE *DIFFICULT*.
YOU'RE ABOUT TO SEE SOME THINGS YOU WON'T LIKE SEEING.
YOU'RE GOING TO SEE A SIDE OF ME I DON'T LIKE SHARING.
YOU'LL BE BRAVE FOR US DESPITE ALL THIS; WON'T YOU, RILEY?

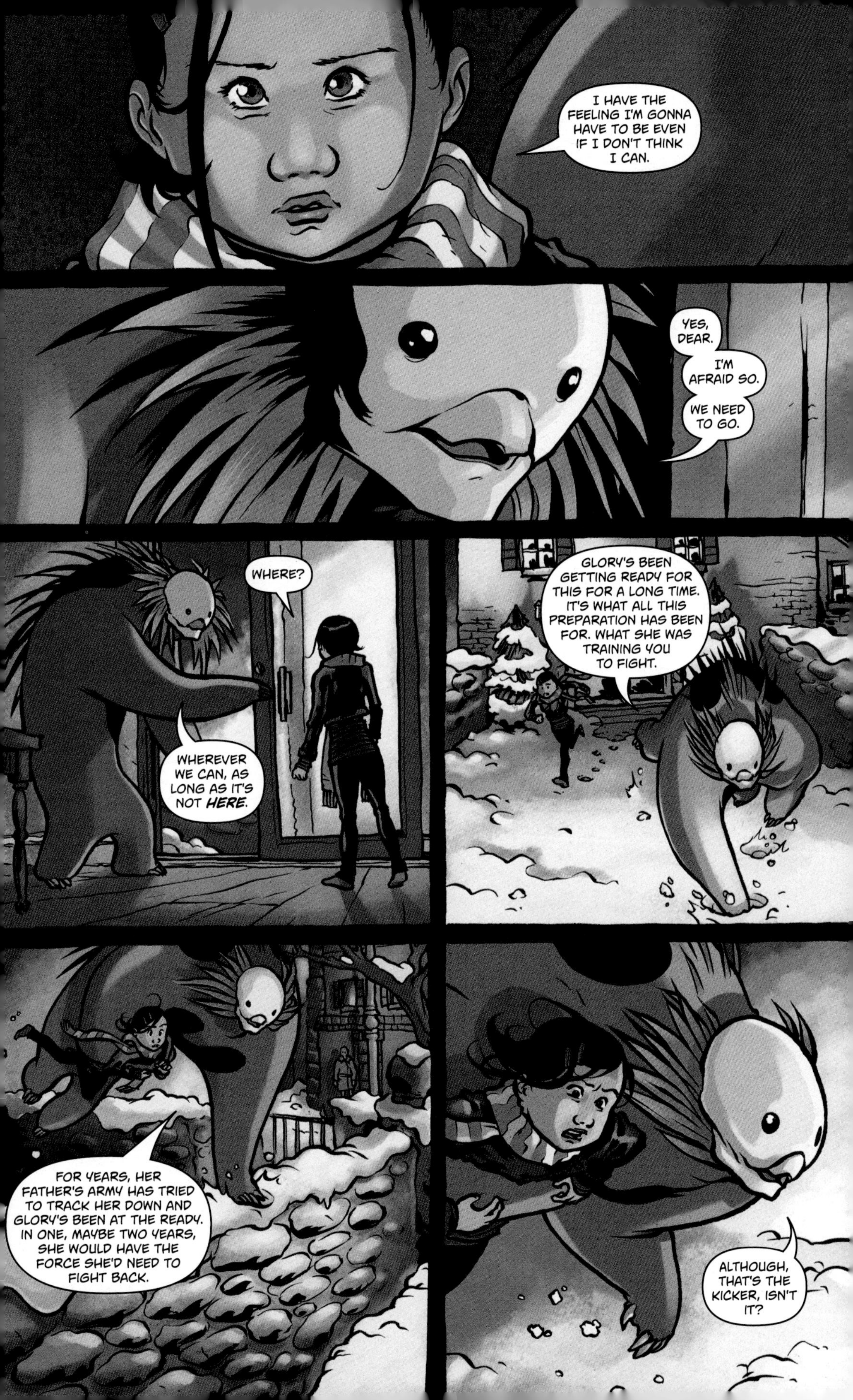
I HAVE THE FEELING I'M GONNA HAVE TO BE EVEN IF I DON'T THINK I CAN.
YES, DEAR.
I'M AFRAID SO.
WE NEED TO GO.
WHERE?
WHEREVER WE CAN, AS LONG AS IT'S NOT *HERE*.
GLORY'S BEEN GETTING READY FOR THIS FOR A LONG TIME. IT'S WHAT ALL THIS PREPARATION HAS BEEN FOR. WHAT SHE WAS TRAINING YOU TO FIGHT.
FOR YEARS, HER FATHER'S ARMY HAS TRIED TO TRACK HER DOWN AND GLORY'S BEEN AT THE READY. IN ONE, MAYBE TWO YEARS, SHE WOULD HAVE THE FORCE SHE'D NEED TO FIGHT BACK.
ALTHOUGH, THAT'S THE KICKER, ISN'T IT?

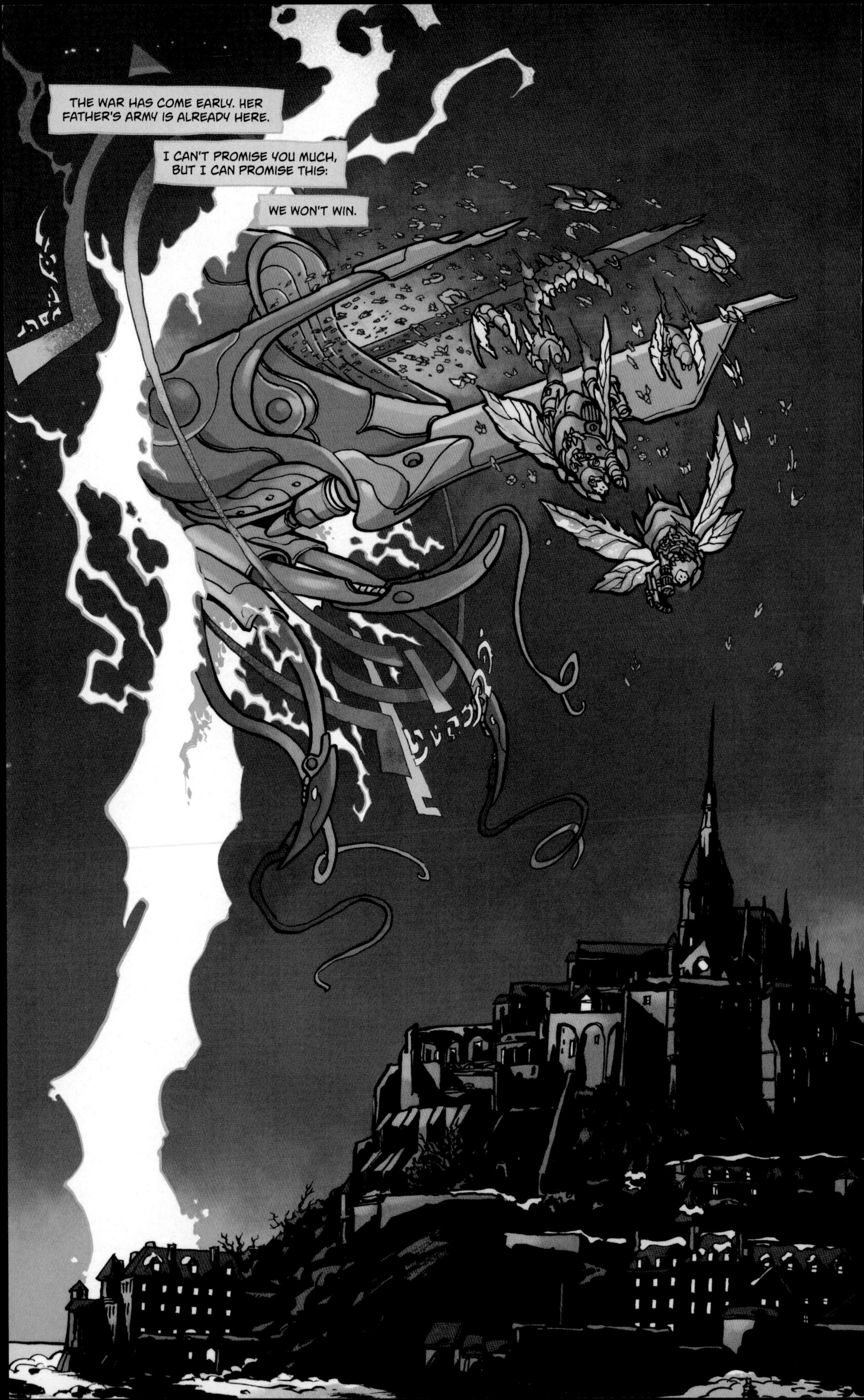
THE WAR HAS COME EARLY. HER FATHER'S ARMY IS ALREADY HERE.
I CAN'T PROMISE YOU MUCH, BUT I CAN PROMISE THIS:
WE WON'T WIN.

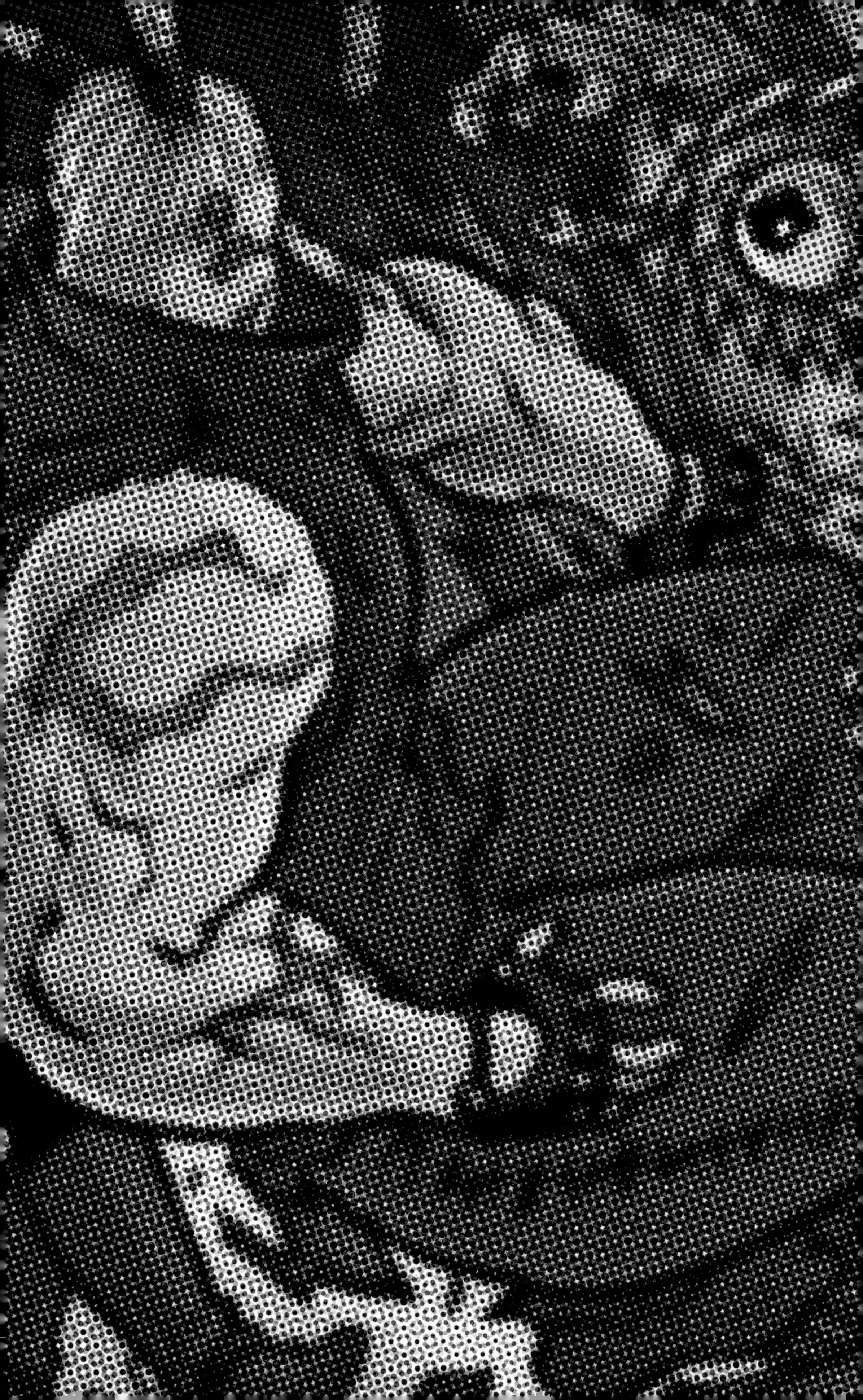

Chapter Five

Cover by Kris Anka

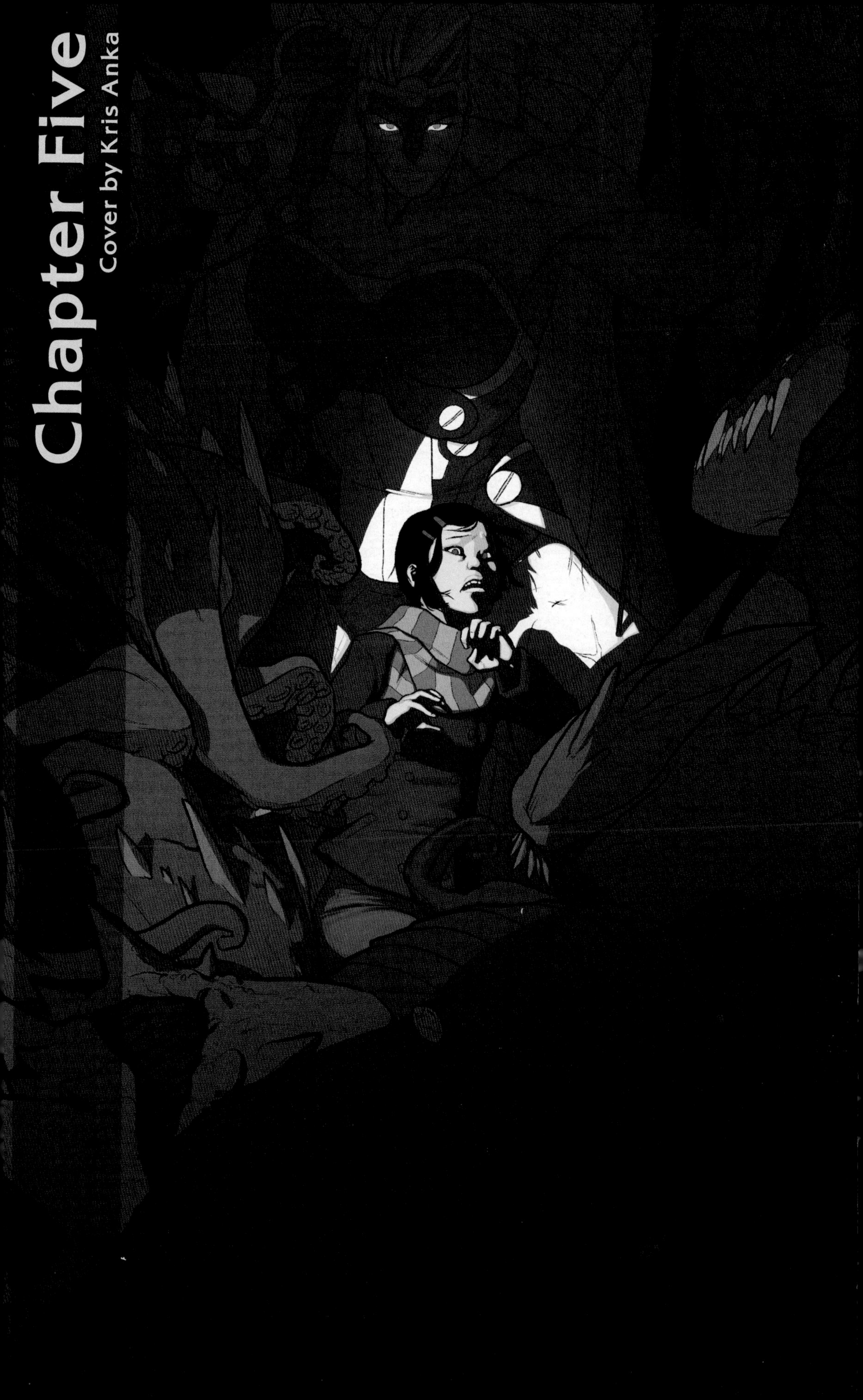

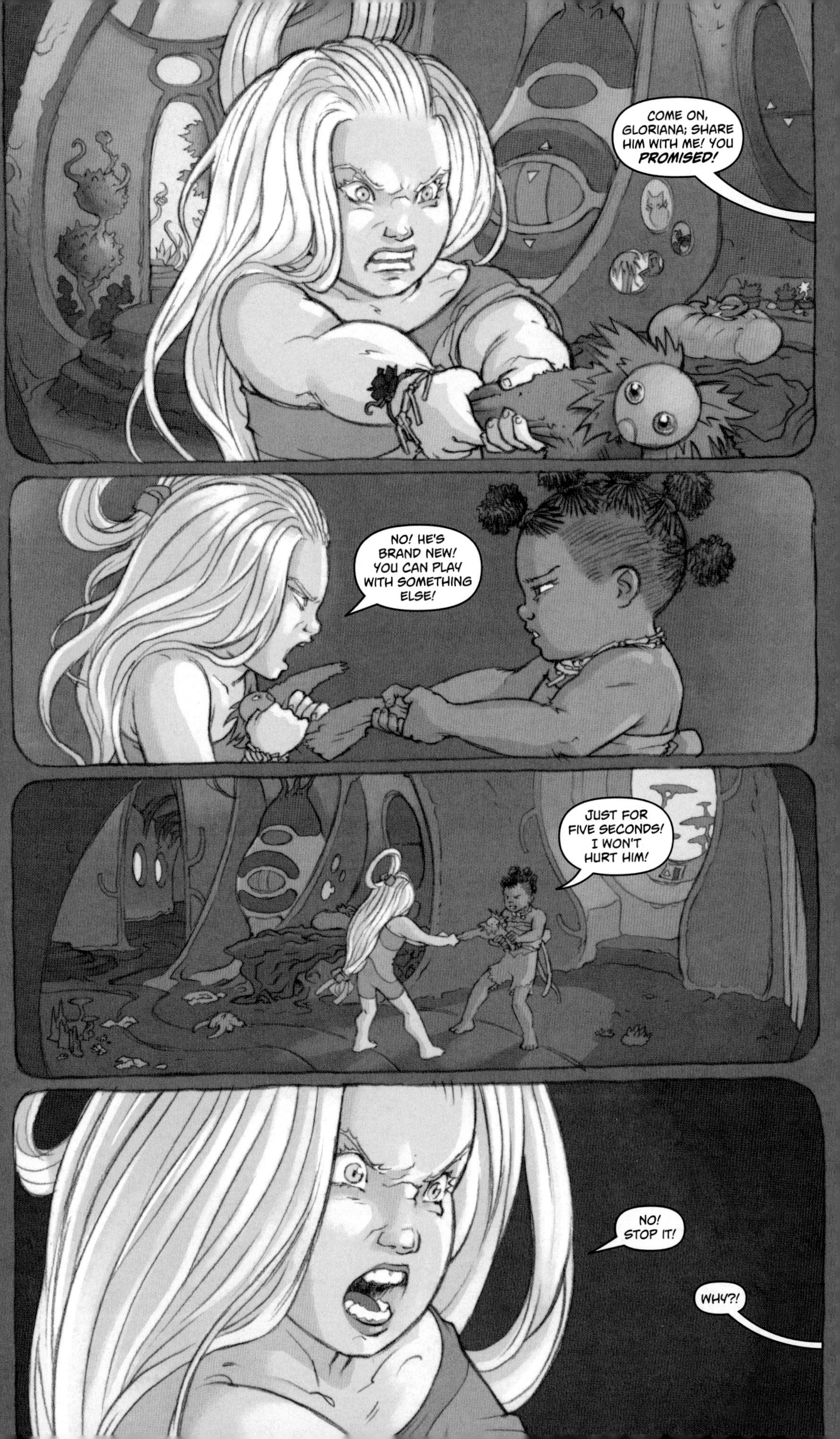
COME ON, GLORIANA; SHARE HIM WITH ME! YOU PROMISED!
NO! HE'S BRAND NEW! YOU CAN PLAY WITH SOMETHING ELSE!
JUST FOR FIVE SECONDS! I WON'T HURT HIM!
NO! STOP IT!
WHY?!

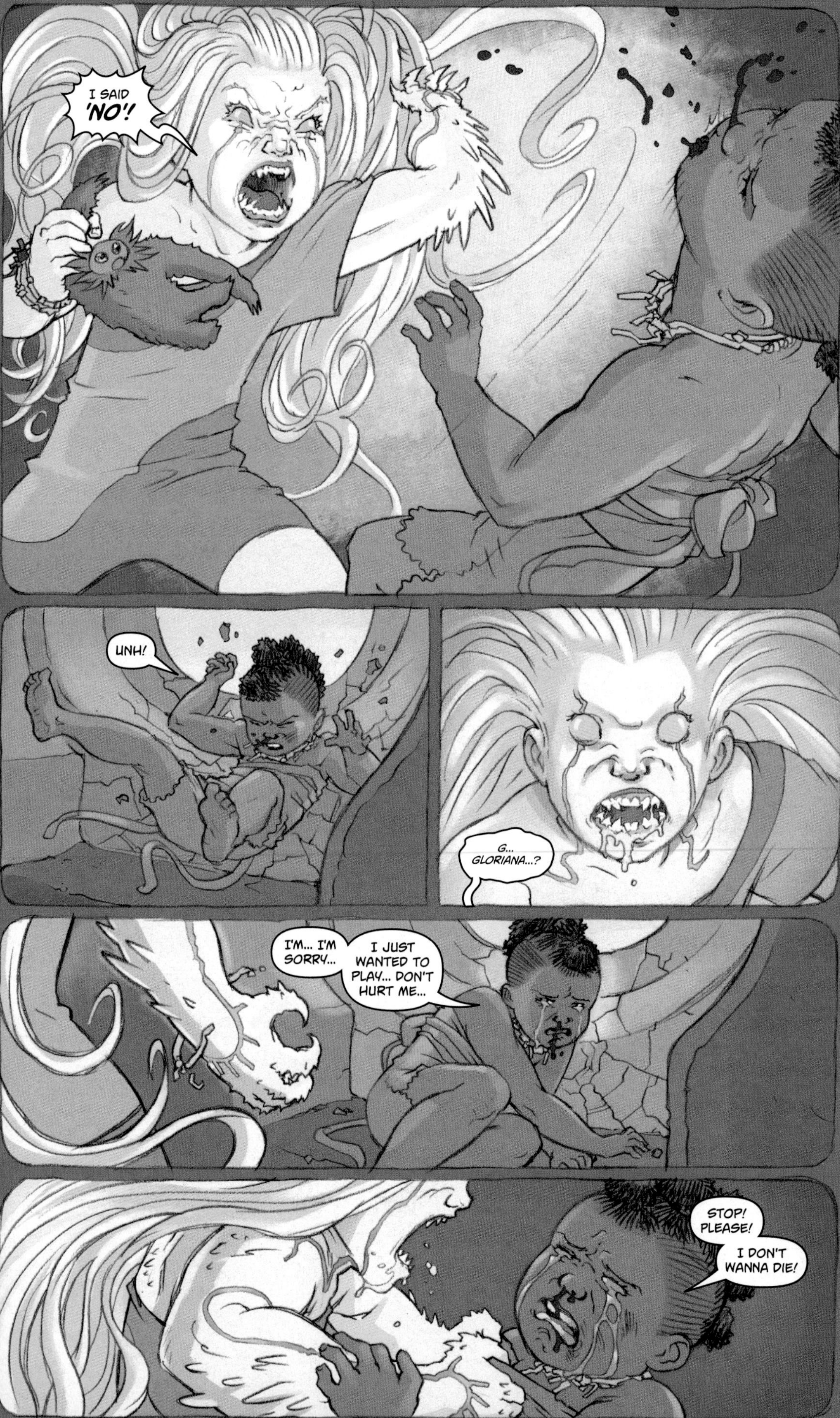
I SAID 'NO'!
UNH!
G... GLORIANA...?
I'M... I'M SORRY...
I JUST WANTED TO PLAY... DON'T HURT ME...
STOP! PLEASE!
I DON'T WANNA DIE!

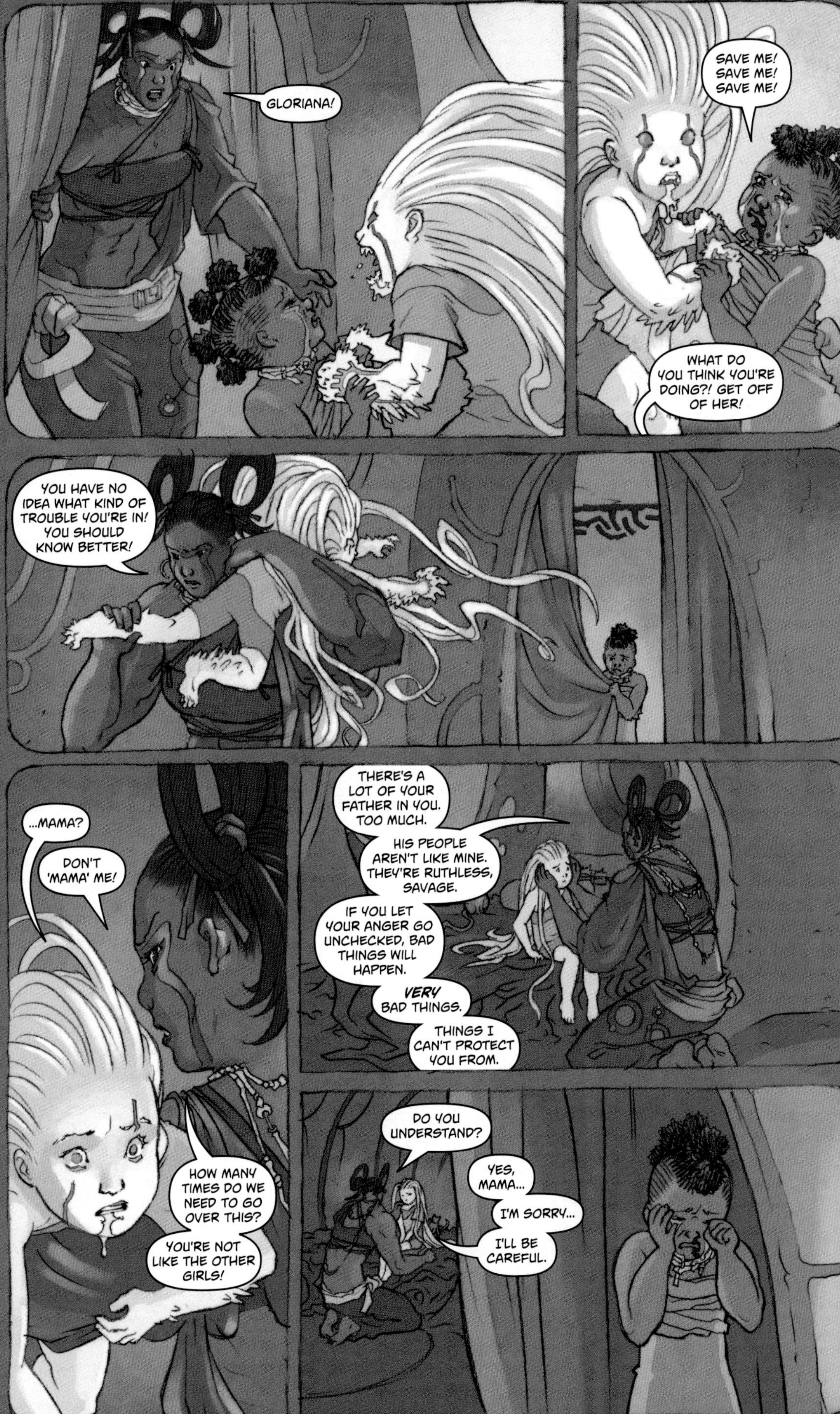
GLORIANA!
SAVE ME! SAVE ME! SAVE ME!
WHAT DO YOU THINK YOU'RE DOING?! GET OFF OF HER!
YOU HAVE NO IDEA WHAT KIND OF TROUBLE YOU'RE IN! YOU SHOULD KNOW BETTER!
...MAMA?
DON'T 'MAMA' ME!
HOW MANY TIMES DO WE NEED TO GO OVER THIS?
YOU'RE NOT LIKE THE OTHER GIRLS!
THERE'S A LOT OF YOUR FATHER IN YOU. TOO MUCH.
HIS PEOPLE AREN'T LIKE MINE. THEY'RE RUTHLESS, SAVAGE.
IF YOU LET YOUR ANGER GO UNCHECKED, BAD THINGS WILL HAPPEN.
VERY BAD THINGS.
THINGS I CAN'T PROTECT YOU FROM.
DO YOU UNDERSTAND?
YES, MAMA...
I'M SORRY...
I'LL BE CAREFUL.

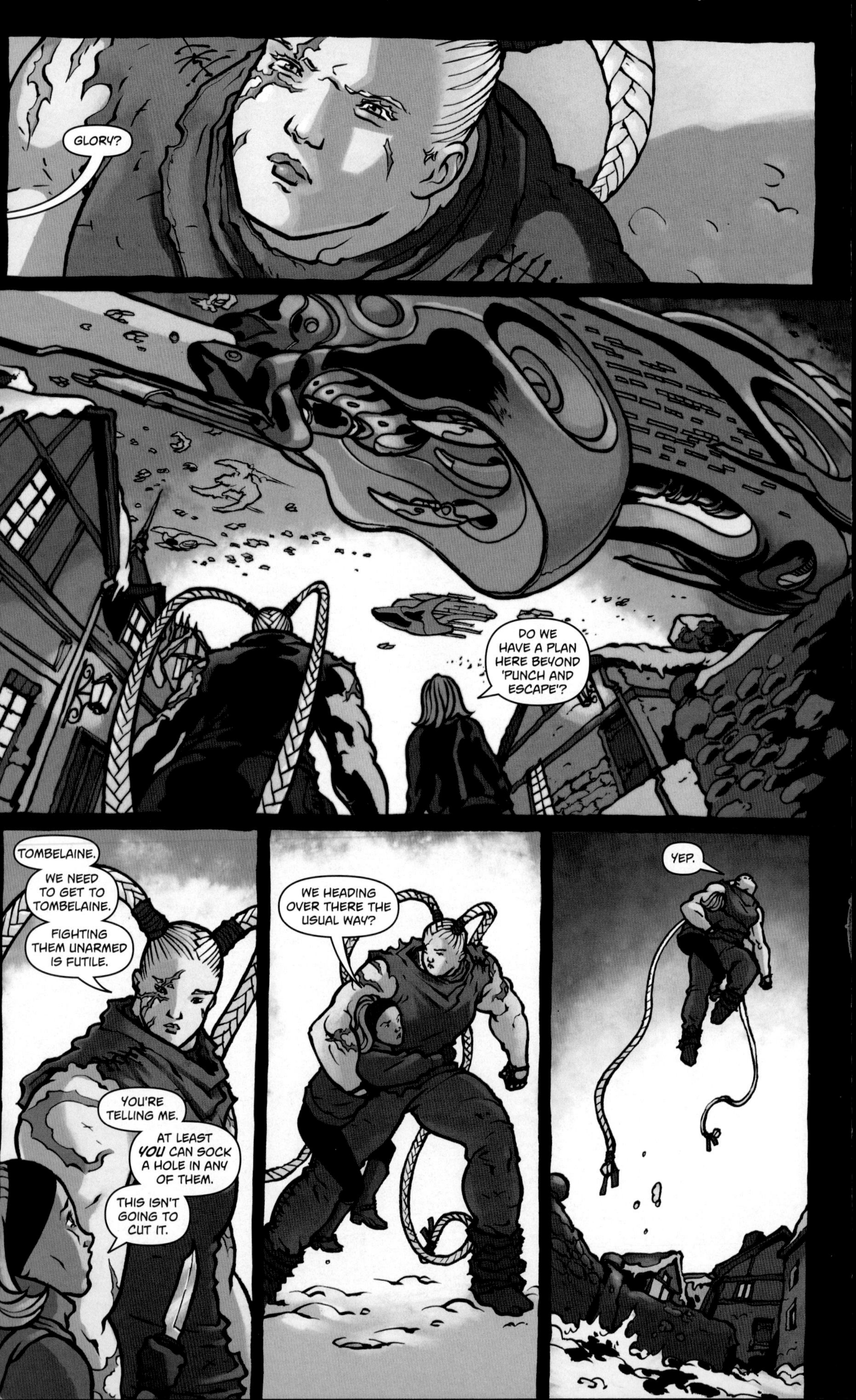
GLORY?
DO WE HAVE A PLAN HERE BEYOND 'PUNCH AND ESCAPE'?
TOMBELAINE.
WE NEED TO GET TO TOMBELAINE.
FIGHTING THEM UNARMED IS FUTILE.
YOU'RE TELLING ME.
AT LEAST *YOU* CAN SOCK A HOLE IN ANY OF THEM.
THIS ISN'T GOING TO CUT IT.
WE HEADING OVER THERE THE USUAL WAY?
YEP.

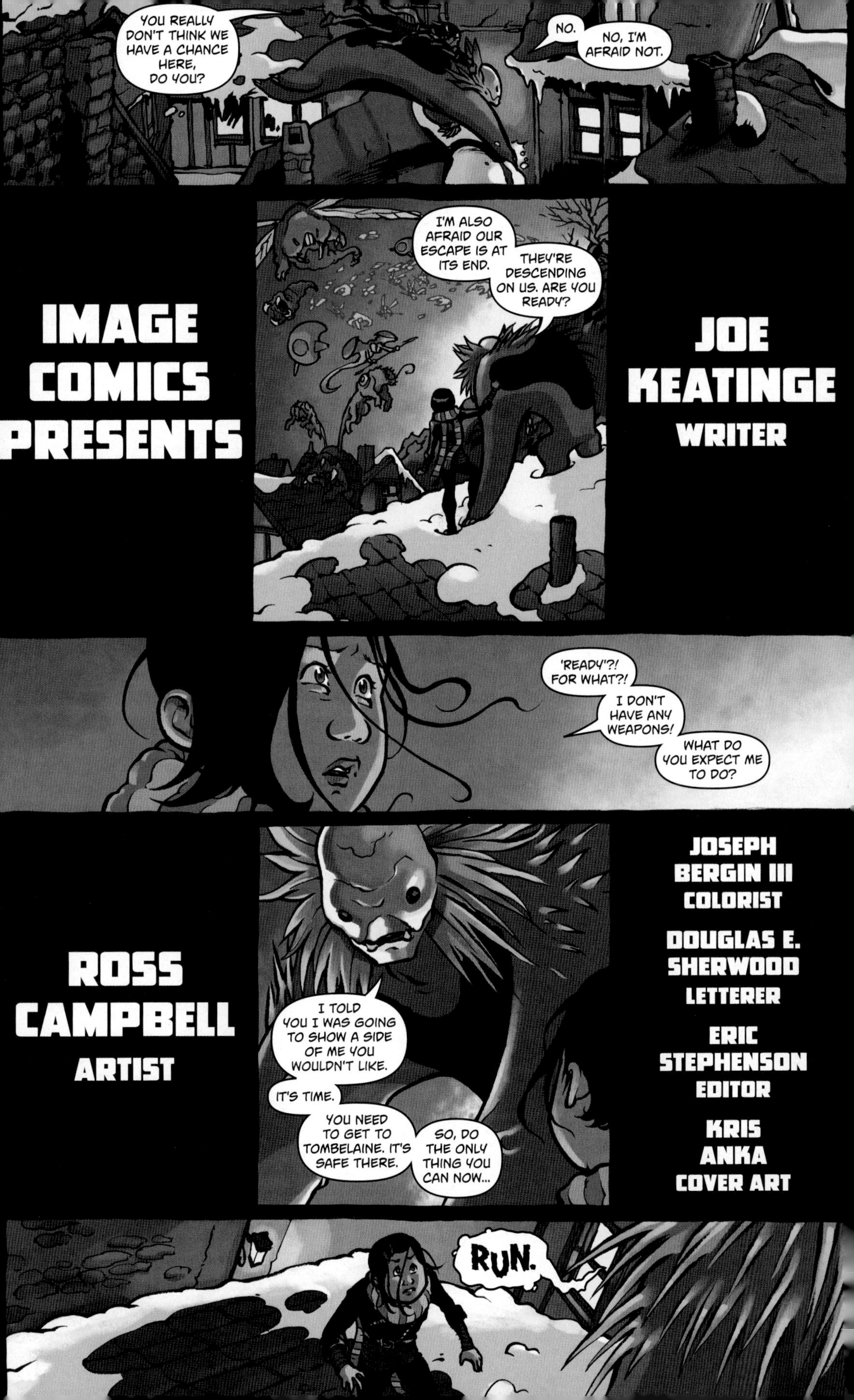
YOU REALLY DON'T THINK WE HAVE A CHANCE HERE, DO YOU?
NO.
NO, I'M AFRAID NOT.
IMAGE COMICS PRESENTS
I'M ALSO AFRAID OUR ESCAPE IS AT ITS END.
THEY'RE DESCENDING ON US. ARE YOU READY?
JOE KEATINGE
WRITER
'READY'?! FOR WHAT?!
I DON'T HAVE ANY WEAPONS!
WHAT DO YOU EXPECT ME TO DO?
ROSS CAMPBELL
ARTIST
I TOLD YOU I WAS GOING TO SHOW A SIDE OF ME YOU WOULDN'T LIKE.
IT'S TIME.
YOU NEED TO GET TO TOMBELAINE. IT'S SAFE THERE.
SO, DO THE ONLY THING YOU CAN NOW...
JOSEPH BERGIN III
COLORIST
DOUGLAS E. SHERWOOD
LETTERER
ERIC STEPHENSON
EDITOR
KRIS ANKA
COVER ART
RUN.

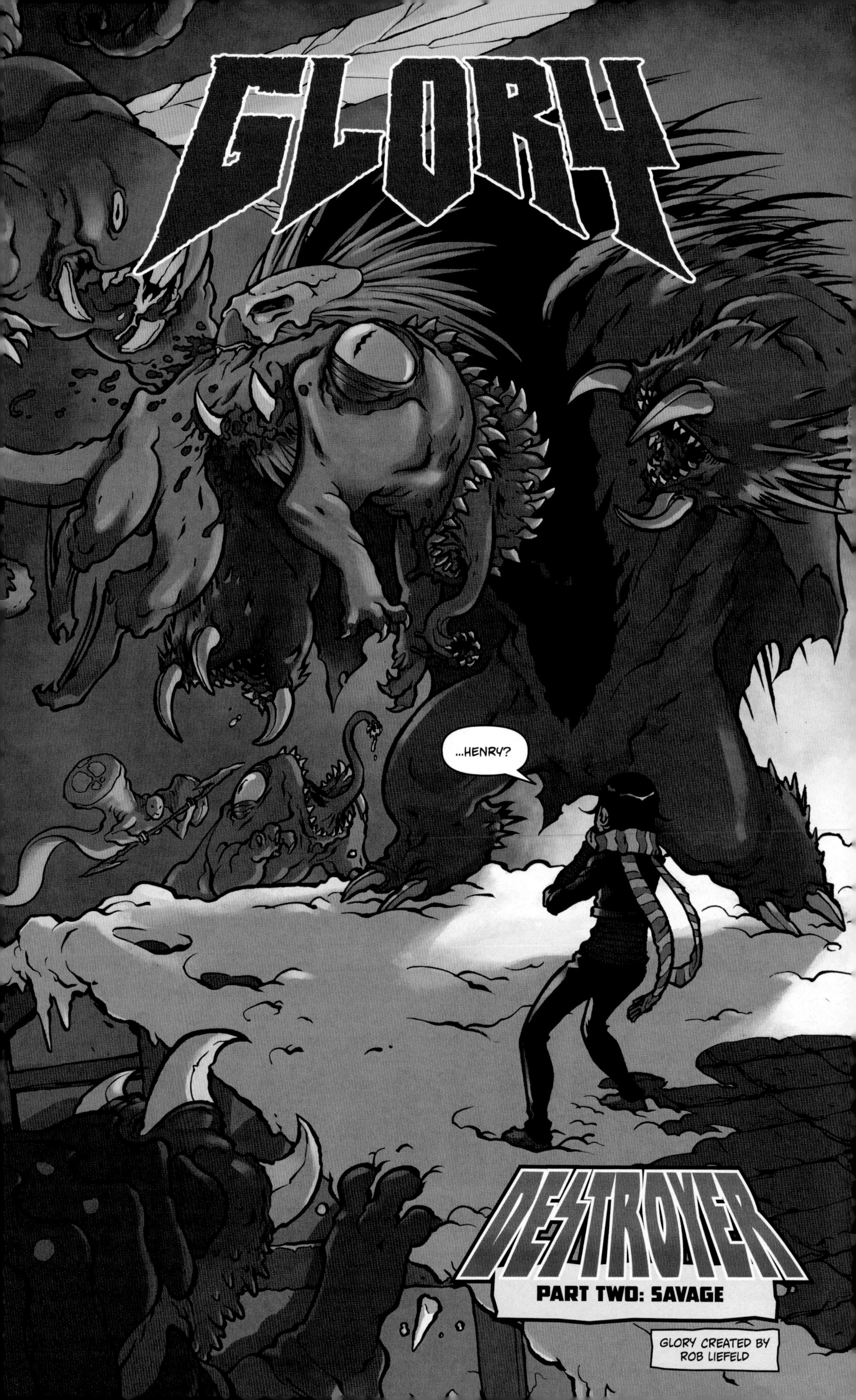
GLORY
...HENRY?
DESTROYER
PART TWO: SAVAGE
GLORY CREATED BY
ROB LIEFELD

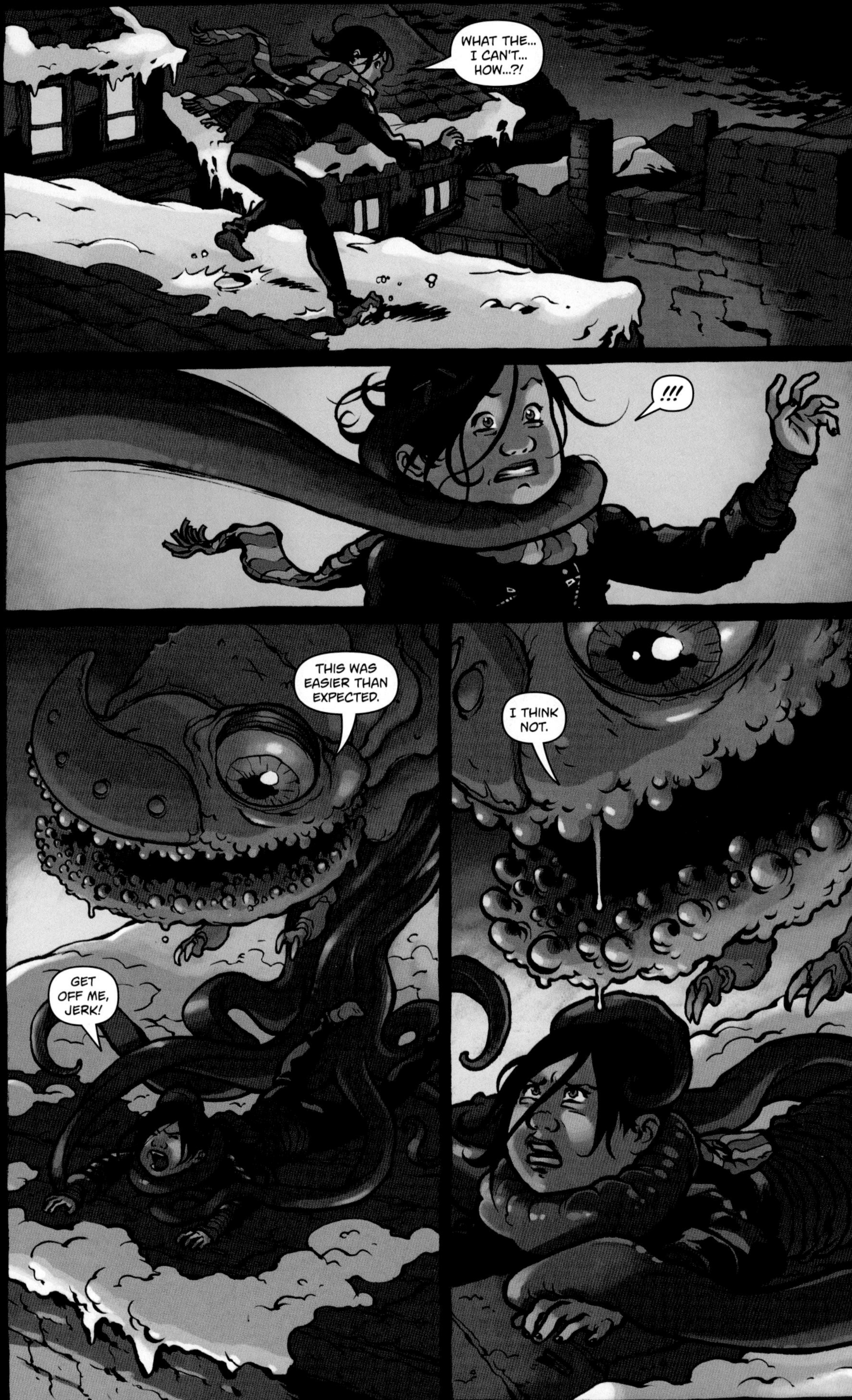
WHAT THE... I CAN'T... HOW...?!
!!!
THIS WAS EASIER THAN EXPECTED.
GET OFF ME, JERK!
I THINK NOT.

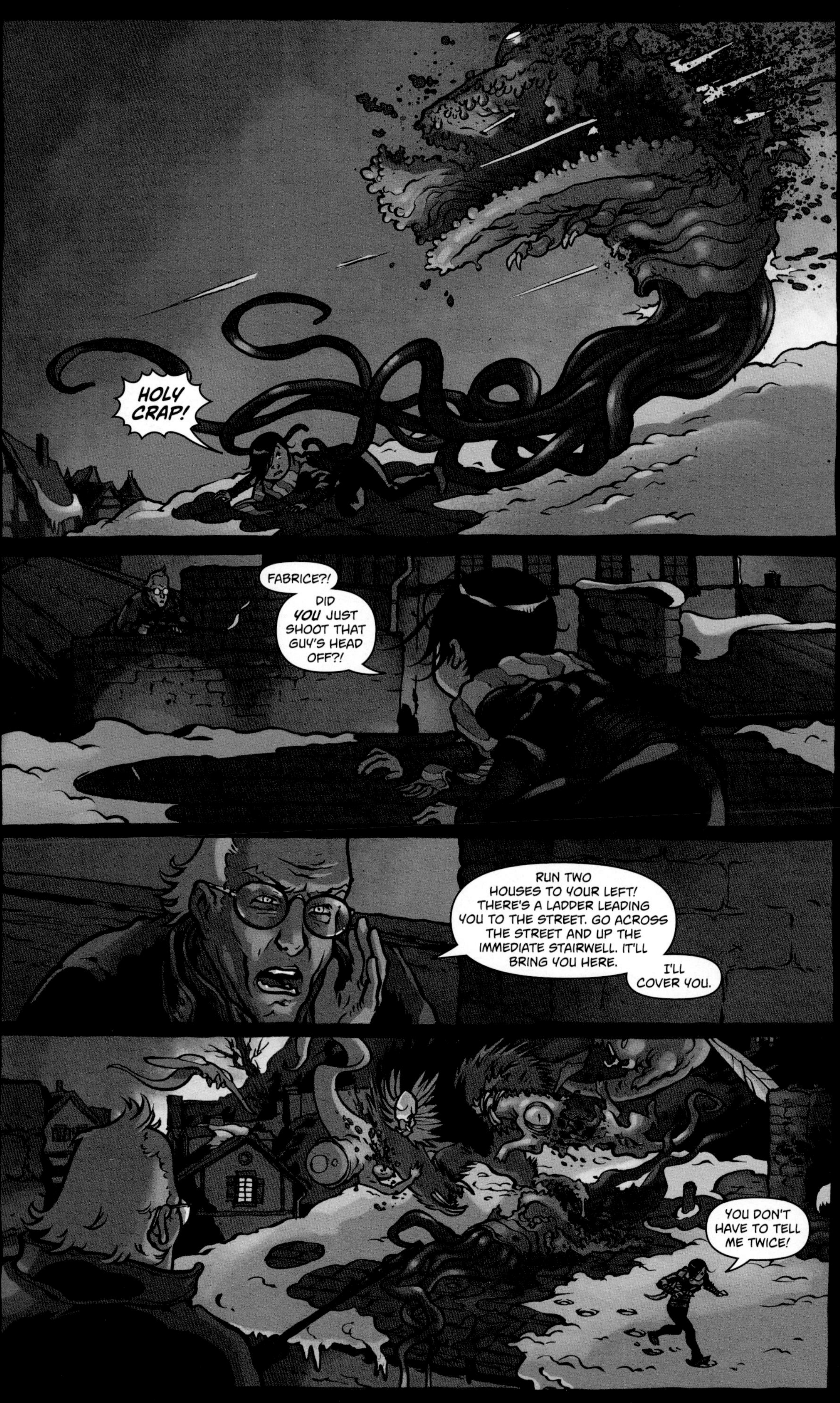
HOLY CRAP!
FABRICE?!
DID YOU JUST SHOOT THAT GUY'S HEAD OFF?!
RUN TWO HOUSES TO YOUR LEFT! THERE'S A LADDER LEADING YOU TO THE STREET. GO ACROSS THE STREET AND UP THE IMMEDIATE STAIRWELL. IT'LL BRING YOU HERE.
I'LL COVER YOU.
YOU DON'T HAVE TO TELL ME TWICE!

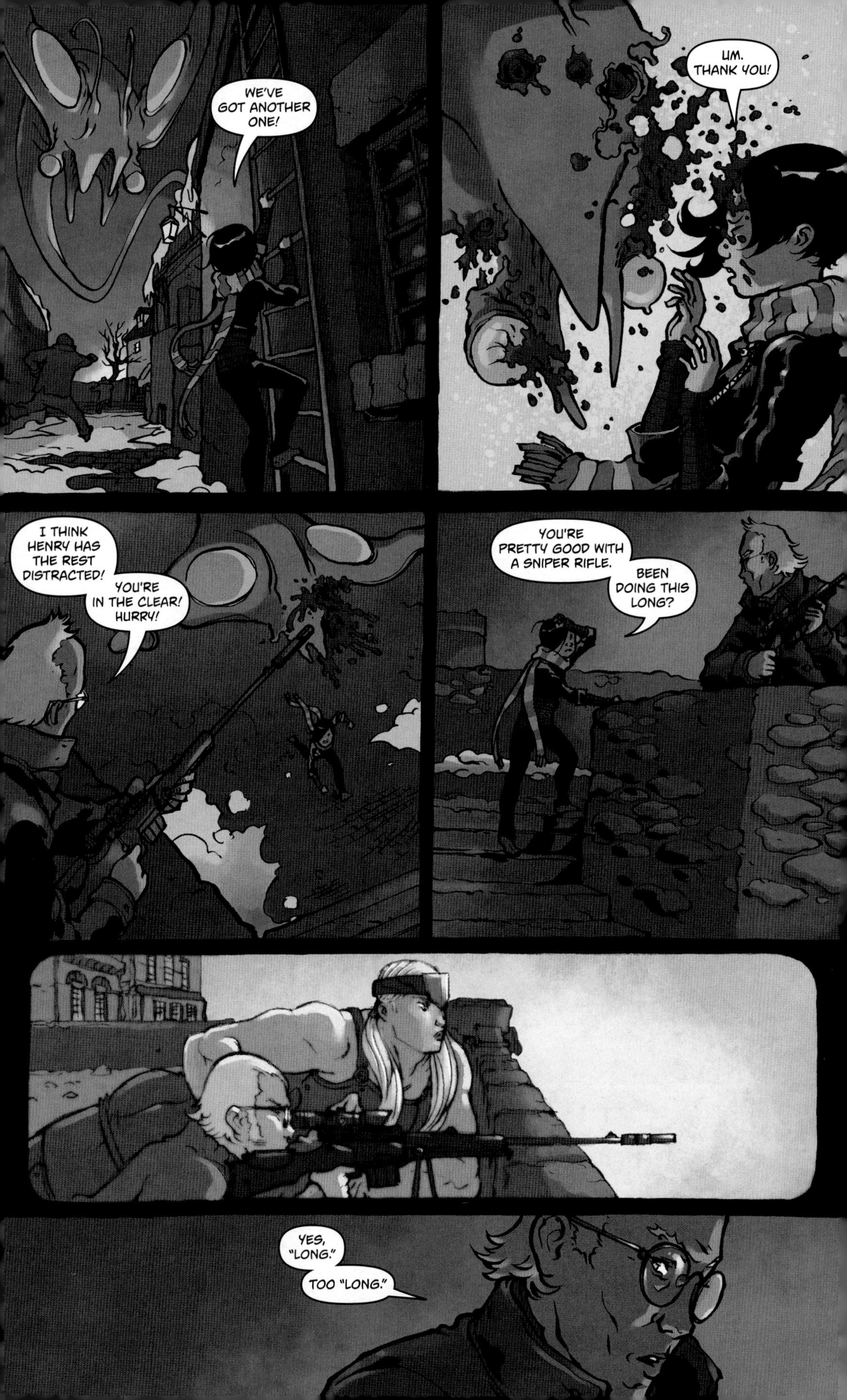
WE'VE GOT ANOTHER ONE!
UM. THANK YOU!
I THINK HENRY HAS THE REST DISTRACTED!
YOU'RE IN THE CLEAR! HURRY!
YOU'RE PRETTY GOOD WITH A SNIPER RIFLE.
BEEN DOING THIS LONG?
YES, "LONG."
TOO "LONG."

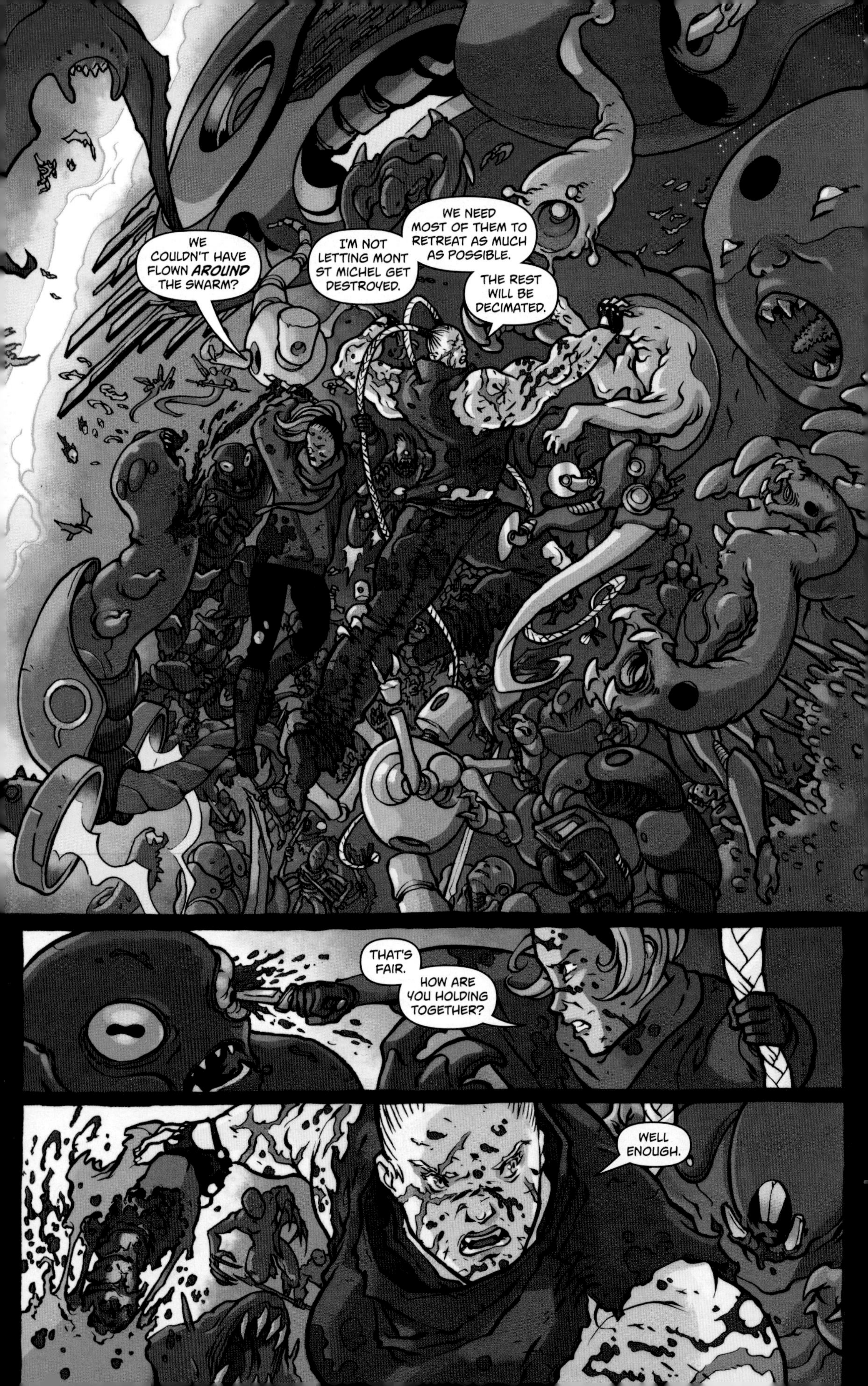

WE COULDN'T HAVE FLOWN AROUND THE SWARM?
I'M NOT LETTING MONT ST MICHEL GET DESTROYED.
WE NEED MOST OF THEM TO RETREAT AS MUCH AS POSSIBLE.
THE REST WILL BE DECIMATED.
THAT'S FAIR.
HOW ARE YOU HOLDING TOGETHER?
WELL ENOUGH.

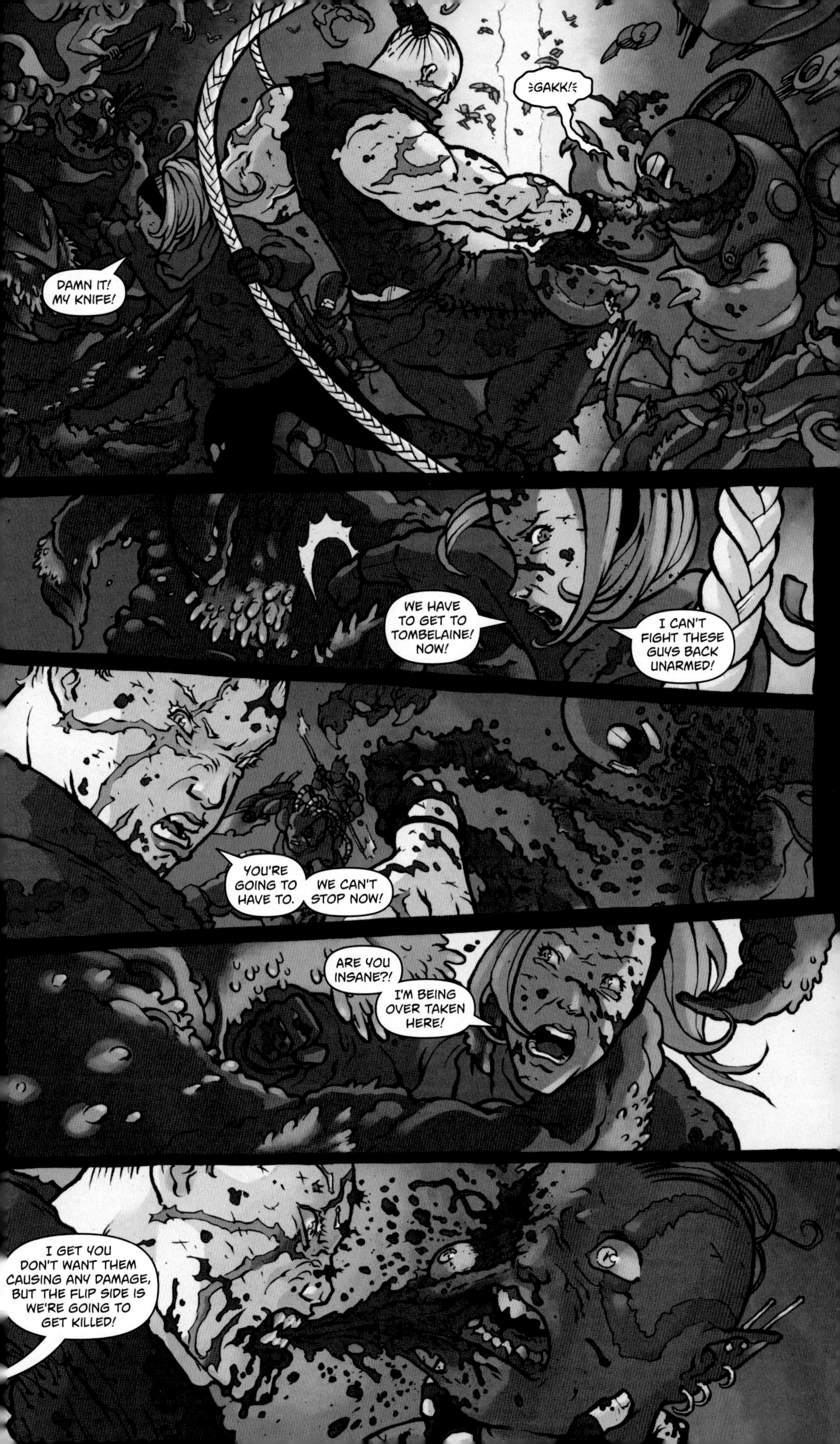
GAKK!
DAMN IT! MY KNIFE!
WE HAVE TO GET TO TOMBELAINE! NOW!
I CAN'T FIGHT THESE GUYS BACK UNARMED!
YOU'RE GOING TO HAVE TO.
WE CAN'T STOP NOW!
ARE YOU INSANE?!
I'M BEING OVER TAKEN HERE!
I GET YOU DON'T WANT THEM CAUSING ANY DAMAGE, BUT THE FLIP SIDE IS WE'RE GOING TO GET KILLED!

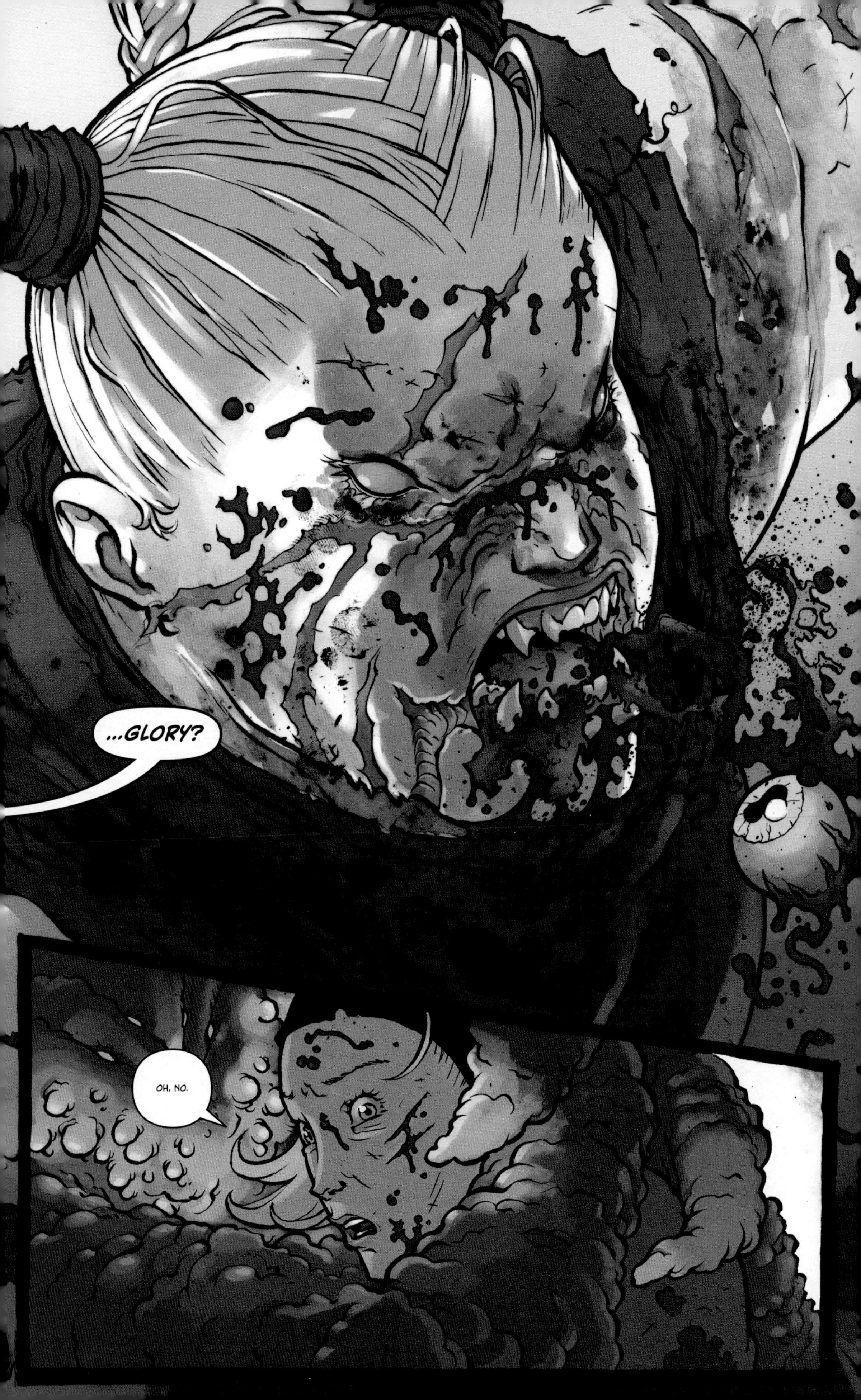
...GLORY?
OH, NO.

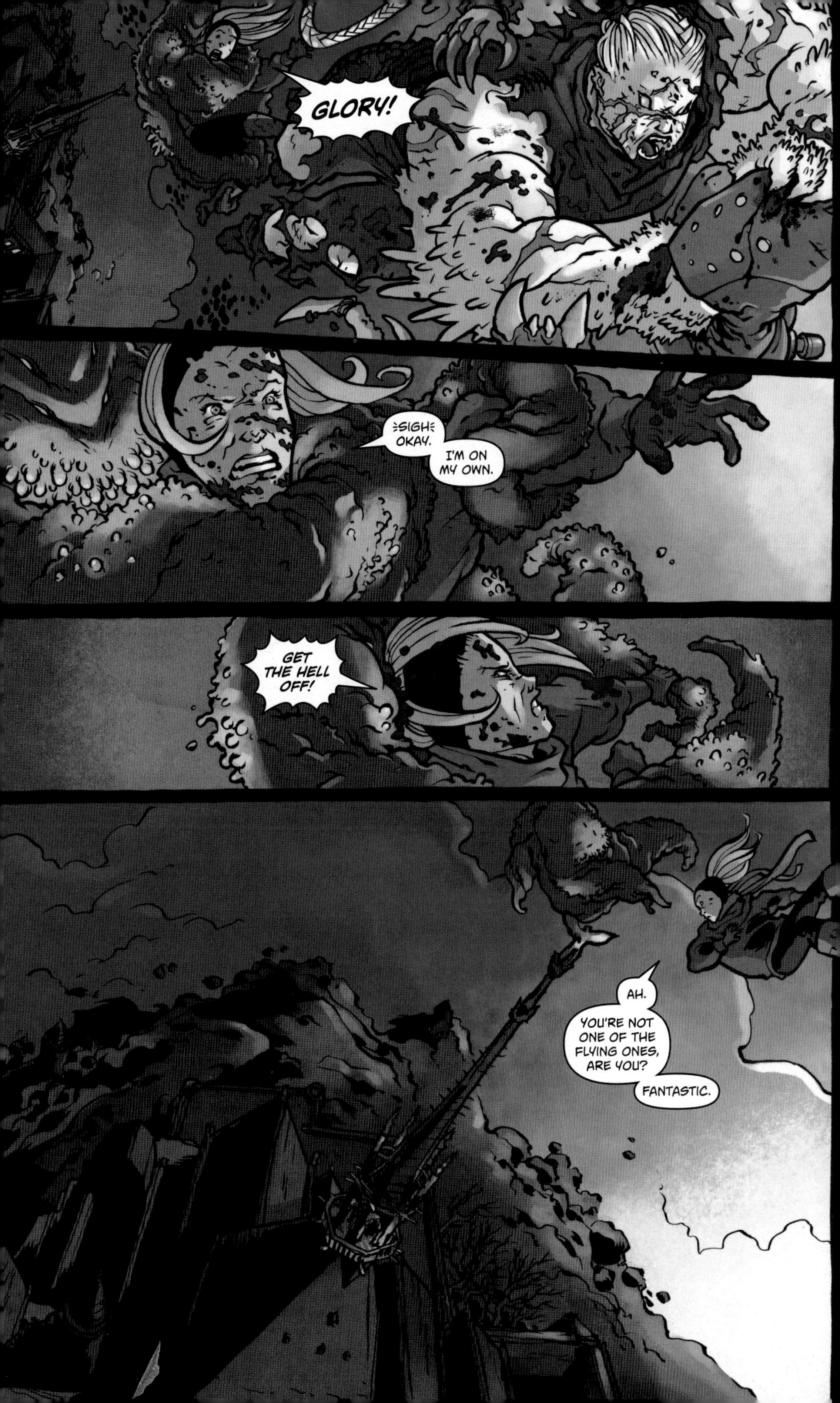
GLORY!
SIGH
OKAY.
I'M ON MY OWN.
GET THE HELL OFF!
AH.
YOU'RE NOT ONE OF THE FLYING ONES, ARE YOU?
FANTASTIC.

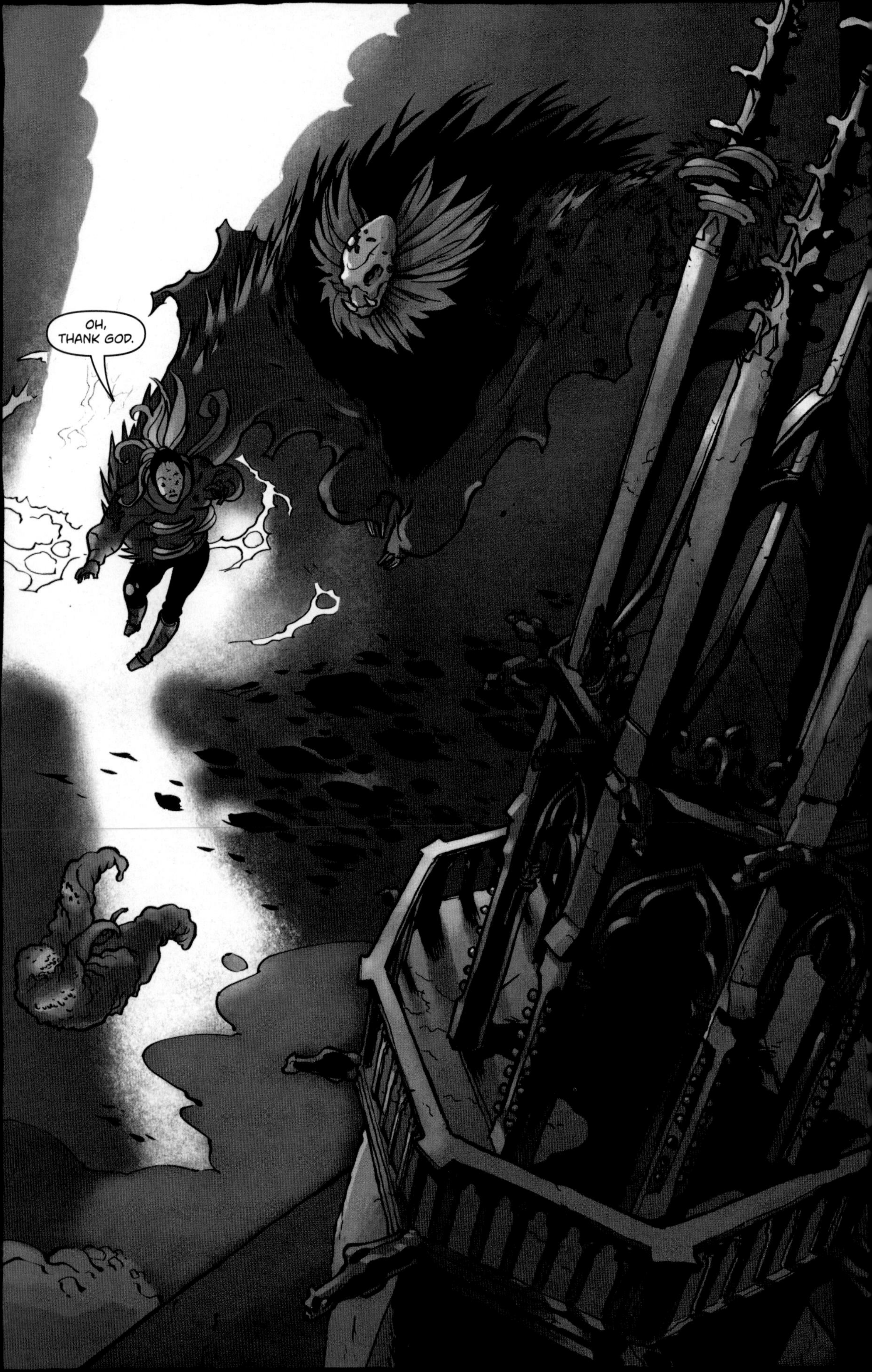
OH, THANK GOD.

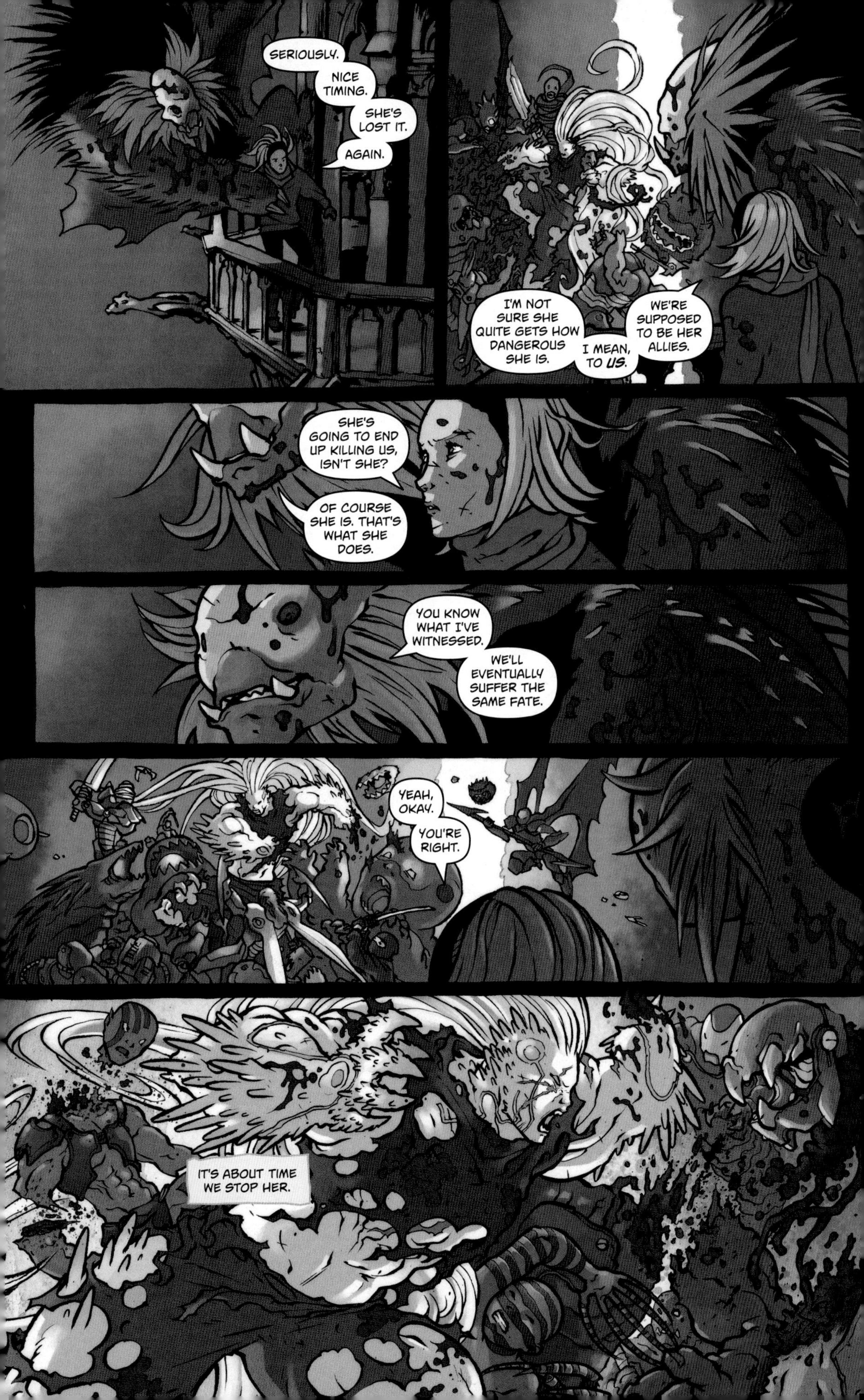
SERIOUSLY.
NICE TIMING.
SHE'S LOST IT.
AGAIN.
I'M NOT SURE SHE QUITE GETS HOW DANGEROUS SHE IS.
I MEAN, TO US.
WE'RE SUPPOSED TO BE HER ALLIES.
SHE'S GOING TO END UP KILLING US, ISN'T SHE?
OF COURSE SHE IS. THAT'S WHAT SHE DOES.
YOU KNOW WHAT I'VE WITNESSED.
WE'LL EVENTUALLY SUFFER THE SAME FATE.
YEAH, OKAY.
YOU'RE RIGHT.
IT'S ABOUT TIME WE STOP HER.

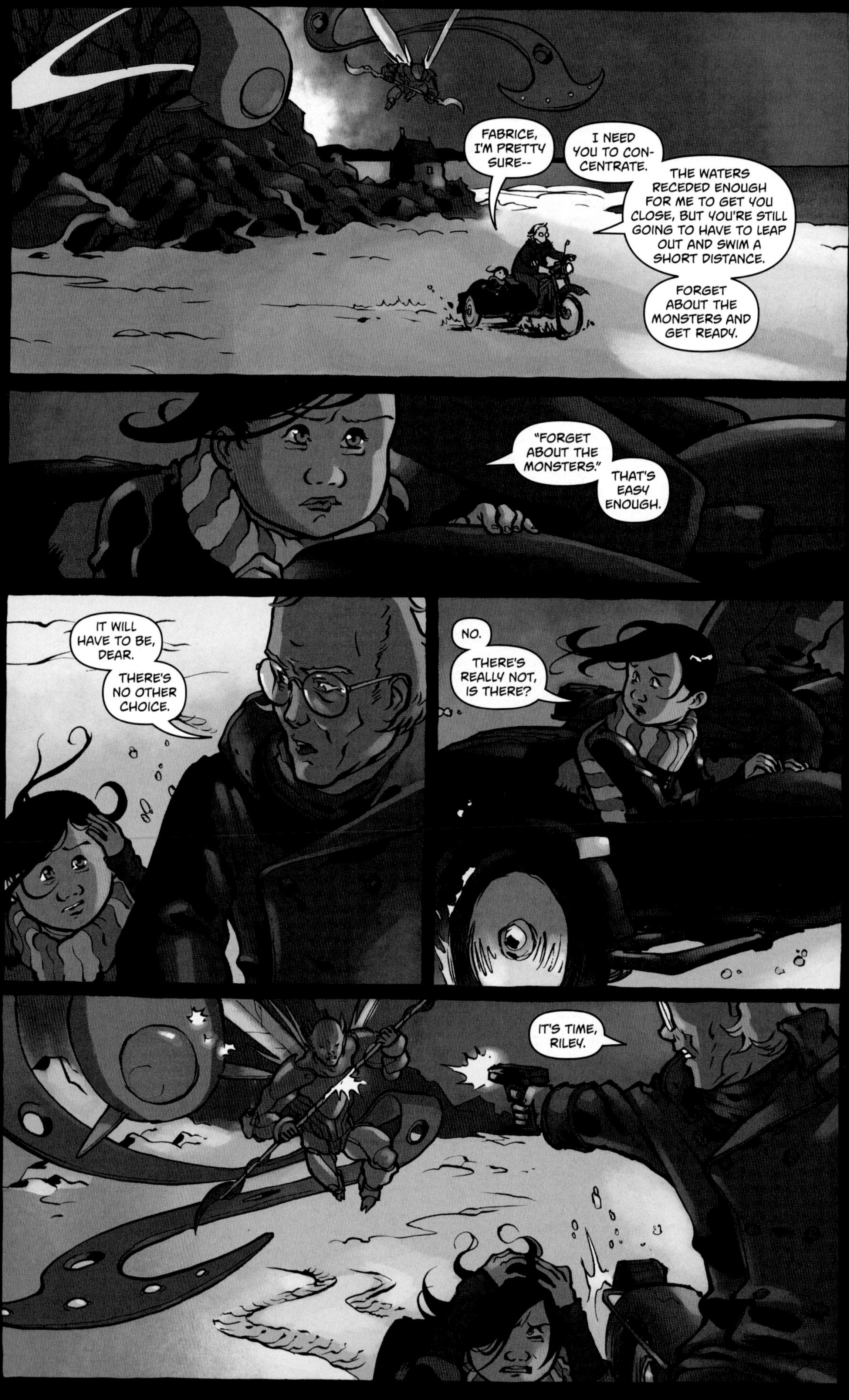
FABRICE, I'M PRETTY SURE--
I NEED YOU TO CON- CENTRATE.
THE WATERS RECEDED ENOUGH FOR ME TO GET YOU CLOSE, BUT YOU'RE STILL GOING TO HAVE TO LEAP OUT AND SWIM A SHORT DISTANCE.
FORGET ABOUT THE MONSTERS AND GET READY.
"FORGET ABOUT THE MONSTERS."
THAT'S EASY ENOUGH.
IT WILL HAVE TO BE, DEAR.
THERE'S NO OTHER CHOICE.
NO.
THERE'S REALLY NOT, IS THERE?
IT'S TIME, RILEY.

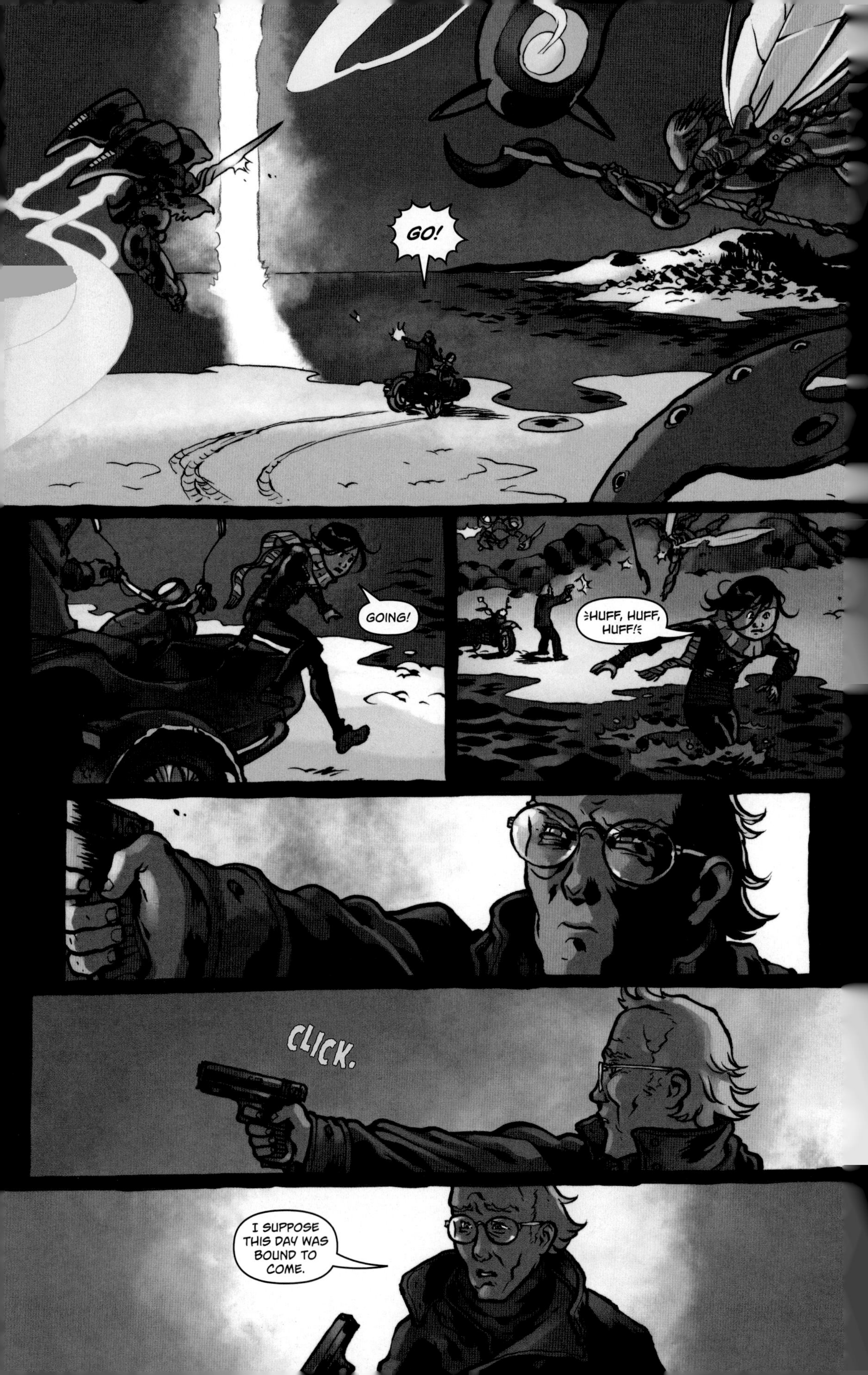
GO!
GOING!
HUFF, HUFF, HUFF!
CLICK.
I SUPPOSE THIS DAY WAS BOUND TO COME.

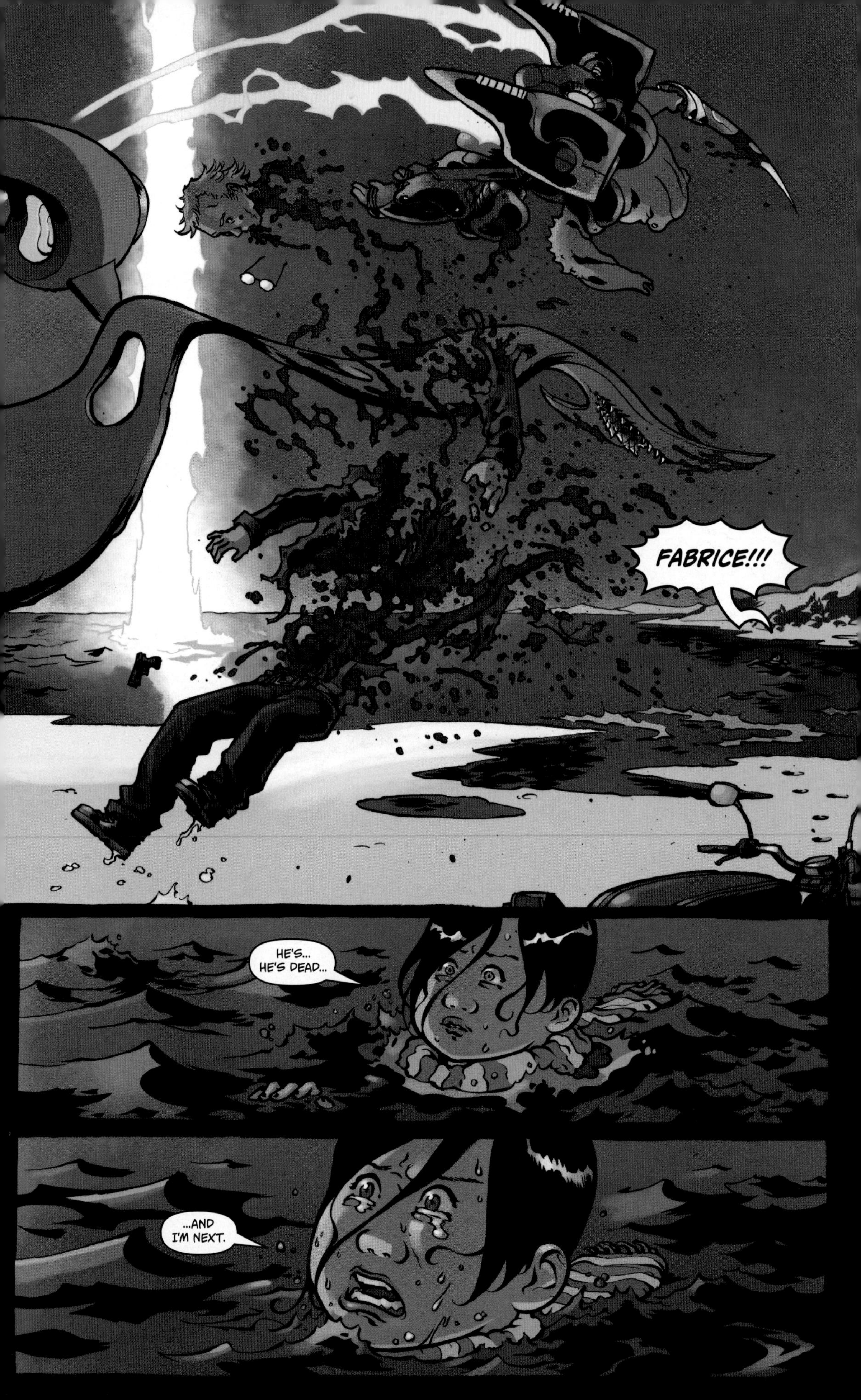
FABRICE!!!
HE'S... HE'S DEAD...
...AND I'M NEXT.

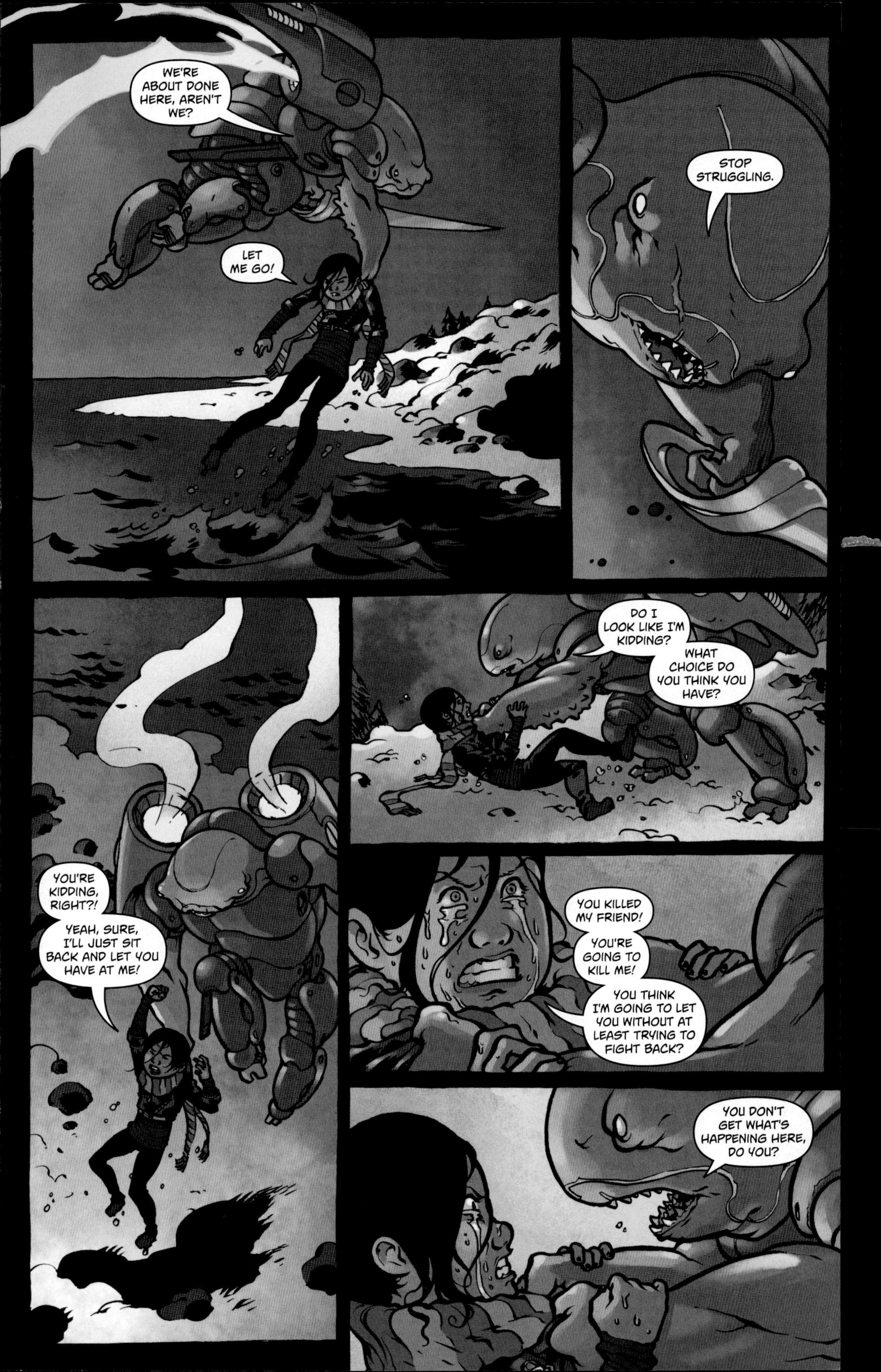
WE'RE ABOUT DONE HERE, AREN'T WE?
LET ME GO!
STOP STRUGGLING.
YOU'RE KIDDING, RIGHT?!
YEAH, SURE, I'LL JUST SIT BACK AND LET YOU HAVE AT ME!
DO I LOOK LIKE I'M KIDDING?
WHAT CHOICE DO YOU THINK YOU HAVE?
YOU KILLED MY FRIEND!
YOU'RE GOING TO KILL ME!
YOU THINK I'M GOING TO LET YOU WITHOUT AT LEAST TRYING TO FIGHT BACK?
YOU DON'T GET WHAT'S HAPPENING HERE, DO YOU?

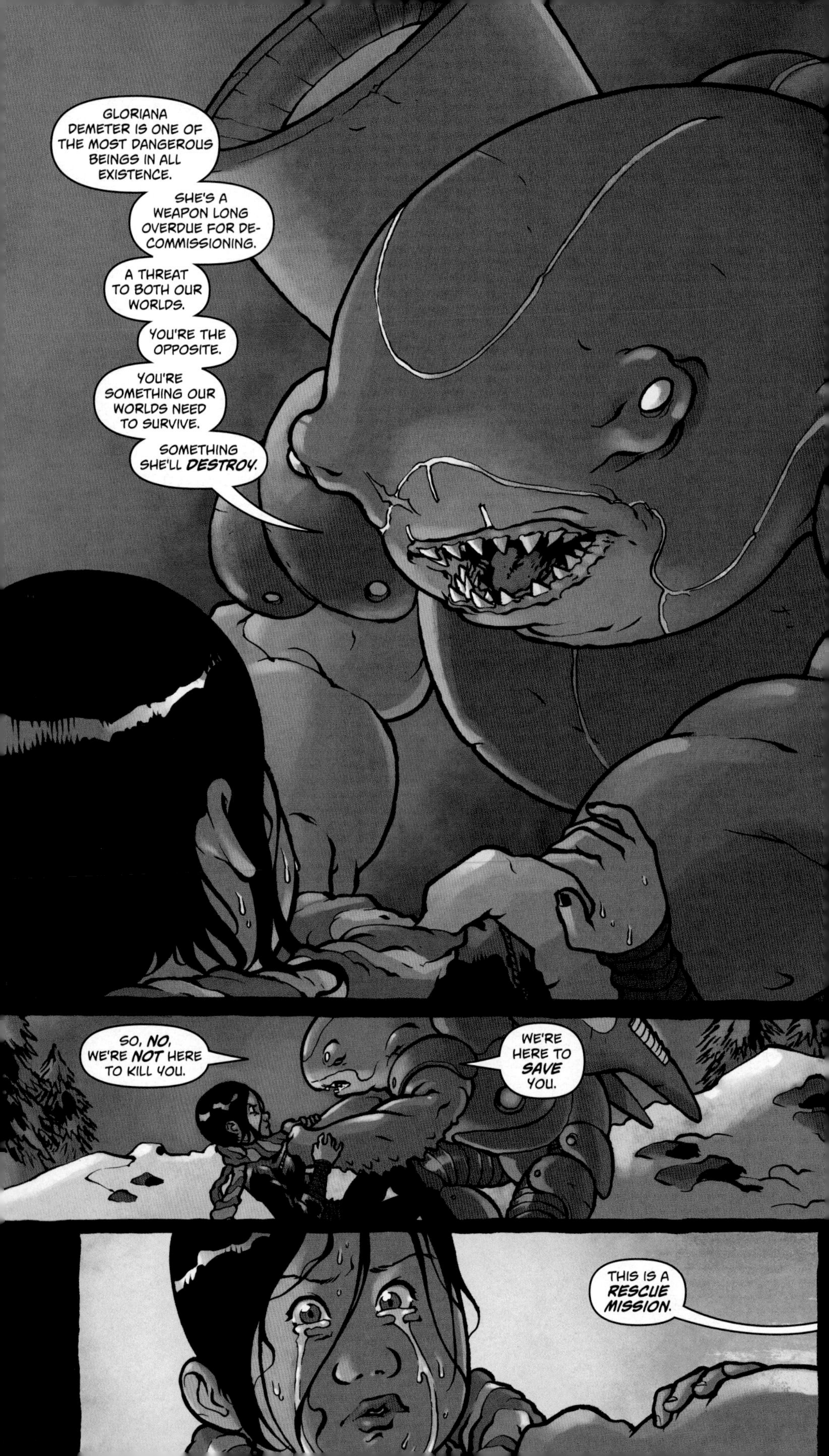
GLORIANA DEMETER IS ONE OF THE MOST DANGEROUS BEINGS IN ALL EXISTENCE.
SHE'S A WEAPON LONG OVERDUE FOR DE-COMMISSIONING.
A THREAT TO BOTH OUR WORLDS.
YOU'RE THE OPPOSITE.
YOU'RE SOMETHING OUR WORLDS NEED TO SURVIVE.
SOMETHING SHE'LL DESTROY.
SO, NO, WE'RE NOT HERE TO KILL YOU.
WE'RE HERE TO SAVE YOU.
THIS IS A RESCUE MISSION.

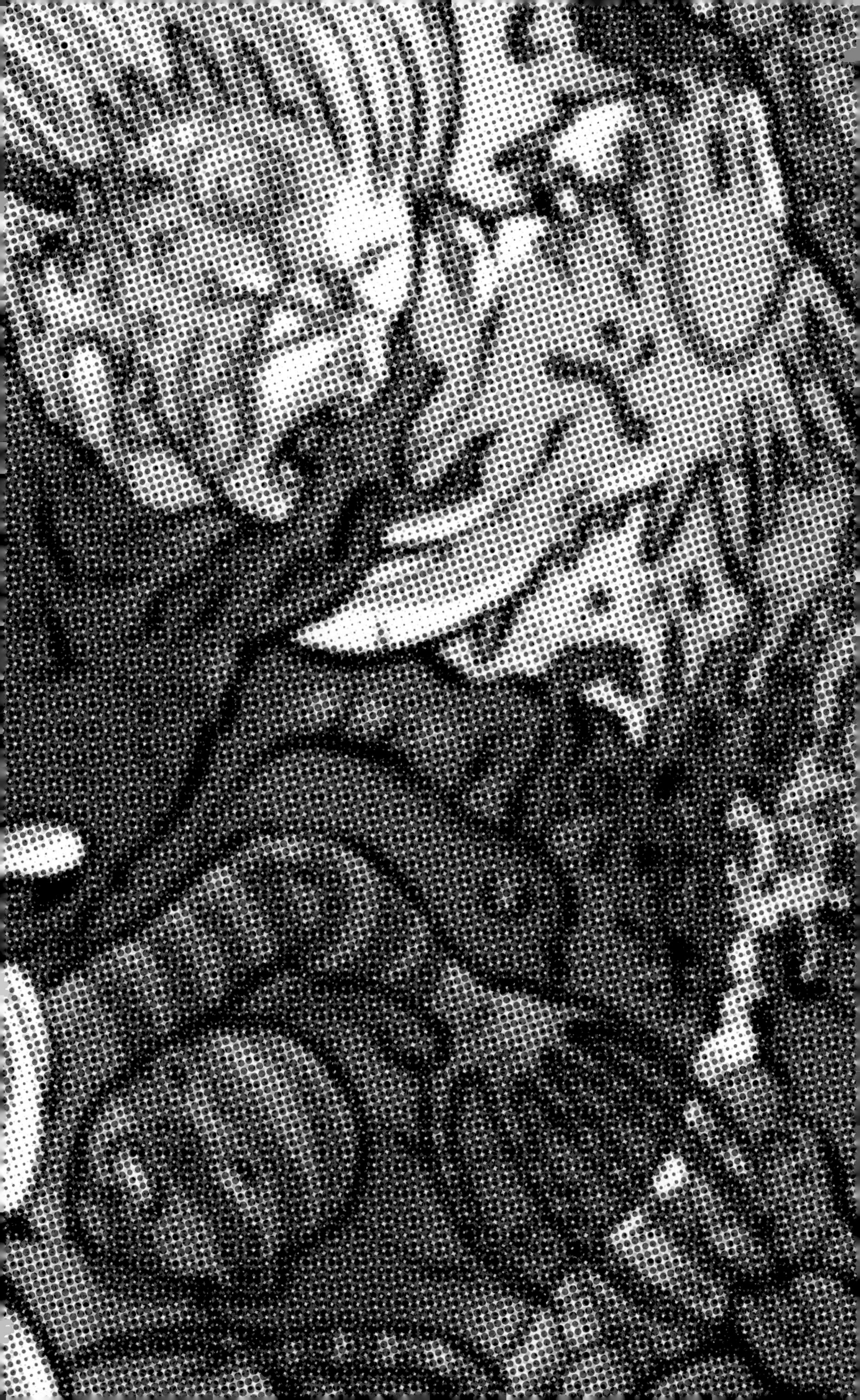

Chapter Six

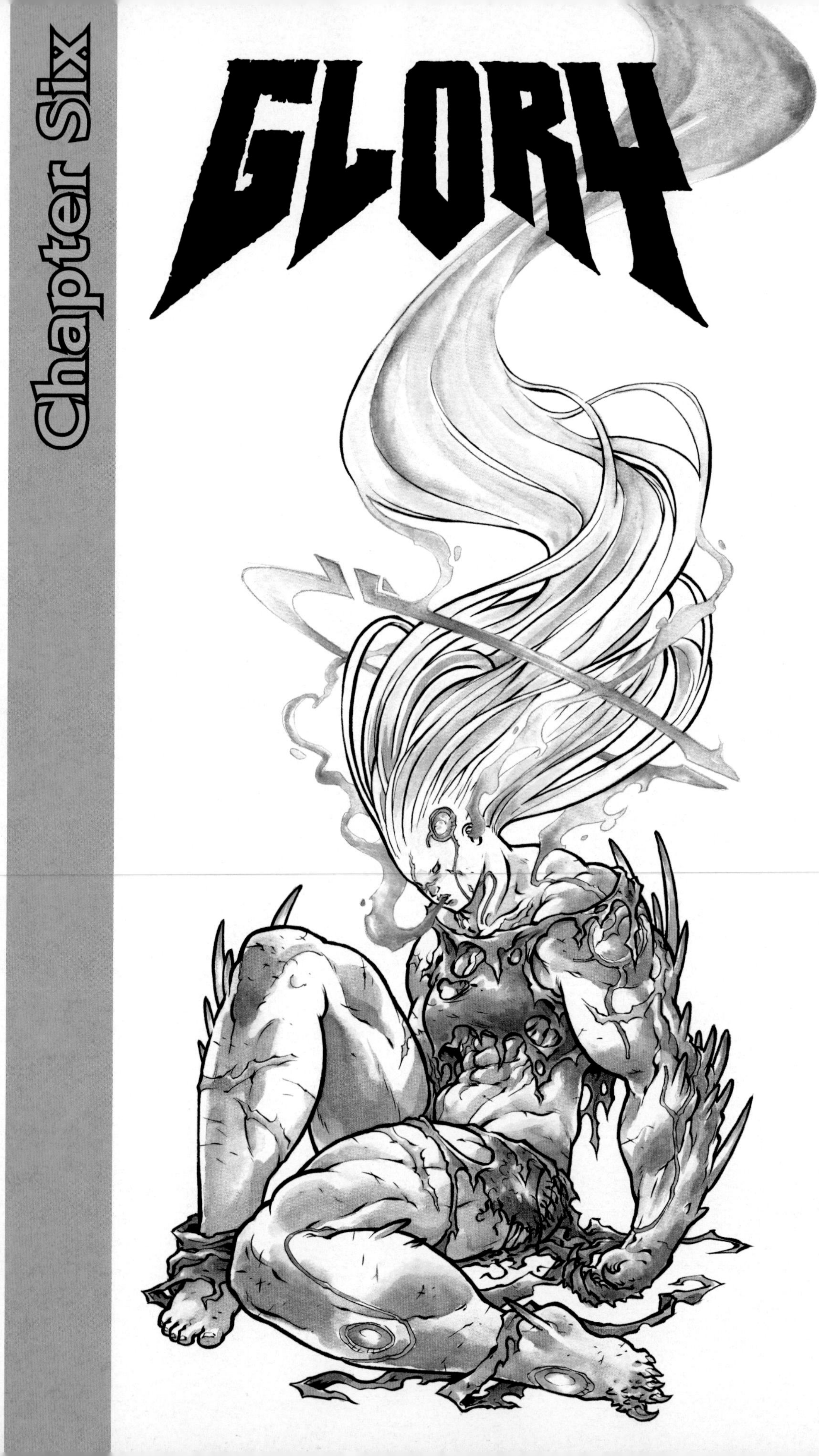
GLORY

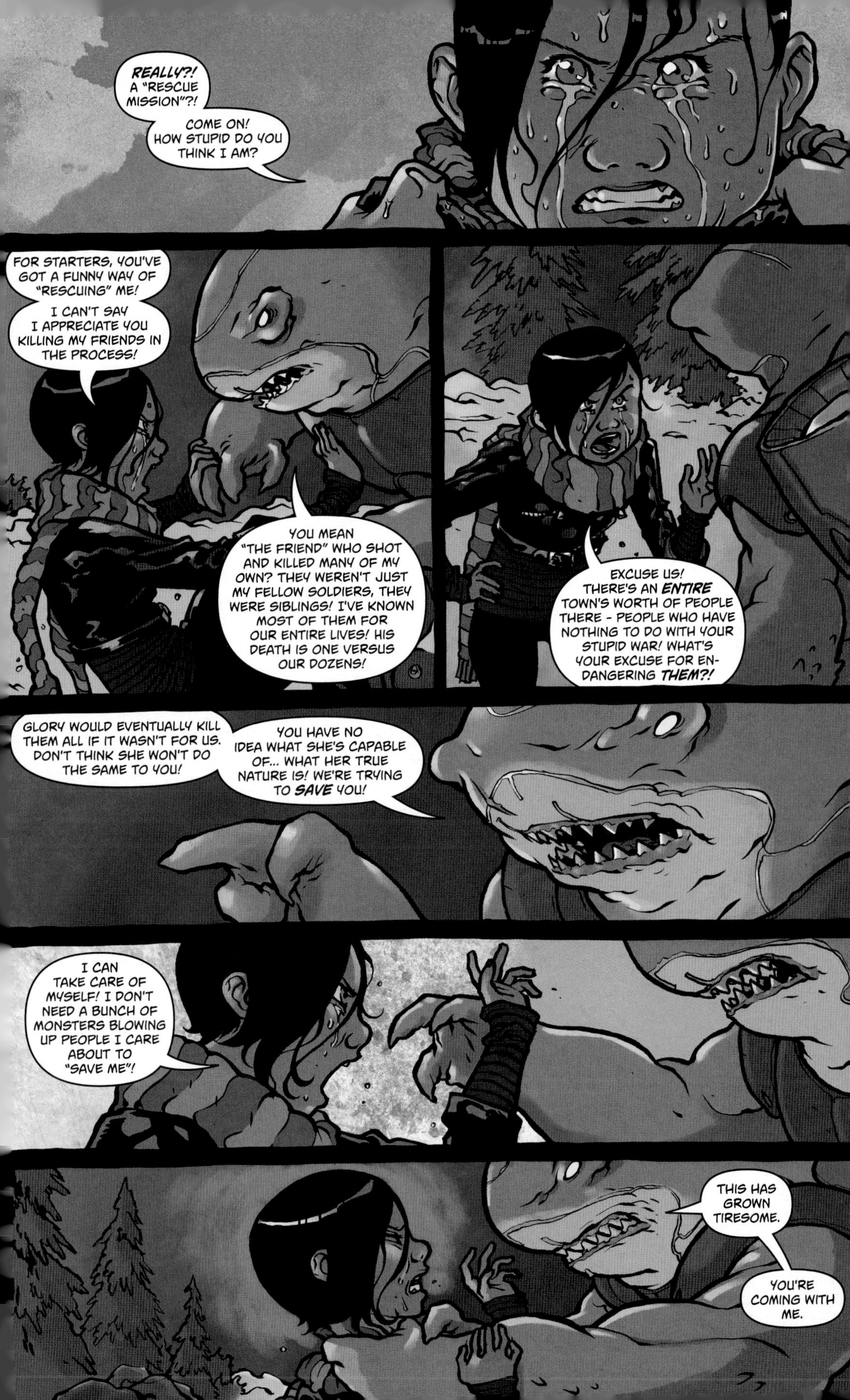
REALLY?! A "RESCUE MISSION"?!
COME ON! HOW STUPID DO YOU THINK I AM?
FOR STARTERS, YOU'VE GOT A FUNNY WAY OF "RESCUING" ME!
I CAN'T SAY I APPRECIATE YOU KILLING MY FRIENDS IN THE PROCESS!
YOU MEAN "THE FRIEND" WHO SHOT AND KILLED MANY OF MY OWN? THEY WEREN'T JUST MY FELLOW SOLDIERS, THEY WERE SIBLINGS! I'VE KNOWN MOST OF THEM FOR OUR ENTIRE LIVES! HIS DEATH IS ONE VERSUS OUR DOZENS!
EXCUSE US! THERE'S AN ENTIRE TOWN'S WORTH OF PEOPLE THERE - PEOPLE WHO HAVE NOTHING TO DO WITH YOUR STUPID WAR! WHAT'S YOUR EXCUSE FOR ENDANGERING THEM?!
GLORY WOULD EVENTUALLY KILL THEM ALL IF IT WASN'T FOR US. DON'T THINK SHE WON'T DO THE SAME TO YOU!
YOU HAVE NO IDEA WHAT SHE'S CAPABLE OF... WHAT HER TRUE NATURE IS! WE'RE TRYING TO SAVE YOU!
I CAN TAKE CARE OF MYSELF! I DON'T NEED A BUNCH OF MONSTERS BLOWING UP PEOPLE I CARE ABOUT TO "SAVE ME"!
THIS HAS GROWN TIRESOME.
YOU'RE COMING WITH ME.

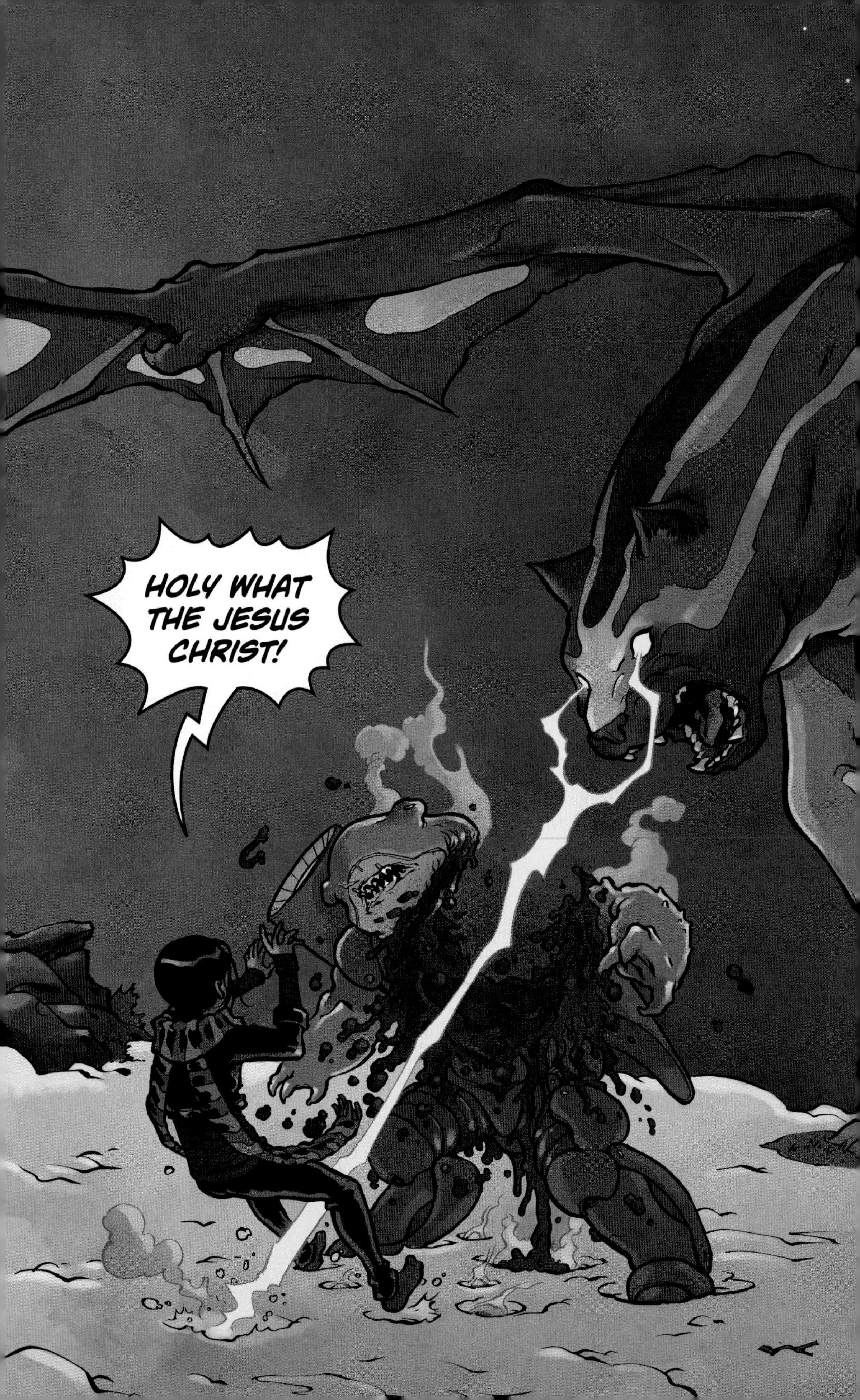
HOLY WHAT THE JESUS CHRIST!

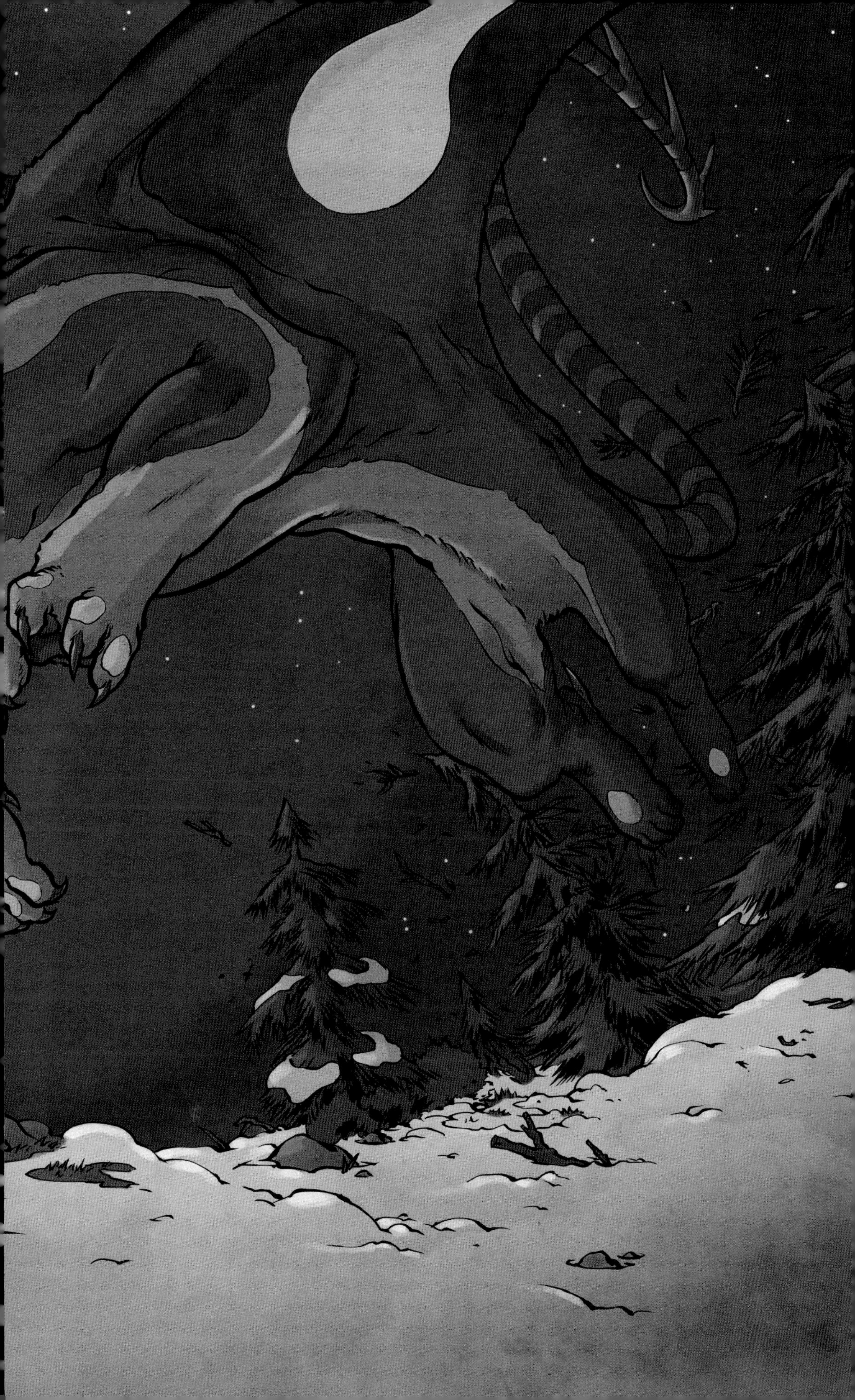

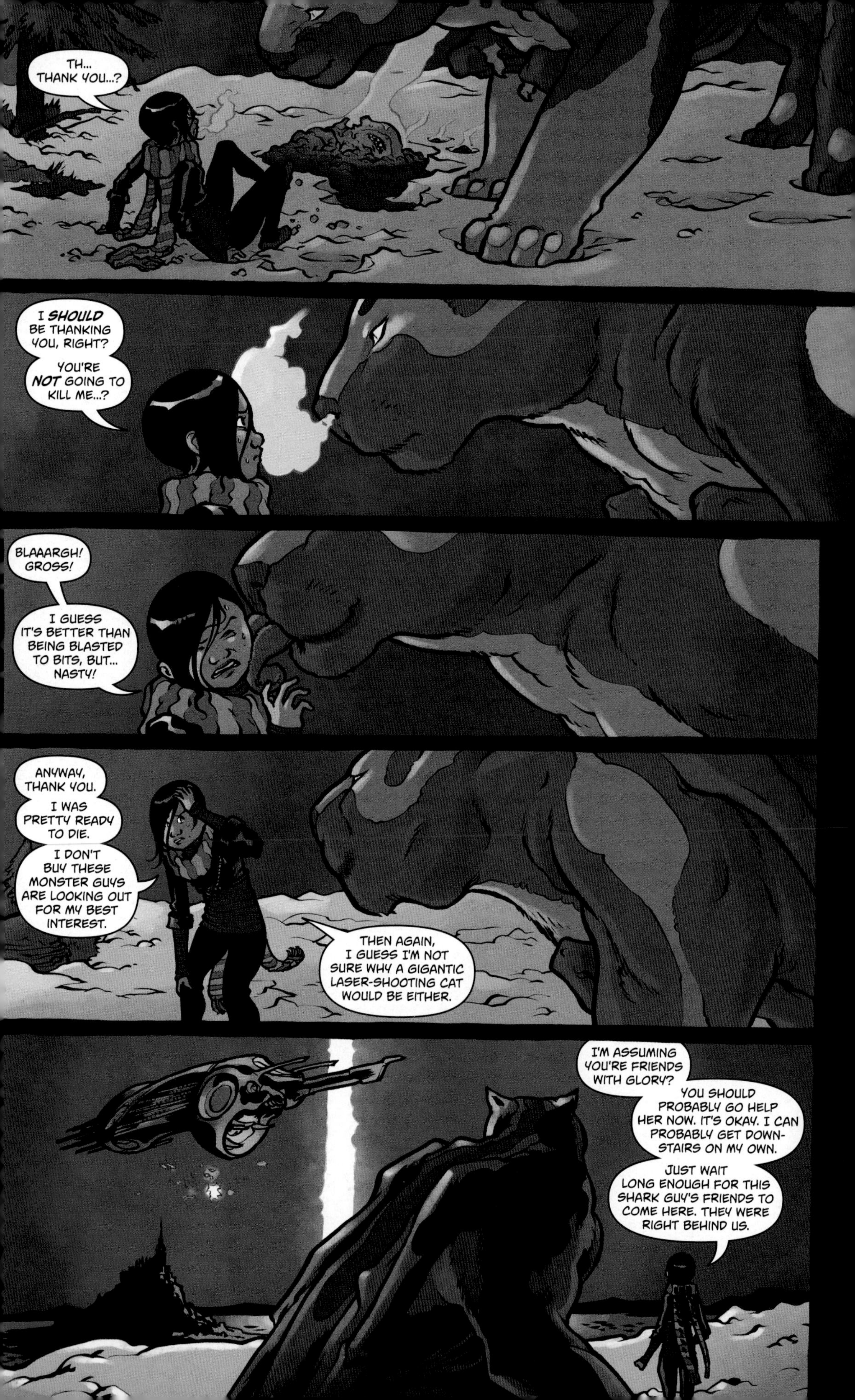
TH... THANK YOU...?
I SHOULD BE THANKING YOU, RIGHT?
YOU'RE NOT GOING TO KILL ME...?
BLAAARGH! GROSS!
I GUESS IT'S BETTER THAN BEING BLASTED TO BITS, BUT... NASTY!
ANYWAY, THANK YOU.
I WAS PRETTY READY TO DIE.
I DON'T BUY THESE MONSTER GUYS ARE LOOKING OUT FOR MY BEST INTEREST.
THEN AGAIN, I GUESS I'M NOT SURE WHY A GIGANTIC LASER-SHOOTING CAT WOULD BE EITHER.
I'M ASSUMING YOU'RE FRIENDS WITH GLORY?
YOU SHOULD PROBABLY GO HELP HER NOW. IT'S OKAY. I CAN PROBABLY GET DOWN-STAIRS ON MY OWN.
JUST WAIT LONG ENOUGH FOR THIS SHARK GUY'S FRIENDS TO COME HERE. THEY WERE RIGHT BEHIND US.

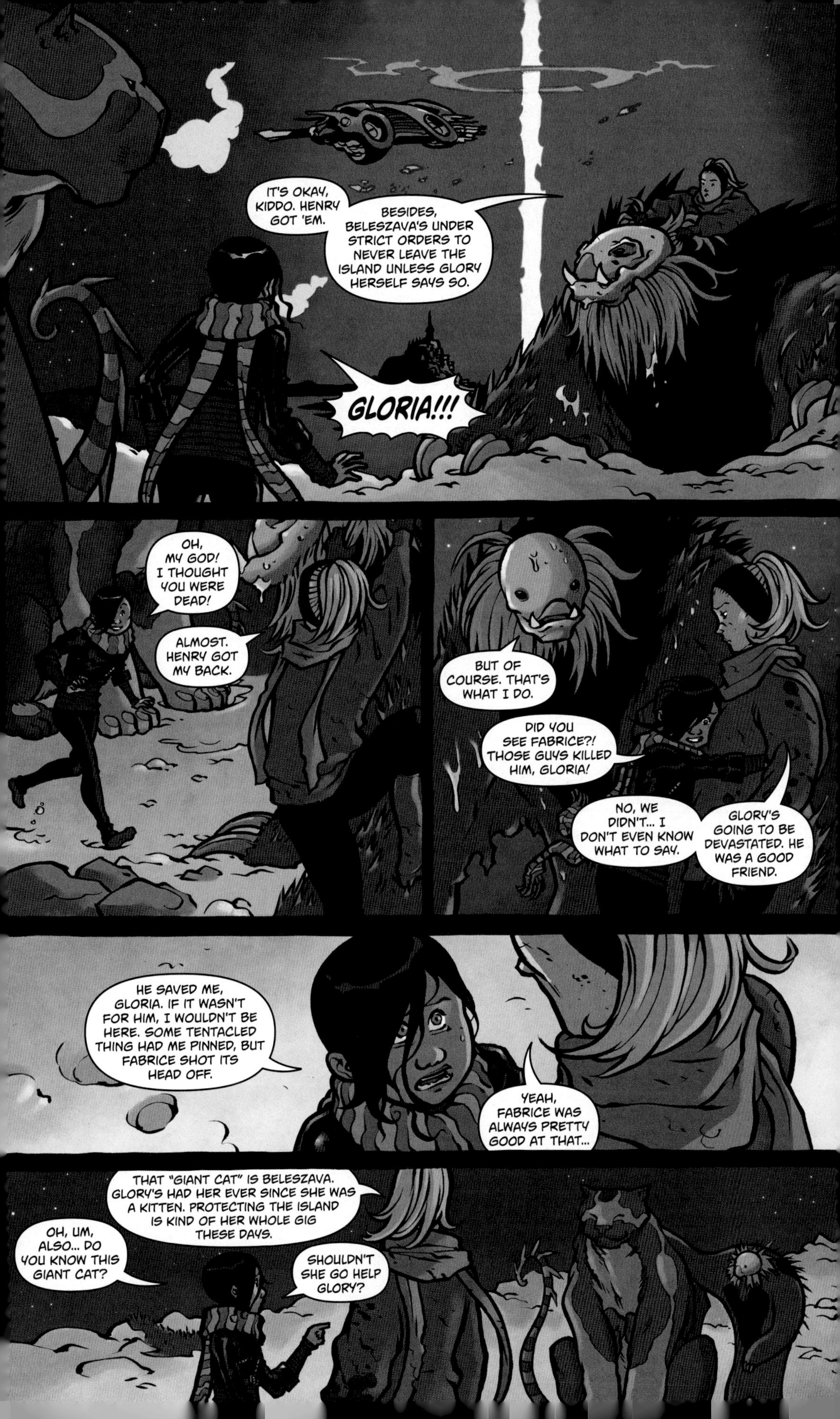
IT'S OKAY, KIDDO. HENRY GOT 'EM.
BESIDES, BELESZAVA'S UNDER STRICT ORDERS TO NEVER LEAVE THE ISLAND UNLESS GLORY HERSELF SAYS SO.
GLORIA!!!
OH, MY GOD! I THOUGHT YOU WERE DEAD!
ALMOST. HENRY GOT MY BACK.
BUT OF COURSE. THAT'S WHAT I DO.
DID YOU SEE FABRICE?! THOSE GUYS KILLED HIM, GLORIA!
NO, WE DIDN'T... I DON'T EVEN KNOW WHAT TO SAY.
GLORY'S GOING TO BE DEVASTATED. HE WAS A GOOD FRIEND.
HE SAVED ME, GLORIA. IF IT WASN'T FOR HIM, I WOULDN'T BE HERE. SOME TENTACLED THING HAD ME PINNED, BUT FABRICE SHOT ITS HEAD OFF.
YEAH, FABRICE WAS ALWAYS PRETTY GOOD AT THAT...
OH, UM, ALSO... DO YOU KNOW THIS GIANT CAT?
THAT "GIANT CAT" IS BELESZAVA. GLORY'S HAD HER EVER SINCE SHE WAS A KITTEN. PROTECTING THE ISLAND IS KIND OF HER WHOLE GIG THESE DAYS.
SHOULDN'T SHE GO HELP GLORY?

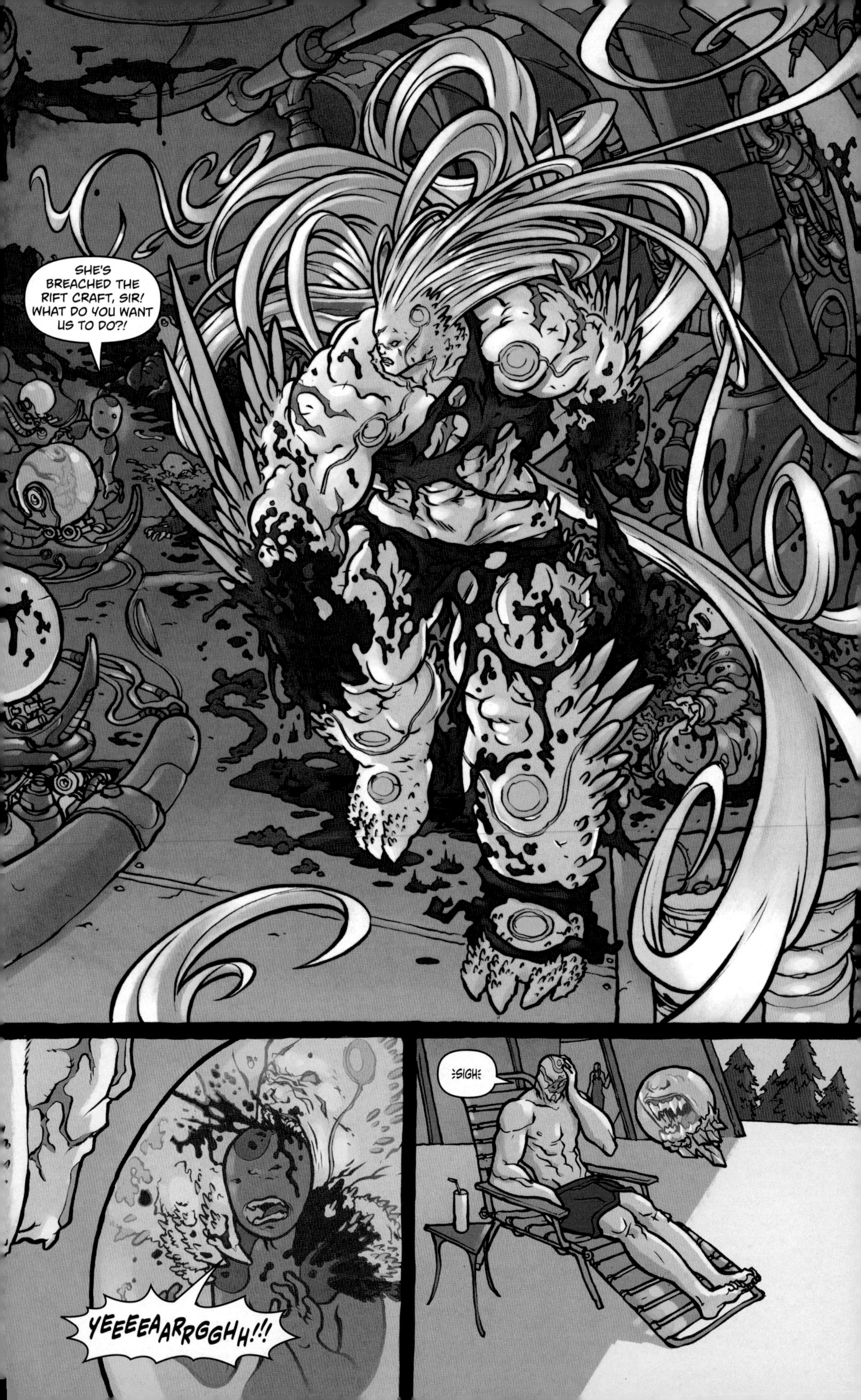
SHE'S BREACHED THE RIFT CRAFT, SIR! WHAT DO YOU WANT US TO DO?!
YEEEEAARRGGHH!!!
SIGH

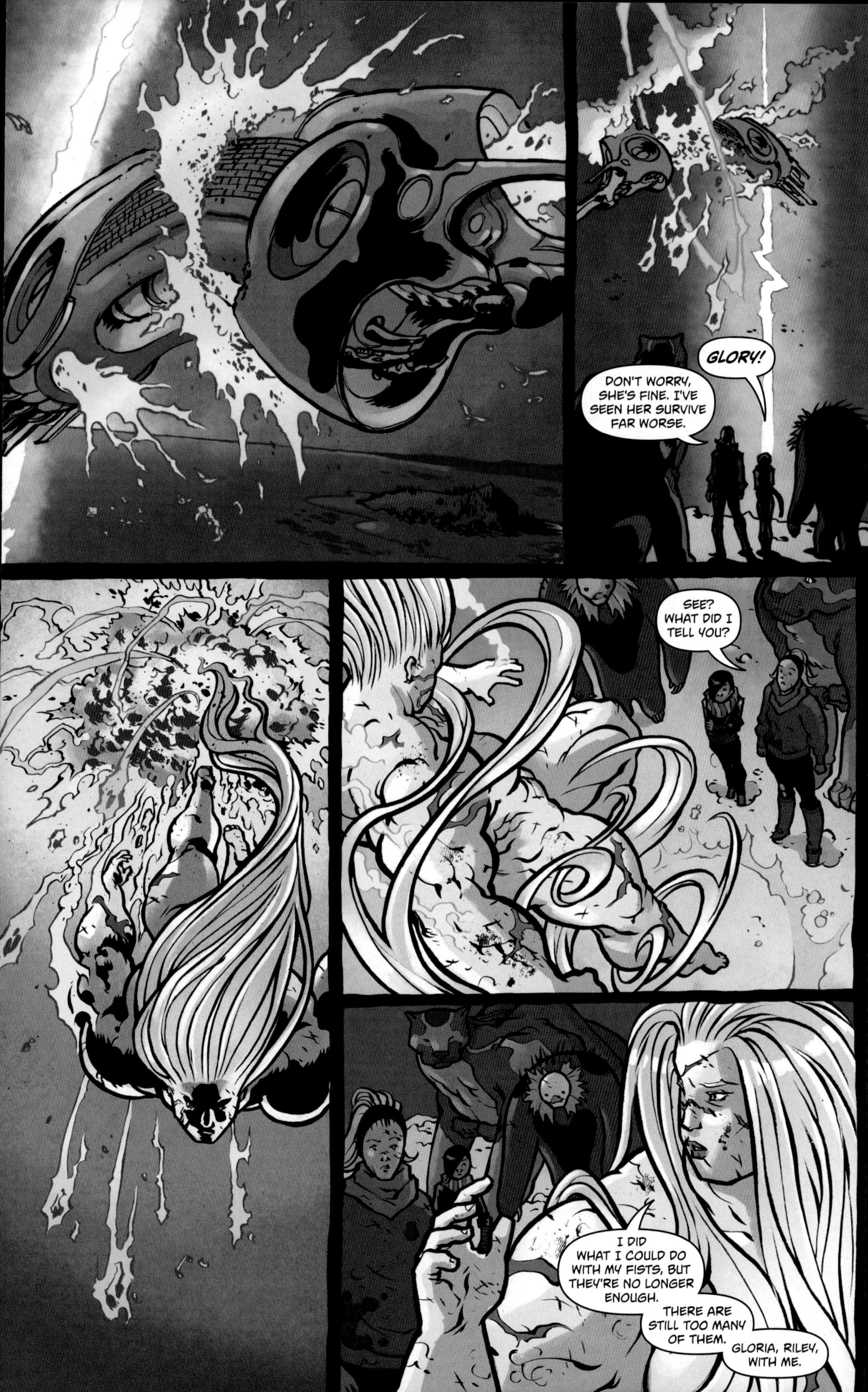
GLORY!
DON'T WORRY, SHE'S FINE. I'VE SEEN HER SURVIVE FAR WORSE.
SEE? WHAT DID I TELL YOU?
I DID WHAT I COULD DO WITH MY FISTS, BUT THEY'RE NO LONGER ENOUGH.
THERE ARE STILL TOO MANY OF THEM.
GLORIA, RILEY, WITH ME.

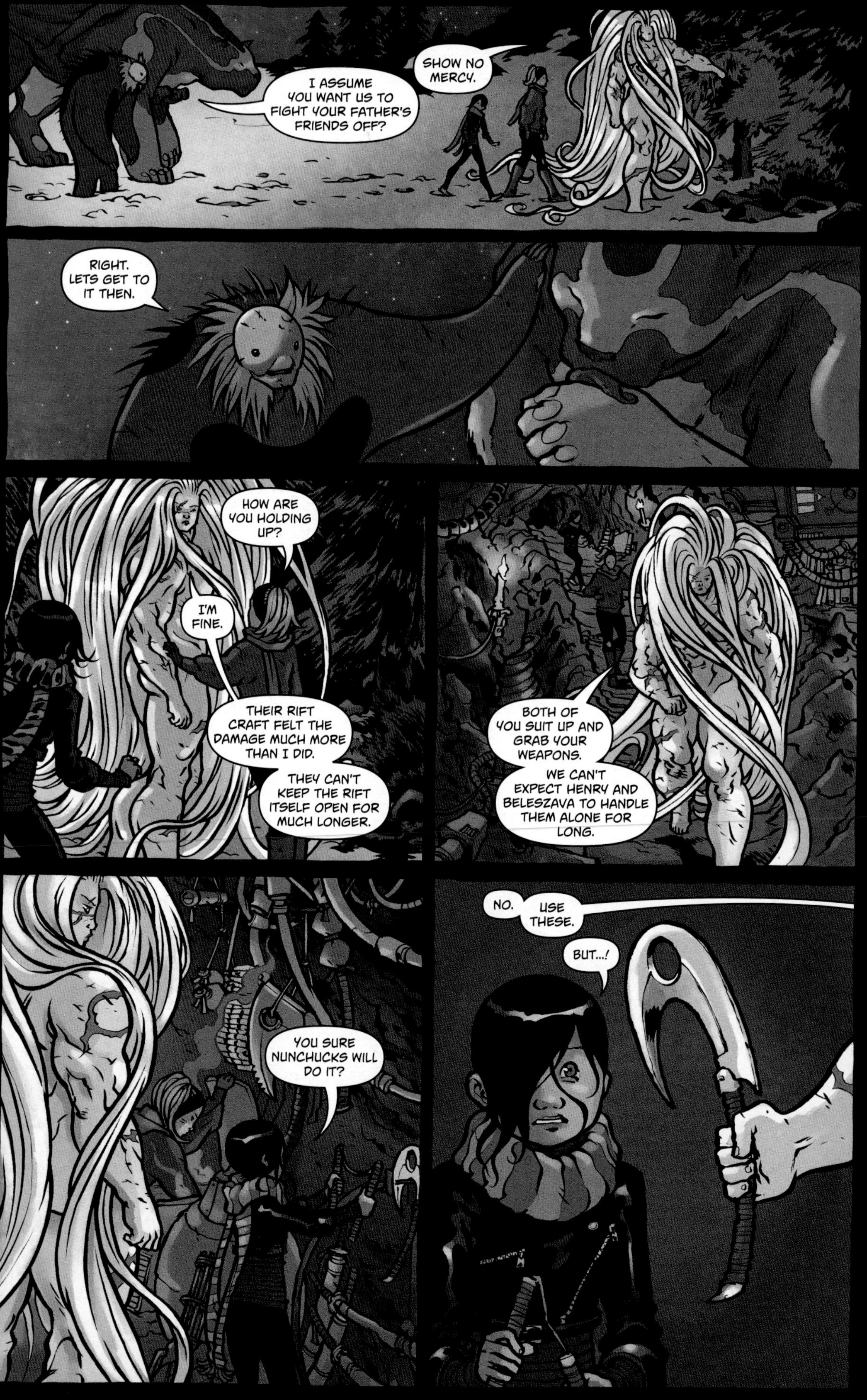
I ASSUME YOU WANT US TO FIGHT YOUR FATHER'S FRIENDS OFF?
SHOW NO MERCY.
RIGHT. LETS GET TO IT THEN.
HOW ARE YOU HOLDING UP?
I'M FINE.
THEIR RIFT CRAFT FELT THE DAMAGE MUCH MORE THAN I DID.
THEY CAN'T KEEP THE RIFT ITSELF OPEN FOR MUCH LONGER.
BOTH OF YOU SUIT UP AND GRAB YOUR WEAPONS.
WE CAN'T EXPECT HENRY AND BELESZAVA TO HANDLE THEM ALONE FOR LONG.
YOU SURE NUNCHUCKS WILL DO IT?
NO.
USE THESE.
BUT...!

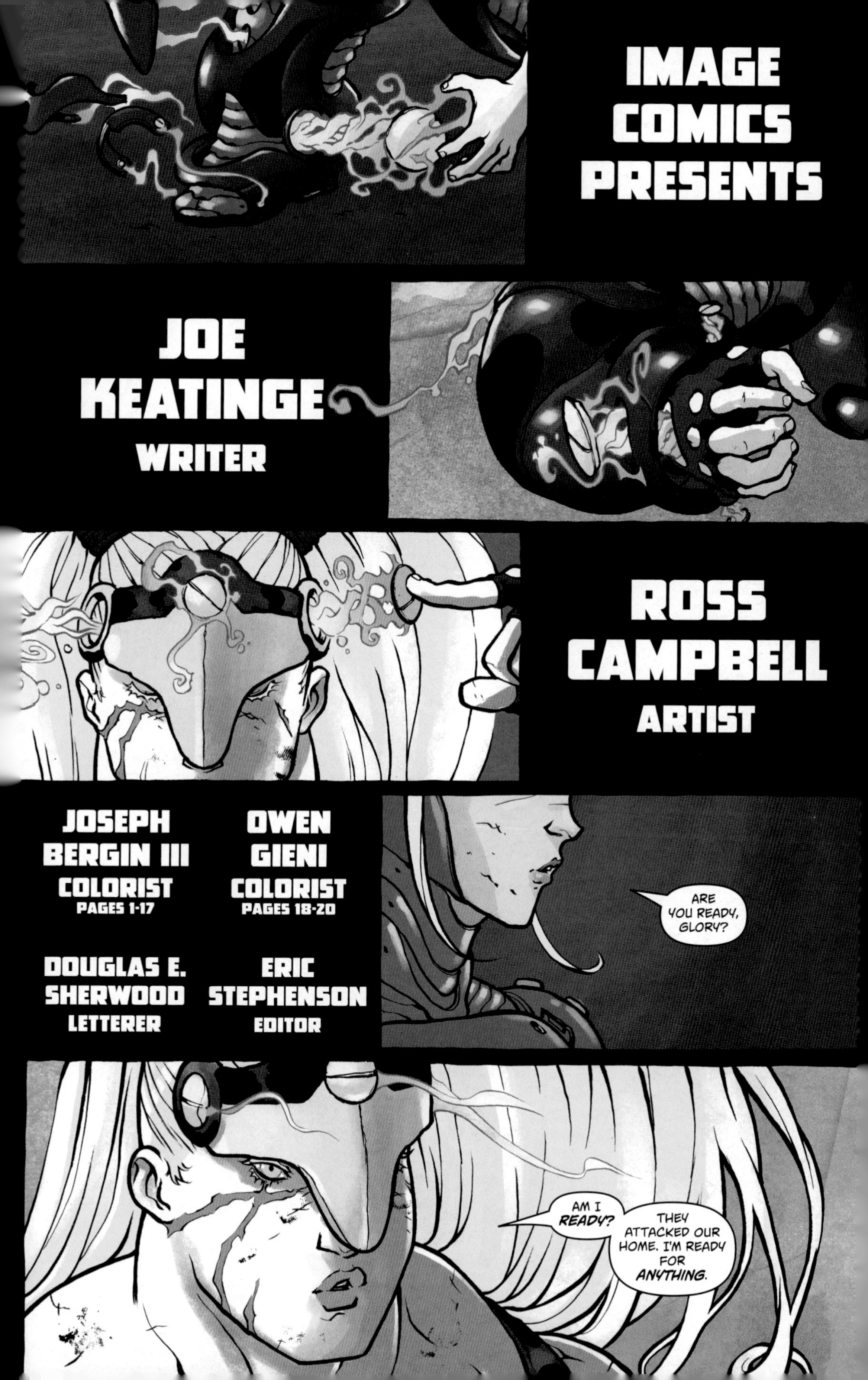

IMAGE COMICS PRESENTS
JOE KEATINGE
WRITER
ROSS CAMPBELL
ARTIST
JOSEPH BERGIN III
COLORIST
PAGES 1-17
OWEN GIENI
COLORIST
PAGES 18-20
DOUGLAS E. SHERWOOD
LETTERER
ERIC STEPHENSON
EDITOR
ARE YOU READY, GLORY?
AM I *READY?*
THEY ATTACKED OUR HOME. I'M READY FOR *ANYTHING.*

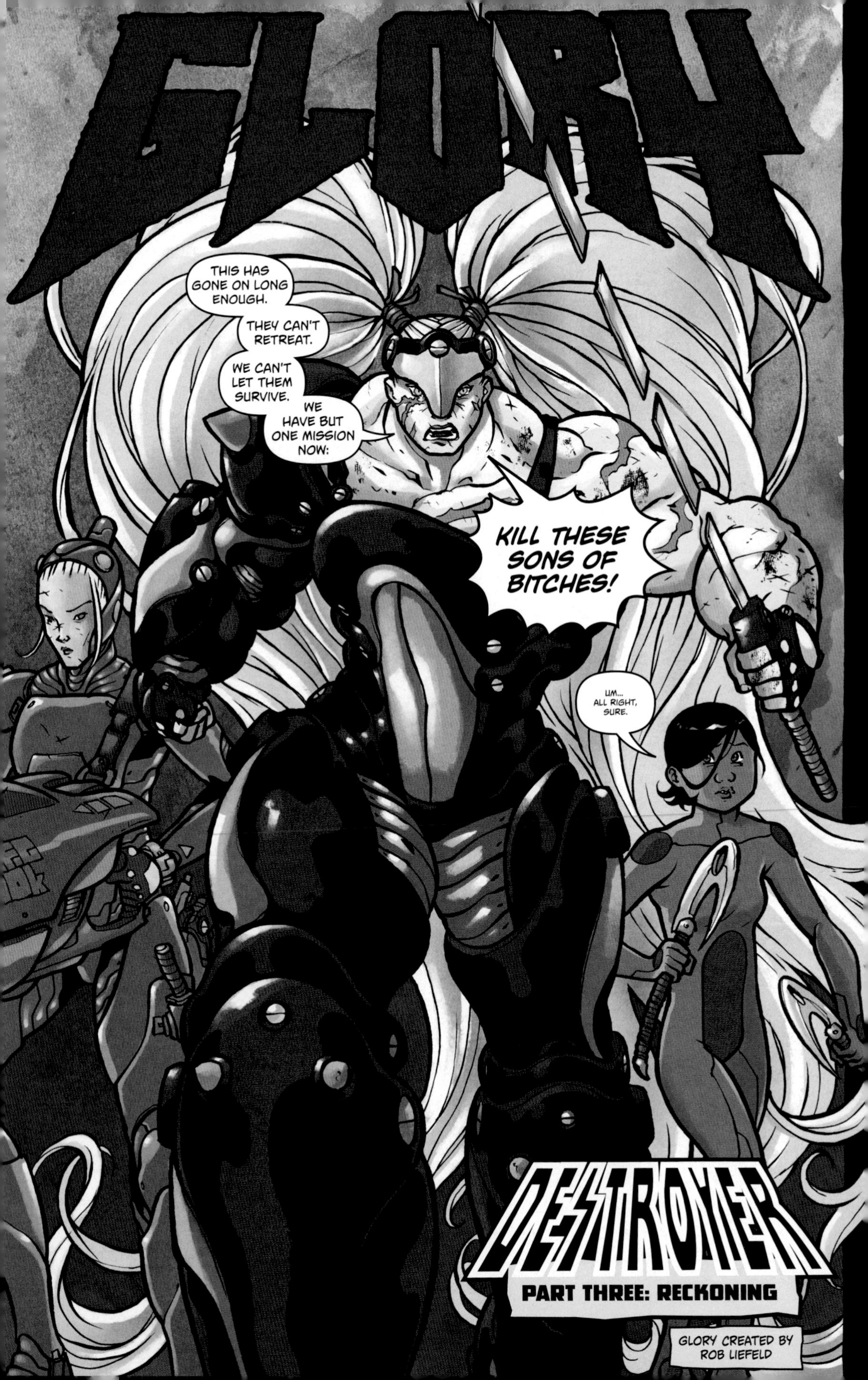
GLORY
THIS HAS GONE ON LONG ENOUGH.
THEY CAN'T RETREAT.
WE CAN'T LET THEM SURVIVE.
WE HAVE BUT ONE MISSION NOW:
KILL THESE SONS OF BITCHES!
UM... ALL RIGHT, SURE.
DESTROYER
PART THREE: RECKONING
GLORY CREATED BY ROB LIEFELD

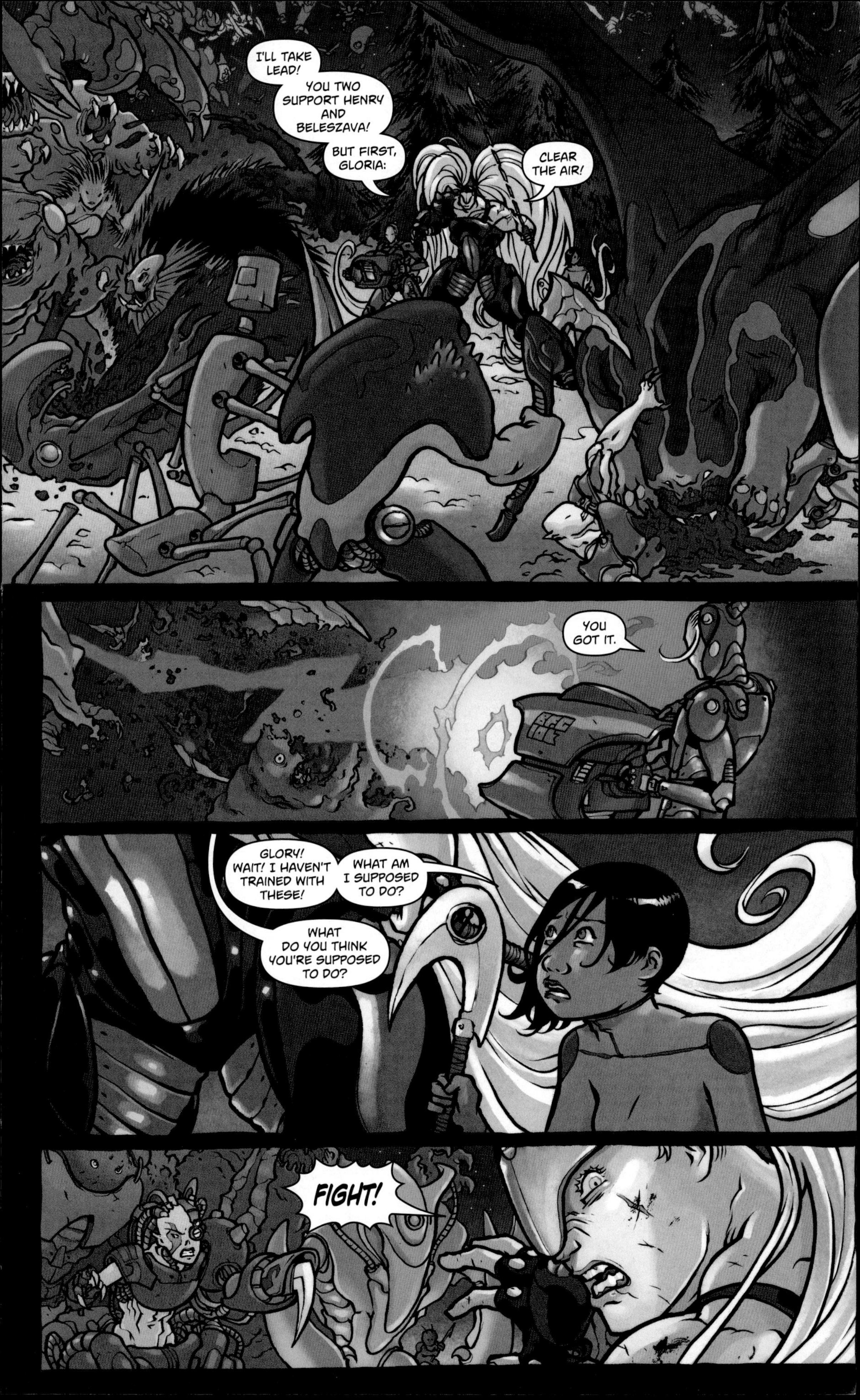
I'LL TAKE LEAD!
YOU TWO SUPPORT HENRY AND BELESZAVA!
BUT FIRST, GLORIA:
CLEAR THE AIR!
YOU GOT IT.
GLORY! WAIT! I HAVEN'T TRAINED WITH THESE!
WHAT AM I SUPPOSED TO DO?
WHAT DO YOU THINK YOU'RE SUPPOSED TO DO?
FIGHT!

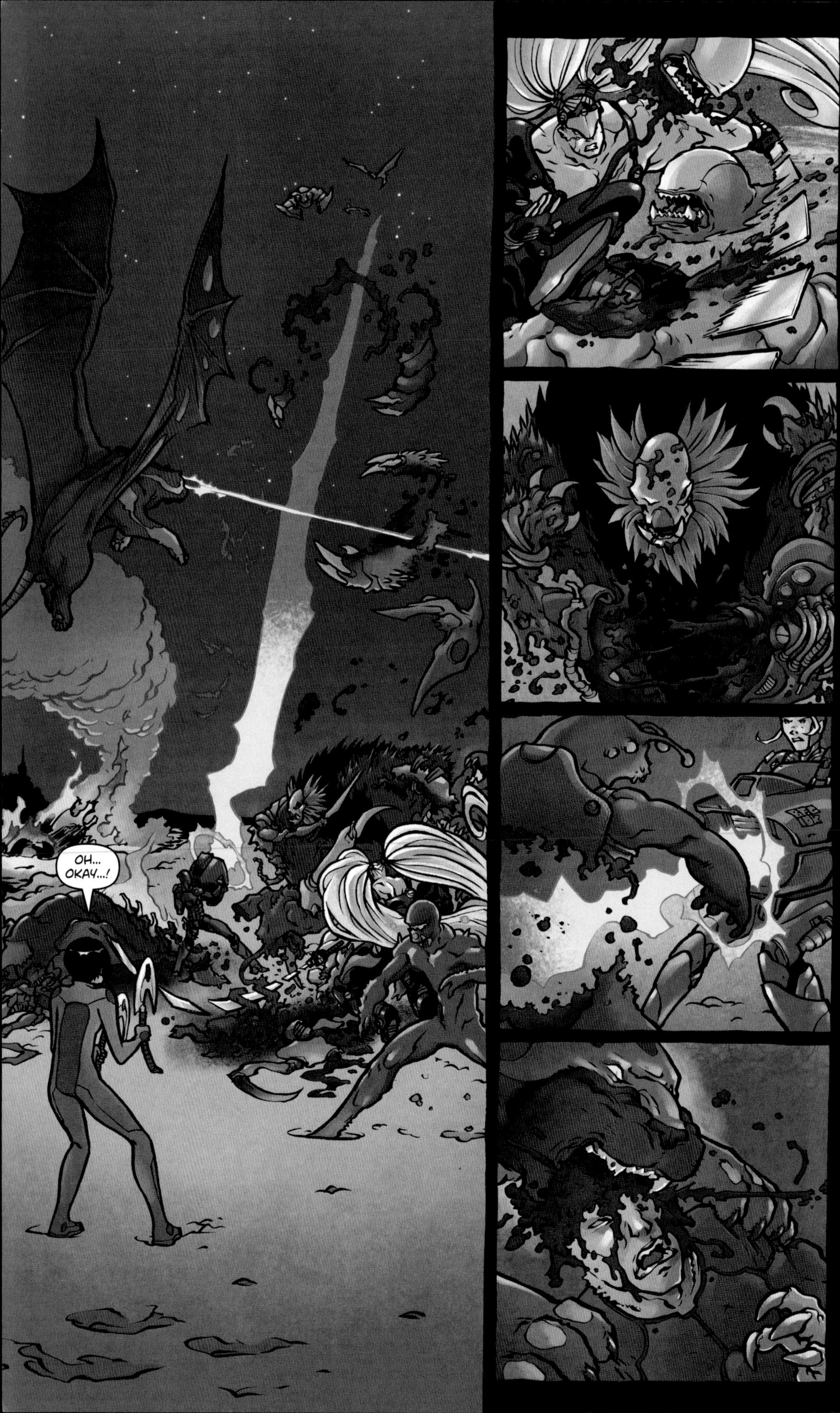
OH... OKAY...!

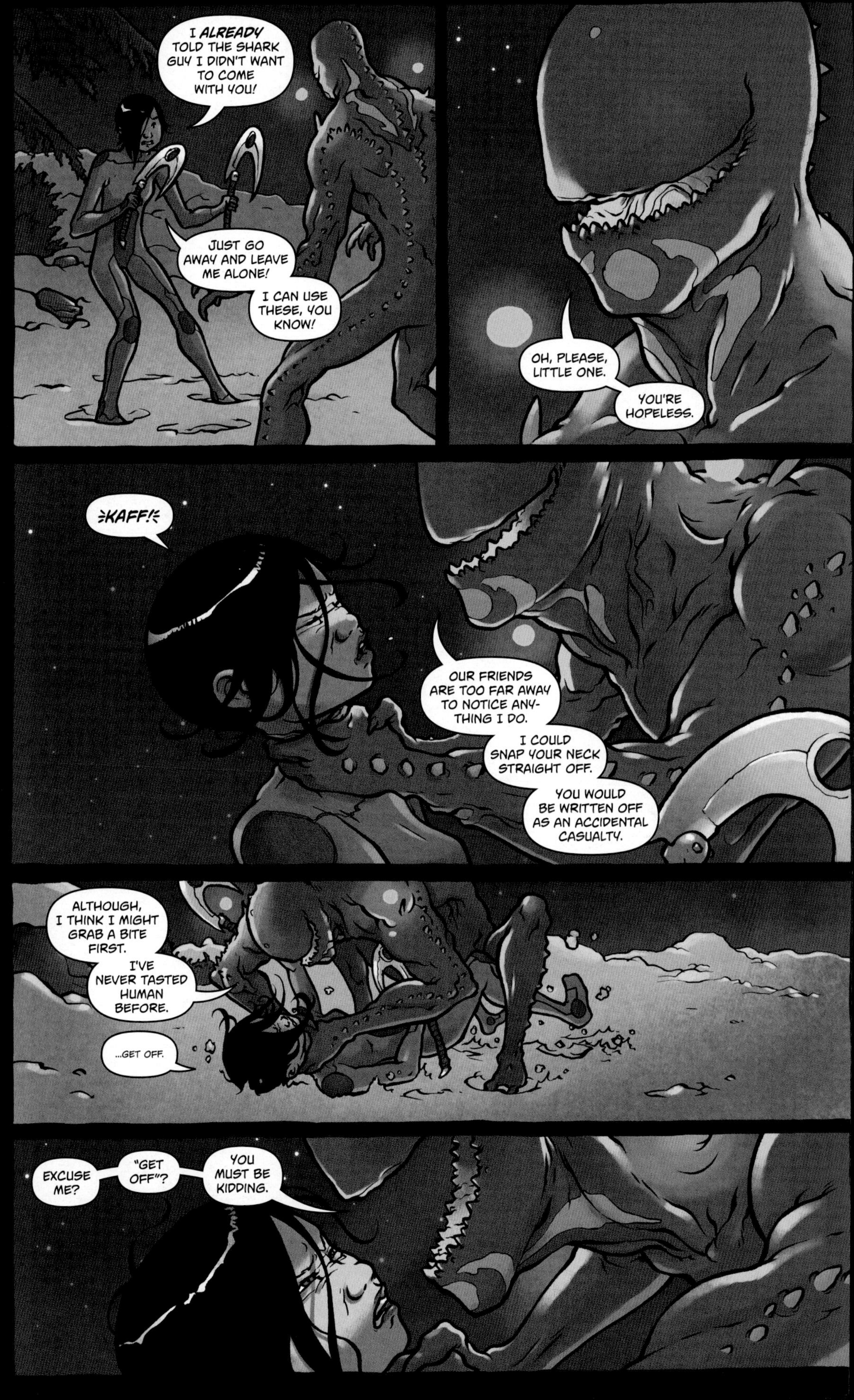
I *ALREADY* TOLD THE SHARK GUY I DIDN'T WANT TO COME WITH YOU!
JUST GO AWAY AND LEAVE ME ALONE!
I CAN USE THESE, YOU KNOW!
OH, PLEASE, LITTLE ONE.
YOU'RE HOPELESS.
KAFF!
OUR FRIENDS ARE TOO FAR AWAY TO NOTICE ANY-THING I DO.
I COULD SNAP YOUR NECK STRAIGHT OFF.
YOU WOULD BE WRITTEN OFF AS AN ACCIDENTAL CASUALTY.
ALTHOUGH, I THINK I MIGHT GRAB A BITE FIRST.
I'VE NEVER TASTED HUMAN BEFORE.
...GET OFF.
EXCUSE ME?
"GET OFF"?
YOU MUST BE KIDDING.

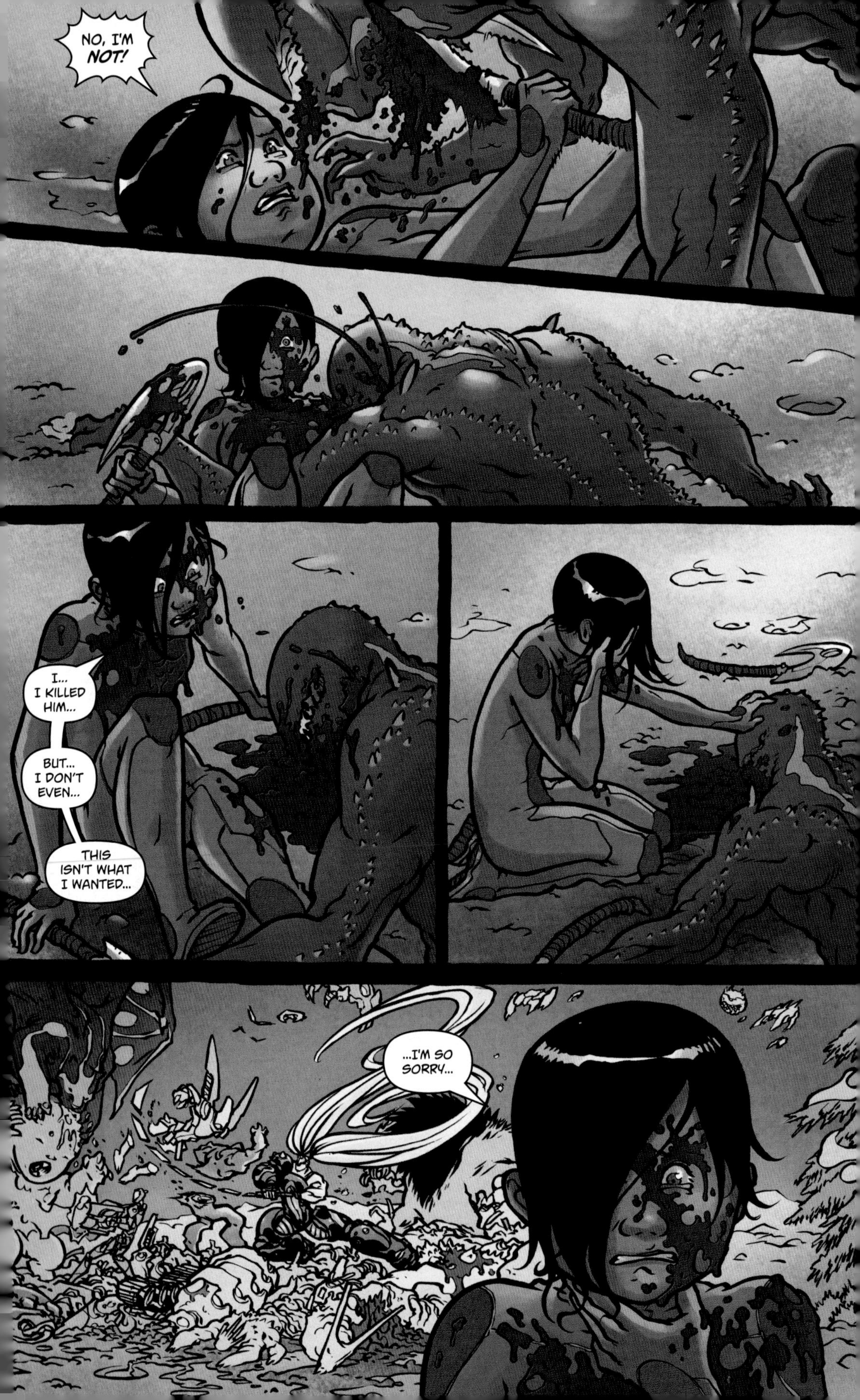
NO, I'M *NOT!*
I... I KILLED HIM...
BUT... I DON'T EVEN...
THIS ISN'T WHAT I WANTED...
...I'M SO SORRY...

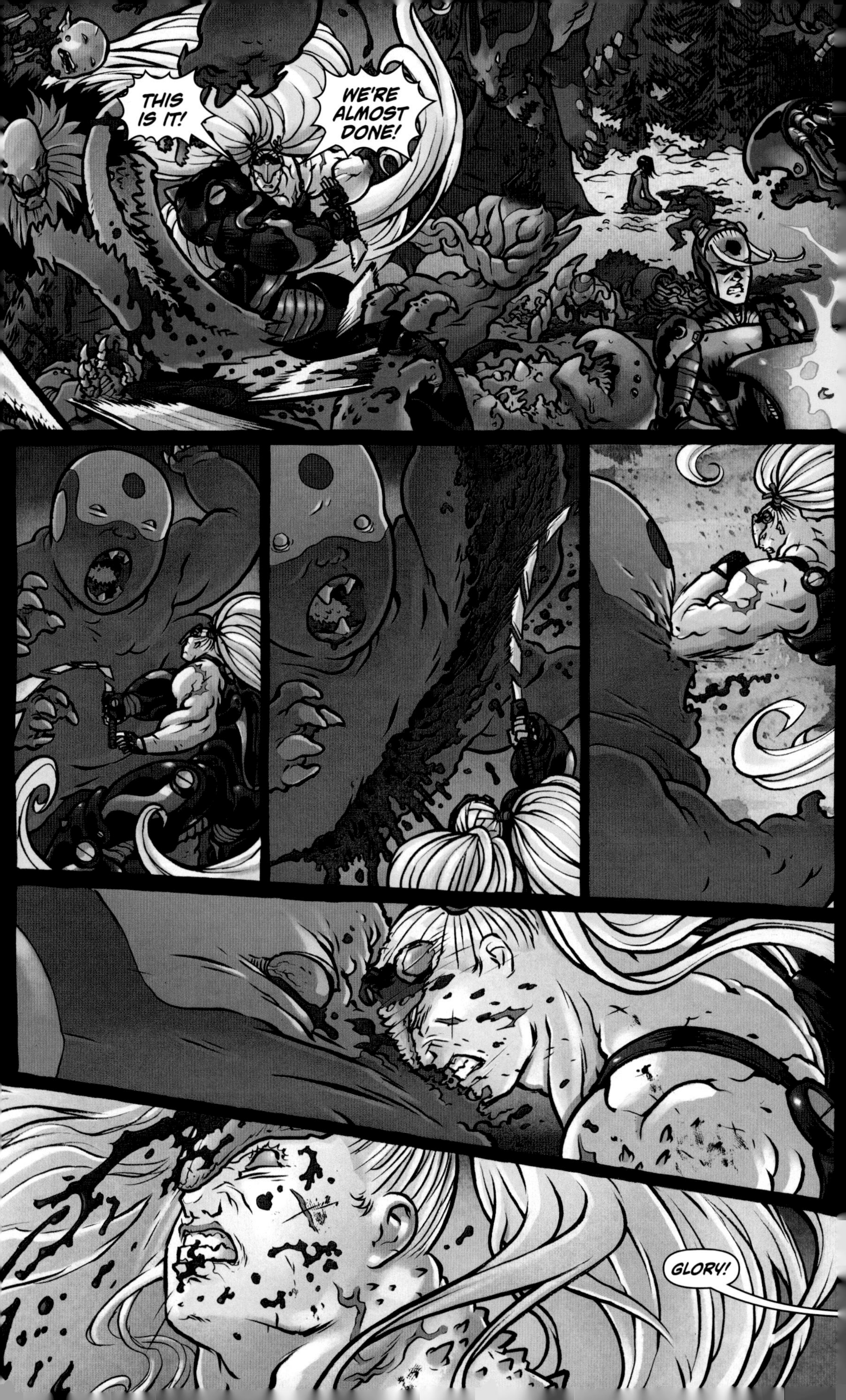
THIS IS IT!
WE'RE ALMOST DONE!
GLORY!

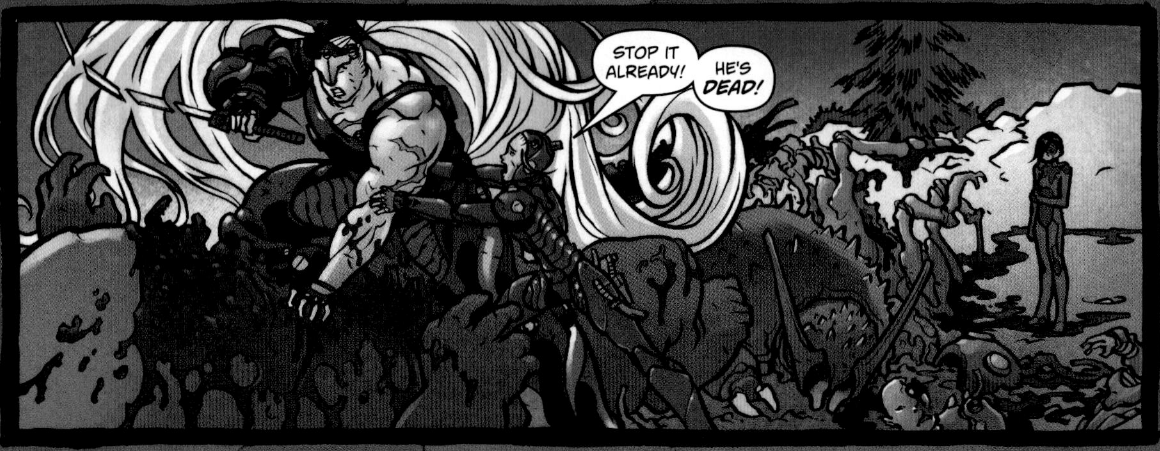
STOP IT ALREADY!
HE'S DEAD!

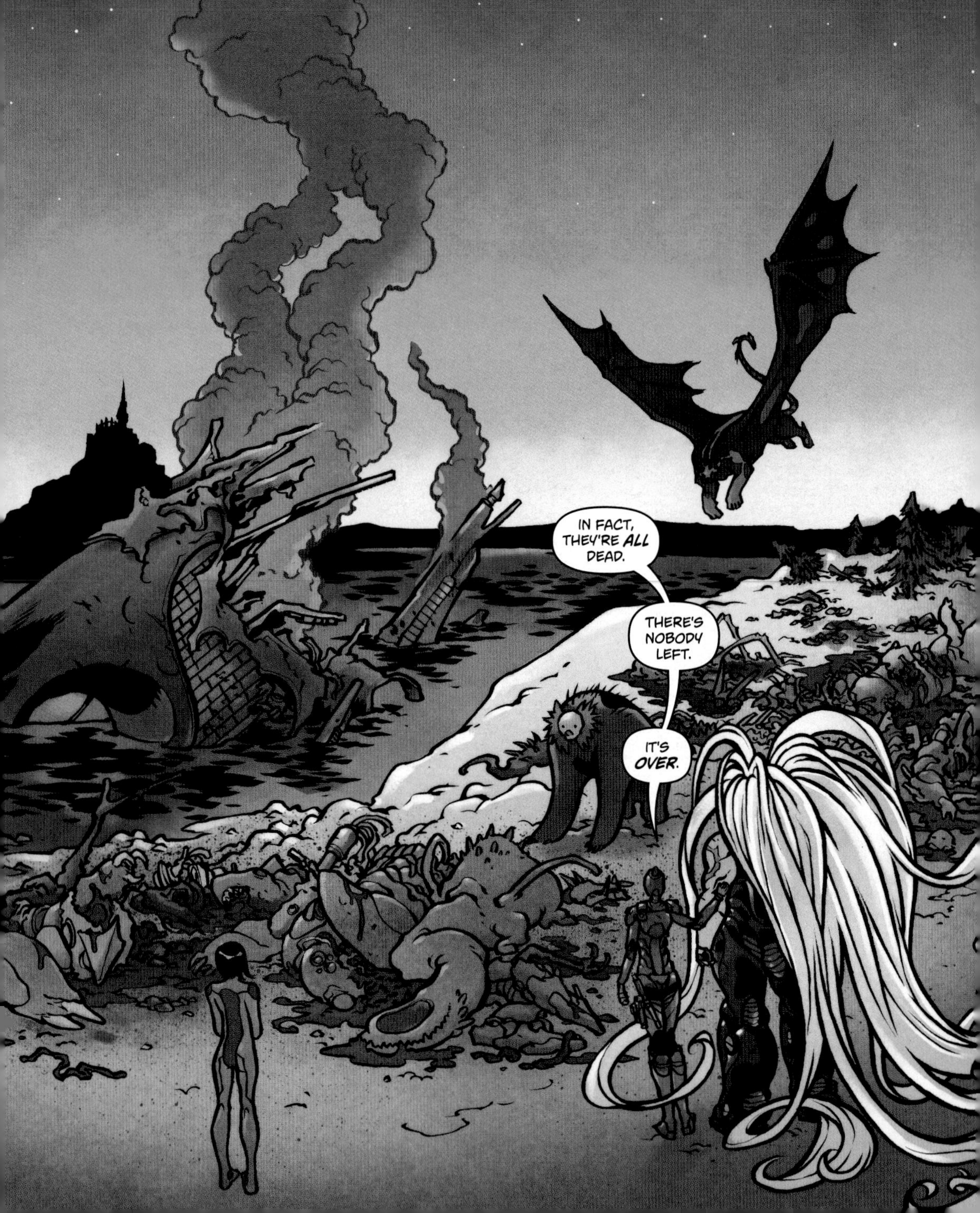
IN FACT, THEY'RE ALL DEAD.
THERE'S NOBODY LEFT.
IT'S OVER.

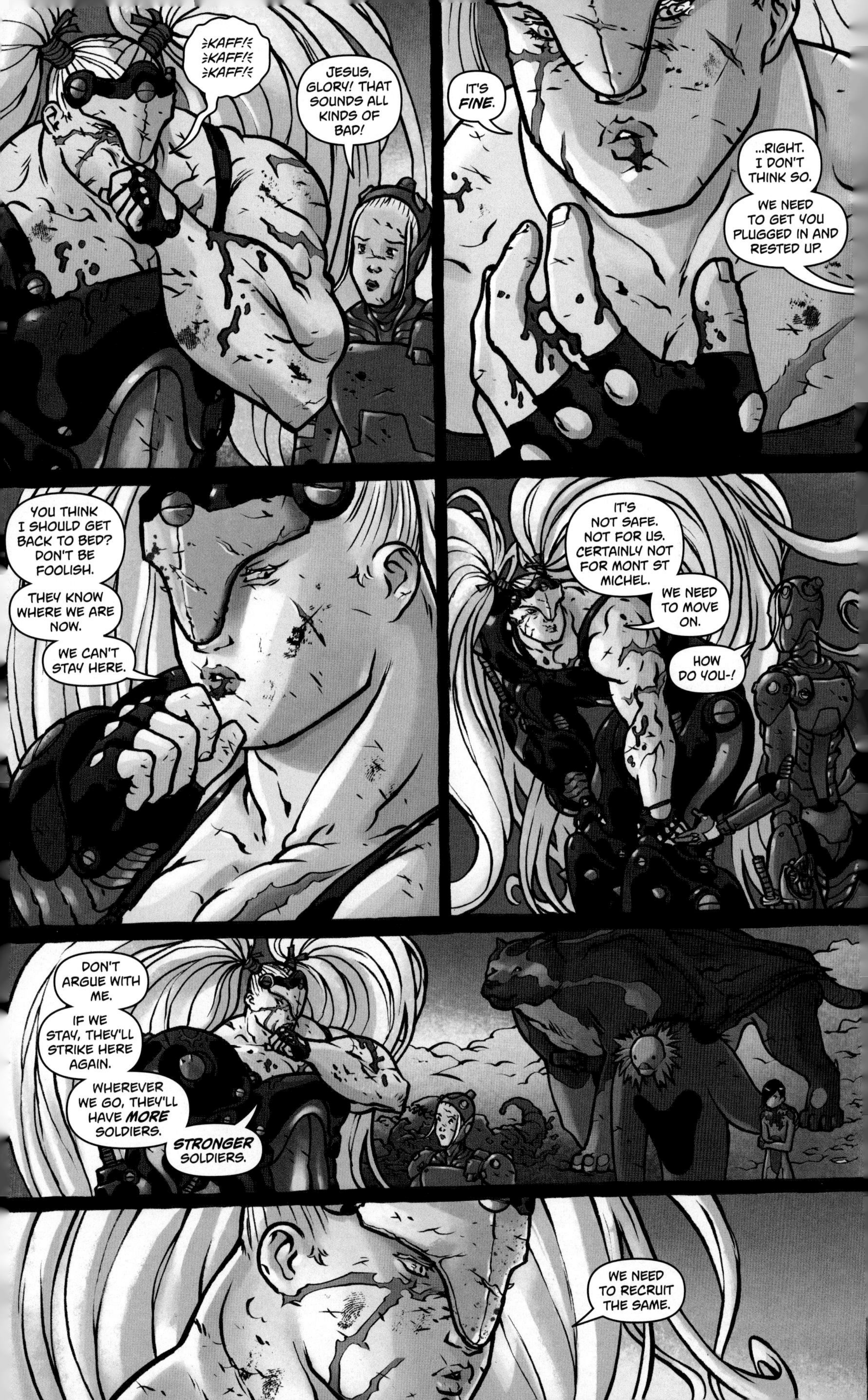

KAFF! KAFF! KAFF!
JESUS, GLORY! THAT SOUNDS ALL KINDS OF BAD!
IT'S FINE.
...RIGHT. I DON'T THINK SO.
WE NEED TO GET YOU PLUGGED IN AND RESTED UP.
YOU THINK I SHOULD GET BACK TO BED? DON'T BE FOOLISH.
THEY KNOW WHERE WE ARE NOW.
WE CAN'T STAY HERE.
IT'S NOT SAFE. NOT FOR US. CERTAINLY NOT FOR MONT ST MICHEL.
WE NEED TO MOVE ON.
HOW DO YOU-!
DON'T ARGUE WITH ME.
IF WE STAY, THEY'LL STRIKE HERE AGAIN.
WHEREVER WE GO, THEY'LL HAVE MORE SOLDIERS.
STRONGER SOLDIERS.
WE NEED TO RECRUIT THE SAME.

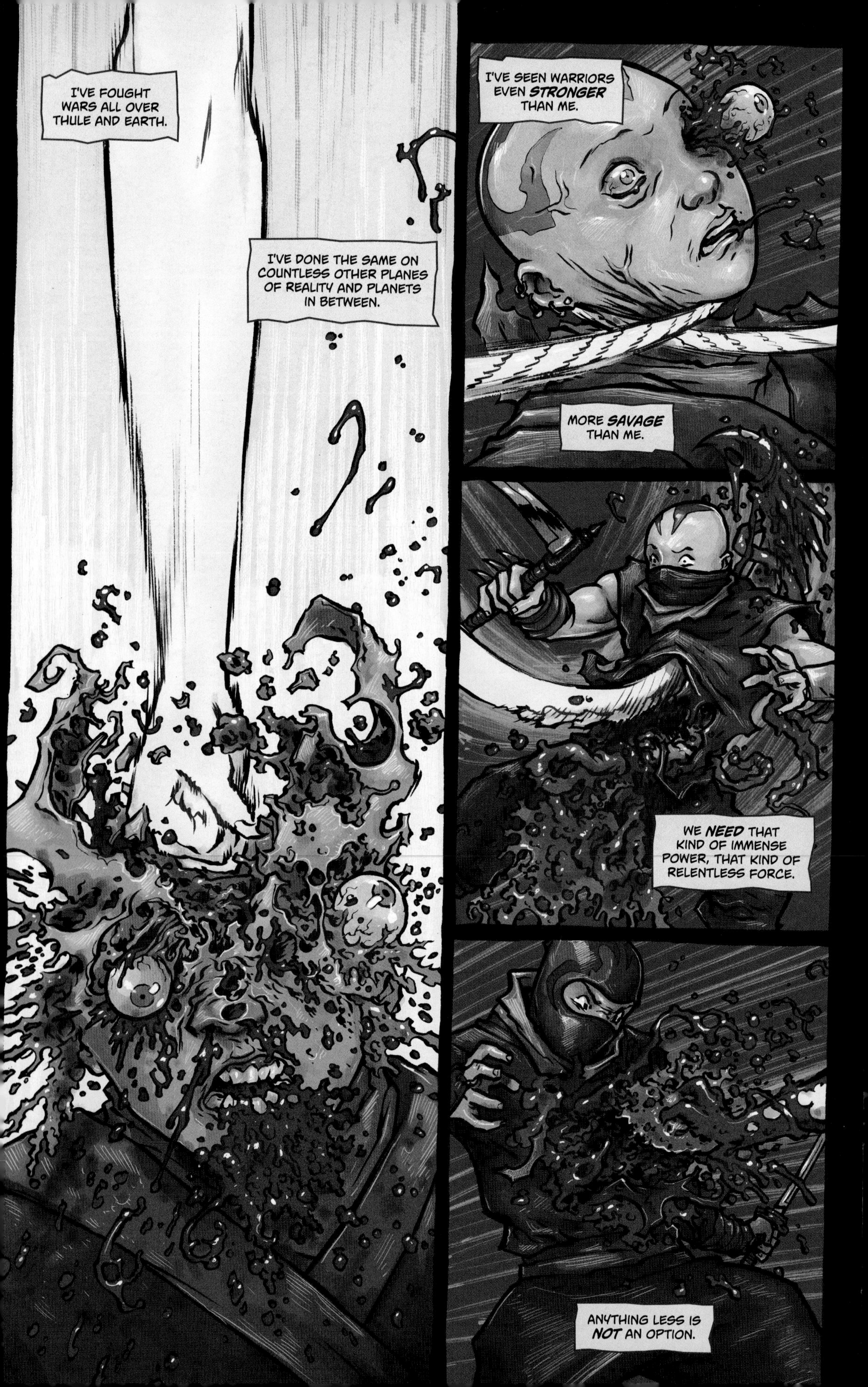

I'VE FOUGHT WARS ALL OVER THULE AND EARTH.
I'VE DONE THE SAME ON COUNTLESS OTHER PLANES OF REALITY AND PLANETS IN BETWEEN.
I'VE SEEN WARRIORS EVEN STRONGER THAN ME.
MORE SAVAGE THAN ME.
WE NEED THAT KIND OF IMMENSE POWER, THAT KIND OF RELENTLESS FORCE.
ANYTHING LESS IS NOT AN OPTION.

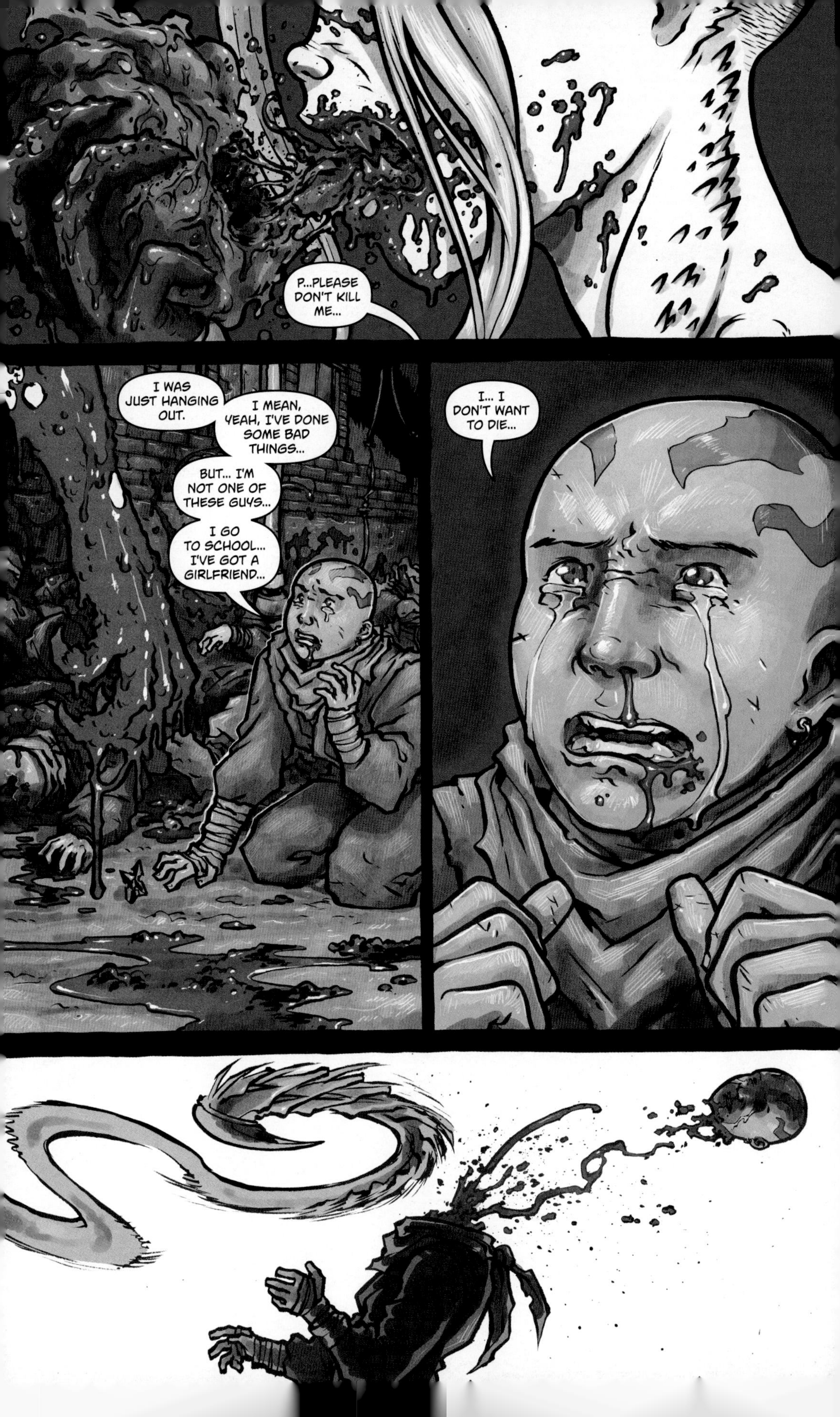
P...PLEASE DON'T KILL ME...
I WAS JUST HANGING OUT.
I MEAN, YEAH, I'VE DONE SOME BAD THINGS...
BUT... I'M NOT ONE OF THESE GUYS...
I GO TO SCHOOL... I'VE GOT A GIRLFRIEND...
I... I DON'T WANT TO DIE...

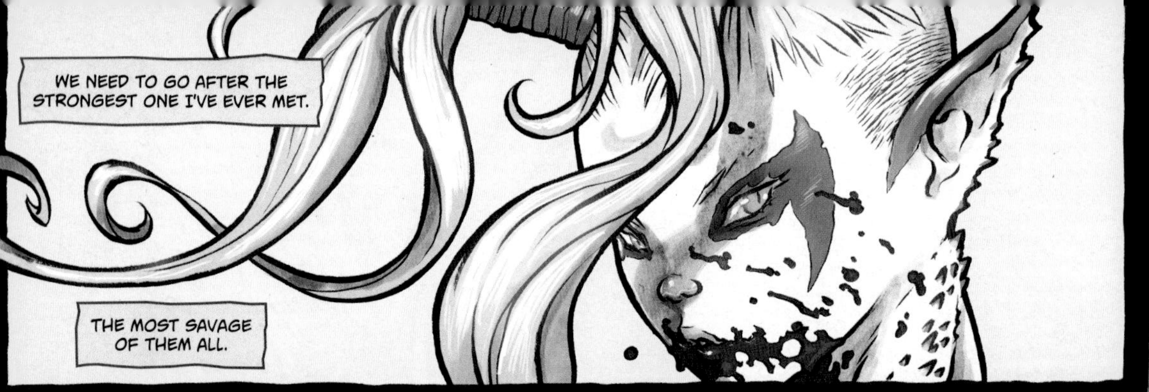
WE NEED TO GO AFTER THE STRONGEST ONE I'VE EVER MET.
THE MOST SAVAGE OF THEM ALL.

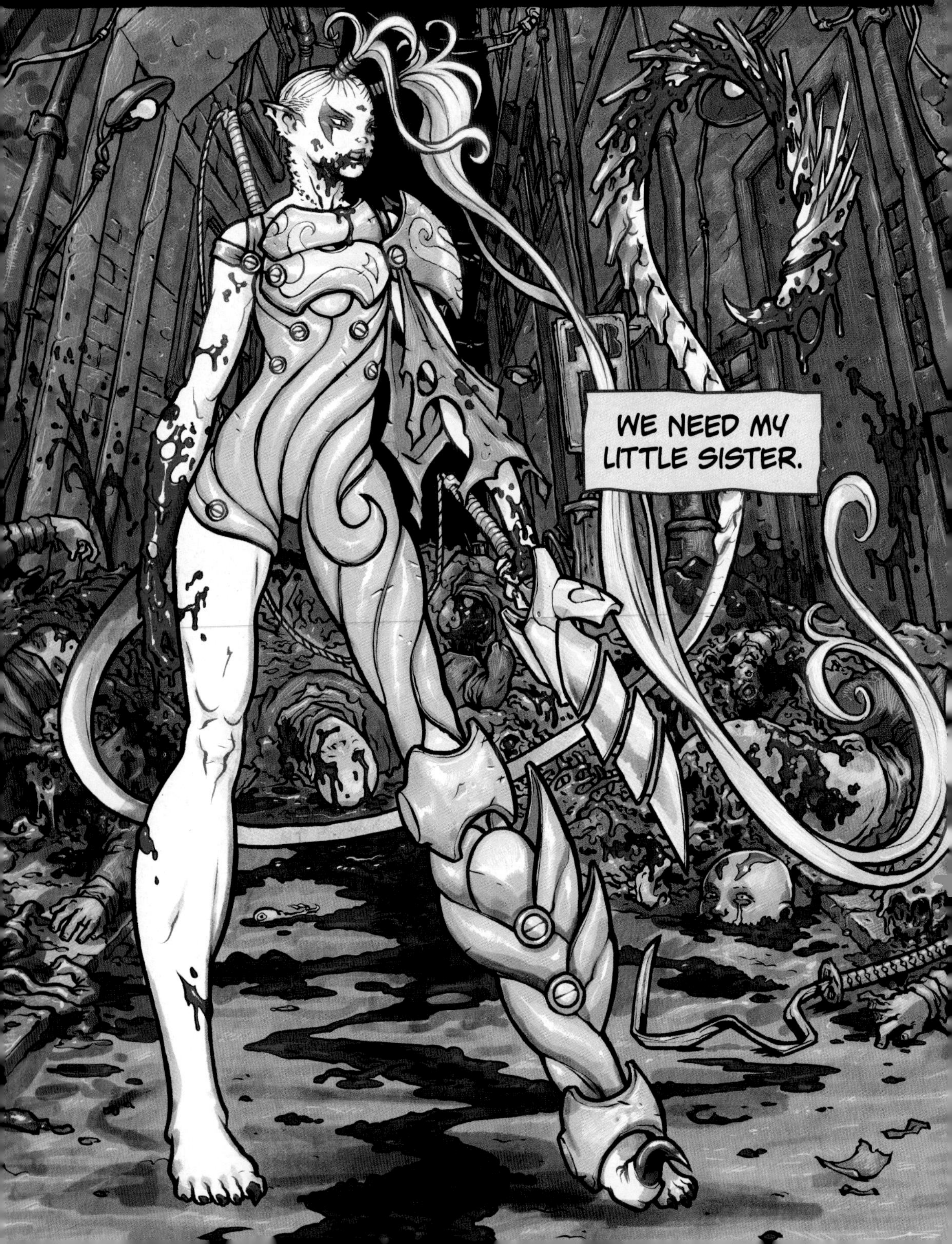
WE NEED MY LITTLE SISTER.

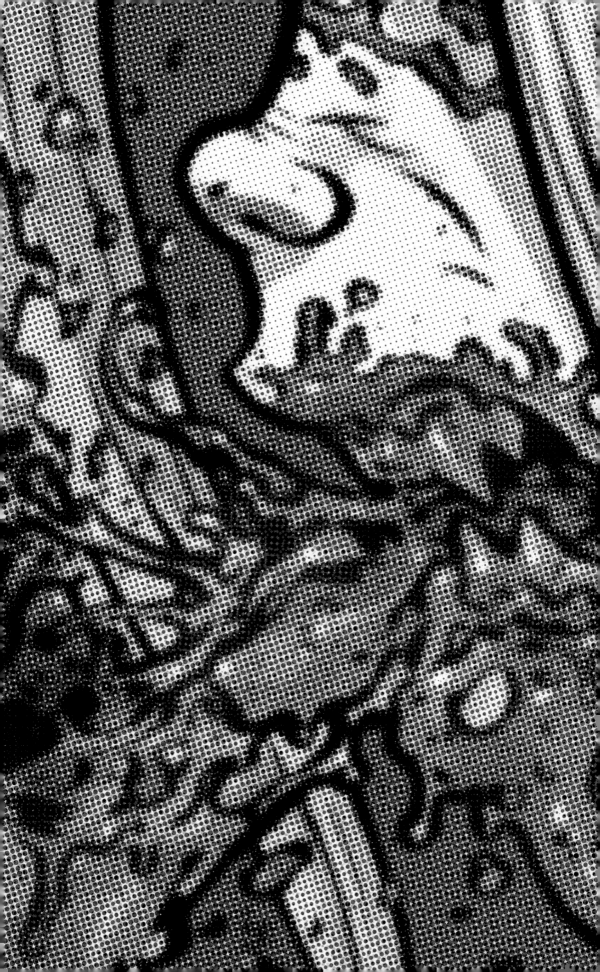

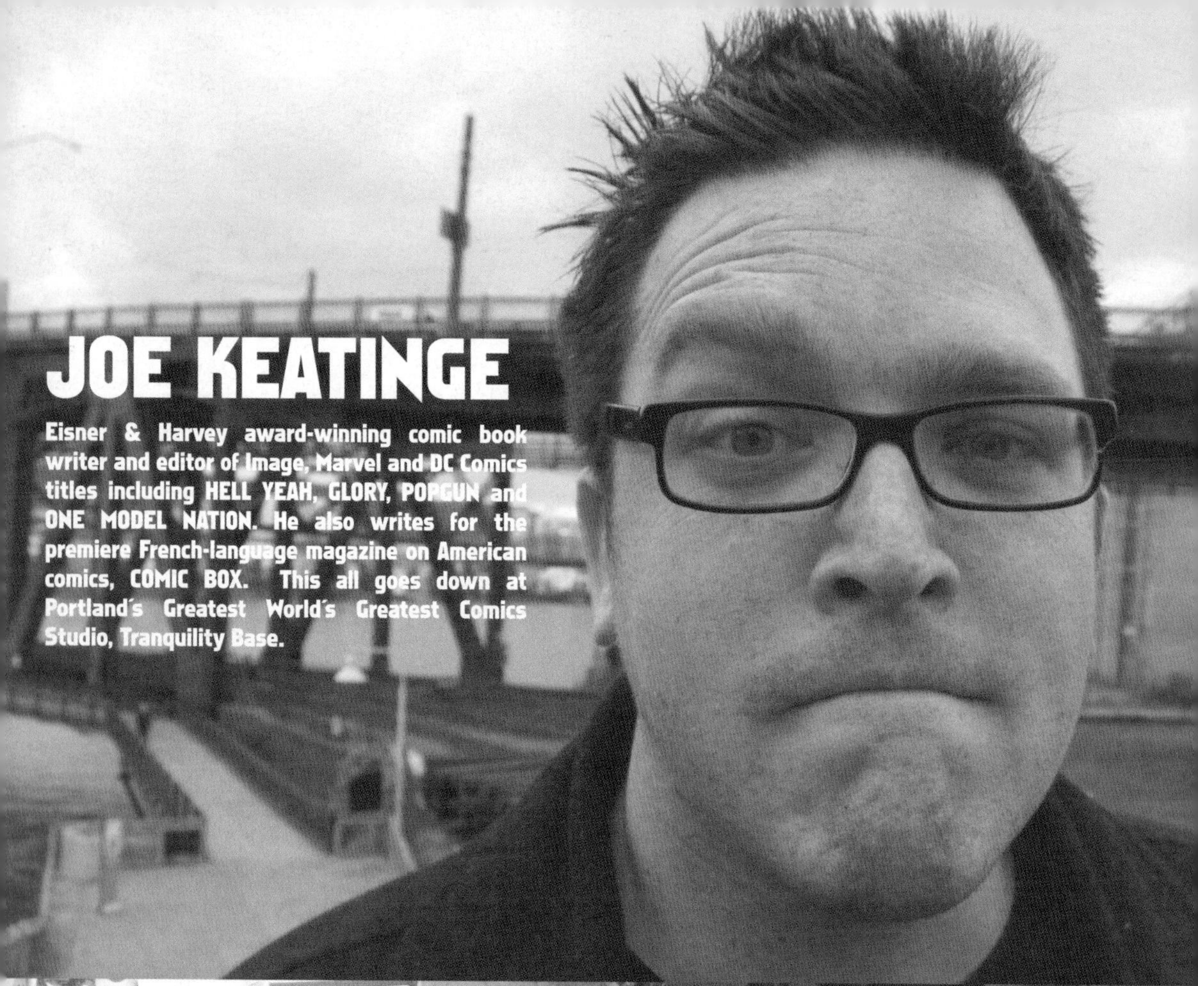

JOE KEATINGE

Eisner & Harvey award-winning comic book writer and editor of Image, Marvel and DC Comics titles including HELL YEAH, GLORY, POPGUN and ONE MODEL NATION. He also writes for the premiere French-language magazine on American comics, COMIC BOX. This all goes down at Portland's Greatest World's Greatest Comics Studio, Tranquility Base.

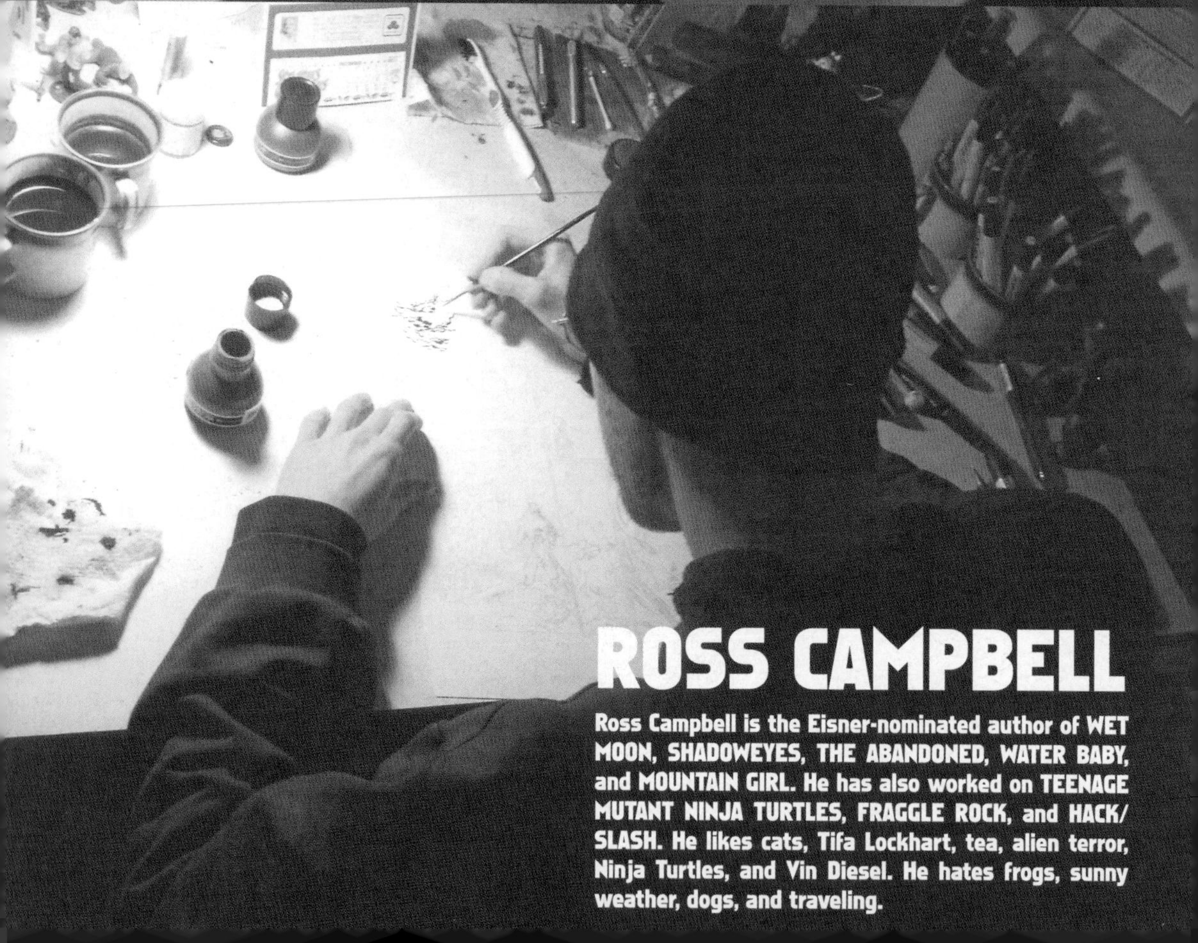

ROSS CAMPBELL

Ross Campbell is the Eisner-nominated author of WET MOON, SHADOWEYES, THE ABANDONED, WATER BABY, and MOUNTAIN GIRL. He has also worked on TEENAGE MUTANT NINJA TURTLES, FRAGGLE ROCK, and HACK/SLASH. He likes cats, Tifa Lockhart, tea, alien terror, Ninja Turtles, and Vin Diesel. He hates frogs, sunny weather, dogs, and traveling.

MS,SHATIA HAMILTON - colorist (23-25)

Ms,Shatia Hamilton is a colorist and the cartoonist of Fungus Grotto.

JOSEPH BERGIN III - colorist (26-28)

Joseph Bergin III is an illustrator and tattoo artist located in Portland, OR. He also colors the Brandon Graham written issues of Prophet.

OWEN GIENI - colorist (28 Epilogue)

Owen Gieni is the illustrator of the other Rob Liefeld demon fighting bad ass, Avengelyne, and colorist on titles such as Debris.

DOUGLAS E. SHERWOOD - letterer

Douglas E. Sherwood was born on the planet hVADOXe in 1984. He has done many things, and now he is here. Deal with it.

CHARO SOLIS - color flatter (26-28)

A few years ago, Charo was immersed in her profession, business administration. She never imagined that someday she'll be working in comics as a color assistant. Now she deeply enjoys being a freelancer and learning about this great industry. Life is full of surprises.

SKETCH GALLERY

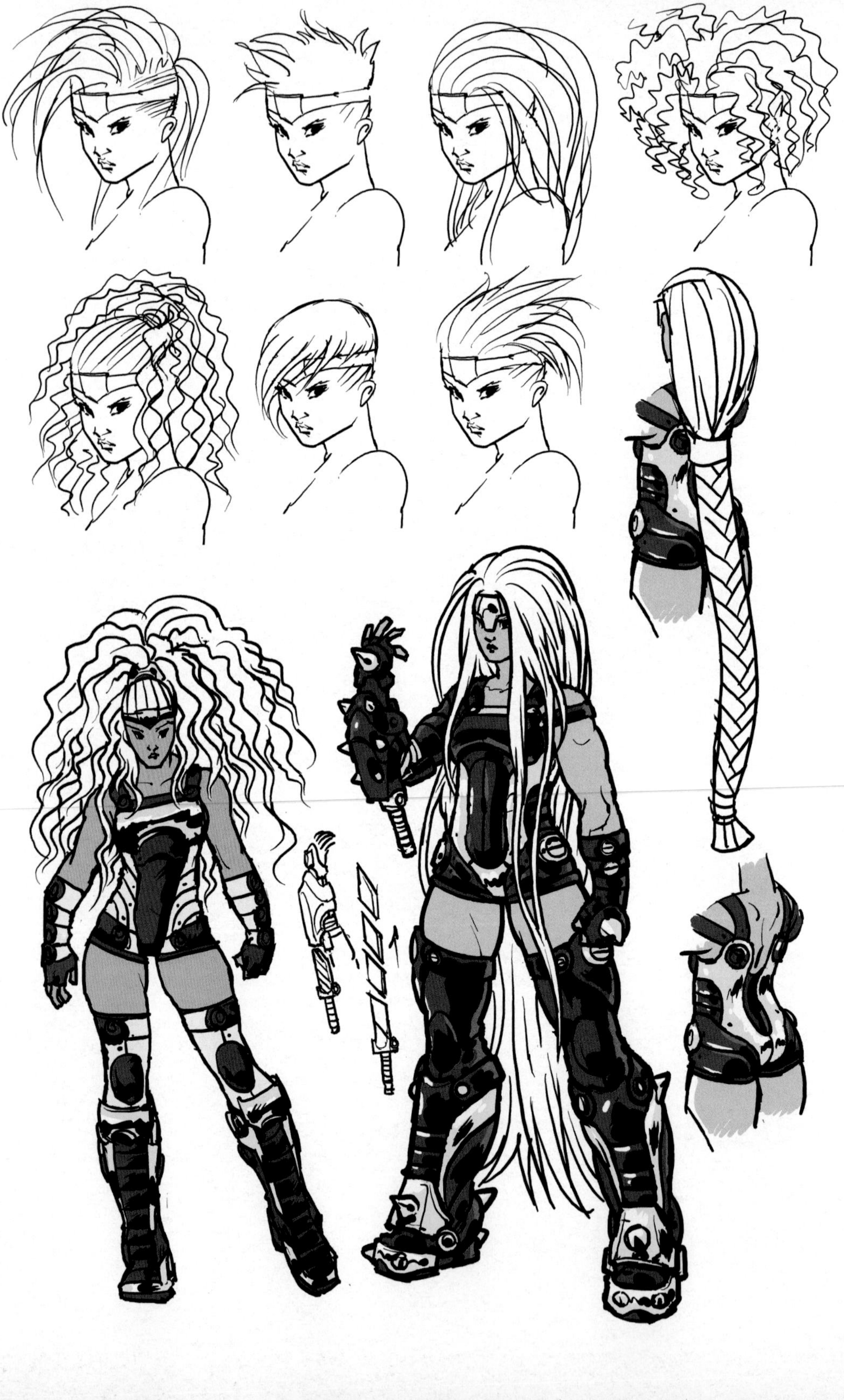

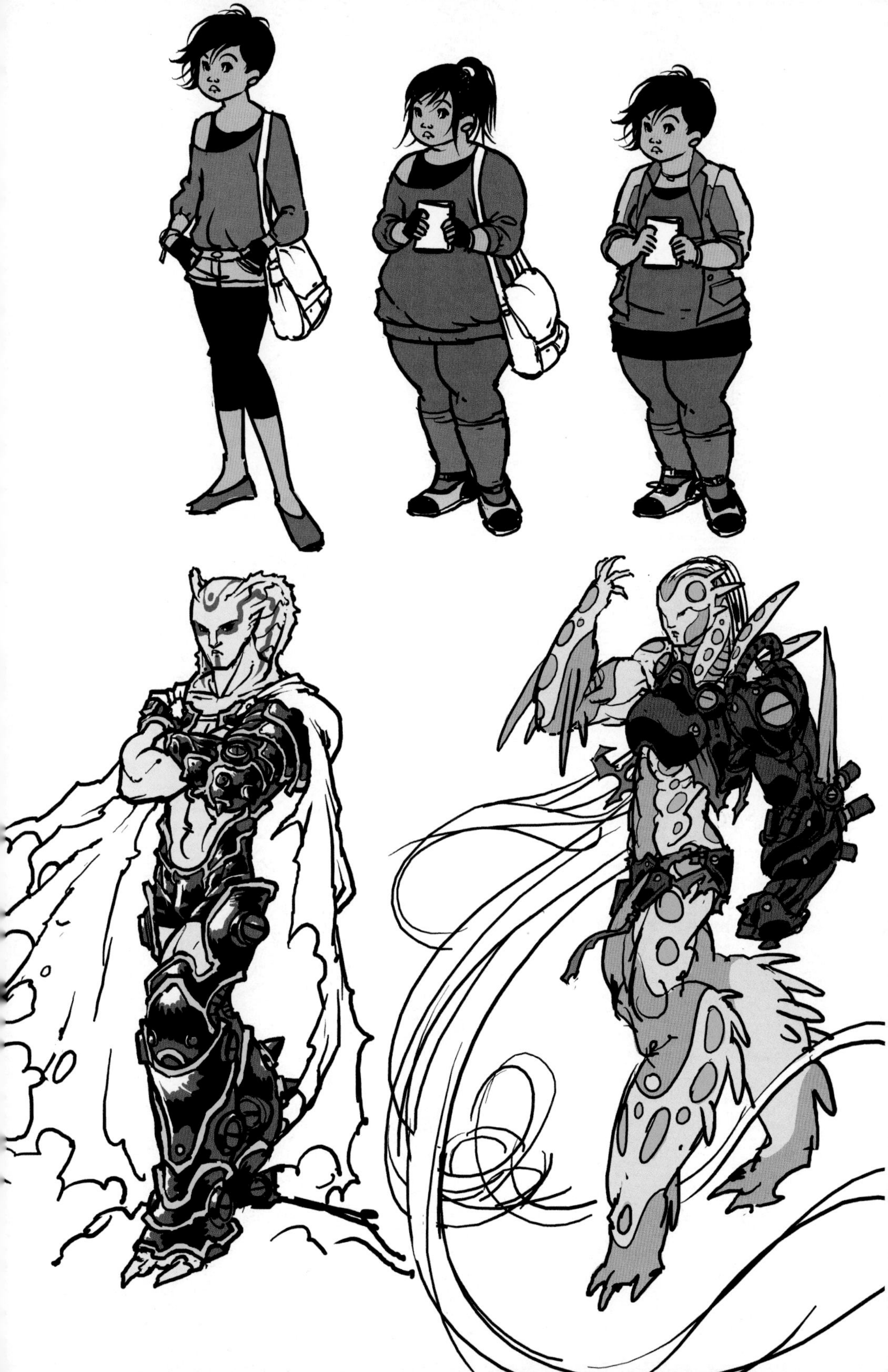

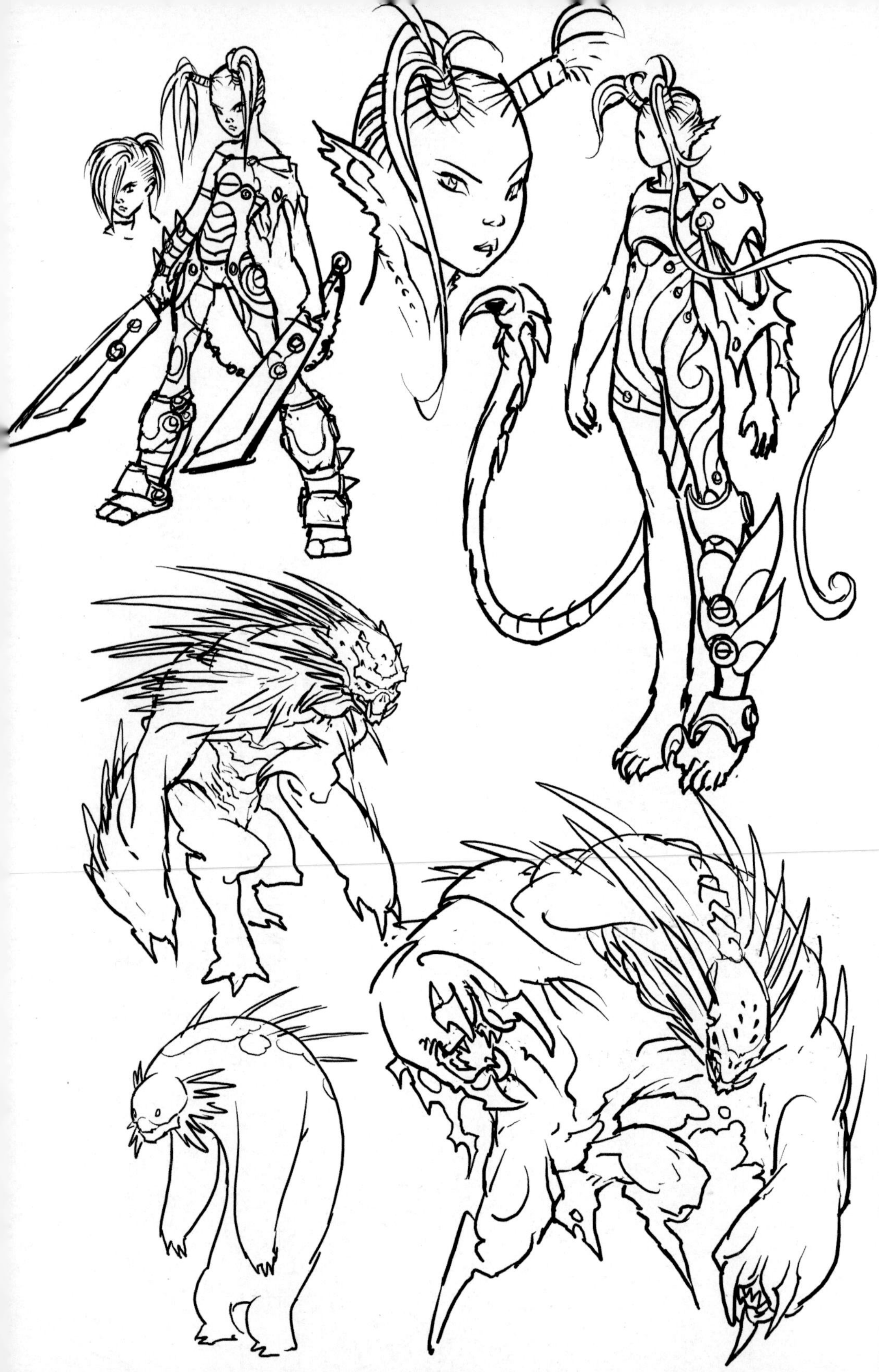